The
Primal Roots
of
American
Philosophy

American and European Philosophy

GENERAL EDITORS: CHARLES E. SCOTT AND JOHN J. STUHR
ASSOCIATE EDITOR: SUSAN M. SCHOENBOHM

Devoted to the contemporary development of American and European philosophy in the pragmatic and Continental traditions, AMERICAN AND EUROPEAN PHILOSOPHY gives expression to uniquely American thought that deepens and advances these traditions and that arises from their mutual encounters. The series will focus on new interpretations of philosophers and philosophical movements within these traditions, original contributions to European or American thought, and issues that arise through the mutual influence of American and European philosophers.

EDITORIAL ADVISORY BOARD

David Farrell Krell, *The Purest of Bastards: Works of Mourning, Art, and Affirmation in the Thought of Jacques Derrida*

Bruce Wilshire, *The Primal Roots of American Philosophy: Pragmatism, Phenomenology, and Native American Thought*

Bruce Wilshire

The Primal Roots of American Philosophy

Pragmatism, Phenomenology,

and

Native American Thought

The Pennsylvania State University Press
University Park, Pennsylvania

Versions of several chapters were previously published in the following journals and collections: Chapter 3: "William James, Black Elk, and the Healing Act," in *Pragmatic Bioethics*, ed. Glenn McGee (Vanderbilt University Press, 1999); Chapter 6: "John Dewey's View on the Subconscious: Difficulties in the Reconstruction of Culture," in *Philosophy and the Reconstruction of Culture: Pragmatic Essays After Dewey*, ed. John Stuhr (SUNY Press, 1993); Chapter 8: "Passion for Meaning: W. E. Hocking's Religious-Philosophical Views," *Transactions of the C. S. Peirce Society* 33 (Fall 1997); Chapter 11: "Pragmatism, Neopragmatism, and Phenomenology: The Richard Rorty Phenomenon," *Human Studies* 20 (1997).

Library of Congress Cataloging-in-Publication Data

Wilshire, Bruce W.
    The primal roots of American philosophy : pragmatism, phenomenology, and Native American thought / Bruce Wilshire.
      p. cm. — (American and European philosophy)
    Includes bibliographical references and index.
    ISBN 0-271-02025-3 (cloth : alk. paper)
    ISBN 0-271-02026-1 (pbk. : alk. paper)
    1. Philosophy, American—19th century.   2. Philosophy, American—20th century.
I. Title. II. Series.
B893 .W55 2000
191—dc21

99-047237

It is the policy of The Pennsylvania State University Press to use acid-free paper for the first printing of all clothbound books. Publications on uncoated stock satisfy the minimum requirements of American National Standard for Information Sciences— Permanence of Paper for Printed Library Materials, ANSI Z39.48–1992.

For my brothers
Leland and Daniel

The very conception of a beginning of conscious life carries with it a paradoxical reference to something prior to that beginning. . . . As we examine our own duration in time . . . we can find no wall of partition between self and prior-to-self. I never know by introspection how old I am, or that I have a finite age. If the impulse which is I is a "racial impulse," there is no reason to ascribe age to it: it is presumably, like energy, always new as on the first day.

—W. E. Hocking, *The Self: Its Body and Freedom*

Contents

Foreword
The Return of the Native in American Philosophy

For a very long time American philosophers have found themselves in a situation of extreme futility. Wanting to be independent thinkers—wanting to articulate an authentically *American* philosophy—they have all too often fallen into epigonic roles and mimetic posturings. This is above all true of twentieth-century American philosophy after World War I, when academic philosophy has been successively positivist, neo-positivist, Wittgensteinian, Austinian, on the one hand, and (after World War II) existential, phenomenological, structuralist, poststructuralist, Heideggerian, Derridean, on the other hand. For all their manifest differences, the two great strands of "analytical" and "continental" philosophy have this much in common: they derive ultimate (and often continuing) inspiration from mainland Europe and England.

It wasn't always so. At the end of the nineteenth century, American pragmatism was a freshly minted style of doing philosophy that was not anticipated by anything comparable elsewhere. This is greatly to the credit of the founders of the movement, Charles Sanders Peirce and William James, who made New World thinking a world-class act. Now, by the beginning of the twenty-first century, philosophers seem to be engaged in very little that is distinctively American.

Bruce Wilshire is not content to accept this simple narrative of decline. A scholar of William James and one of the very first to discern the deep parallels between pragmatism and phenomenology,[1] Wilshire makes bold to claim in this scintillating new book not just that classical pragmatism is an original and unfettered strain of American thought but that, if truth be told, it is far more original than we have ever allowed ourselves to imagine. *It is original because it is also aboriginal.* Pragmatism speaks to us today less because it is forward-looking—as in Cornel West's notion of "prophetic pragmatism"[2]—than because it is covertly and complexly embedded in the only tradition that can rightly be called "native," that is, Native American. Above all in James, but also in Peirce and Dewey, Native American elements can be glimpsed lurking behind the lively prose of the original pragmatists, like tribesmen vanishing soundlessly into the surrounding woods.

Stanley Cavell has eloquently recognized the originality of Emerson and Thoreau—and their uncanny connections with Wittgenstein, Austin, Heidegger, and Derrida.[3] Cavell goes back behind the pragmatists by showing the philosophical importance of the generation just before Peirce and James, as well as the many links that tie that mid-nineteenth-century generation to the mid-twentieth-century thought of leading British and French and German thinkers. Wilshire's drummer is different, and still more radical. He suggests that far further back than the middle of the 1800s there was a truly native strain to American experience and reflection—a strain that was brutally repressed and subsequently ignored. His revolutionary thesis is that we can witness a wholly unexpected return of the repressed in the work of the American pragmatists: the Aboriginal in the Original, the Native in the self-declared "Native Sons." The first day dawns again in the writings of non-native Americans who nonetheless bid fair to being the first distinctively American philosophers.

To appreciate this alarming yet edifying idea, we must set aside our habitual manner of regarding philosophy as a wholly professional matter—as it certainly became after James and Peirce, neither of whom could be called rightly a "professional philosopher." Thoreau had already said famously in *Walden* that "there are nowadays professors of philosophy, but no philosophers." But few philosophers have taken Thoreau's complaint to heart. James and Peirce were themselves ambivalent on this very point: each was half inside and half outside the academy. But if Wilshire's bold thesis is to stand, we must imagine philosophy resituated wholly beyond the academy—not only in Concord just west of Harvard, or New Milford north of Johns Hopkins, but in a different place altogether: in the forests and open plains of North America, where a radically different kind of thought, engendered in a very different kind of life-world, was once to be found.

It takes courage to reconceive philosophy in this way, thereby broadening its horizons to reflect those of the actual landscape of an immense continent. This book calls us both to deprofessionalize American philosophy and to reconnect it with its primal implacement in its own native land. To follow this unaccustomed path is to rediscover what is truly a matter of native genius—the *genius loci* of a terrain whose first inhabitants, still and for the first time, have a great deal to teach us philosophically about what it is to be, and finally to become, American.

Edward S. Casey
SUNY at Stony Brook

Notes

1. See Bruce Wilshire, *William James and Phenomenology: A Study of the Principles of Psychology* (reprint: New York: AMS, 1979).
2. Cornel West, *The American Evasion of Philosophy: A Genealogy of Pragmatism* (Madison: University of Wisconsin Press, 1989), chapter 6.
3. See Stanley Cavell, *The Senses of Walden* (San Francisco: North Point Press, 1981); *This New Yet Unapproachable America: Lectures After Emerson After Wittgenstein* (Albuquerque: Living Batch Press, 1989).

PART ONE

Reclaiming Sources and Possibilities

Looking Forward to the First Day

Europeans crossing the Atlantic in the sixteenth century could smell the New World before they could see it: vegetation's freshness wafted far across the waters. The "classic" American thinkers—Thoreau, Emerson, Peirce, William James, Royce, Dewey—could still smell it, in a real sense. Emerson told us to work out for ourselves an original relation to the universe. Among the connotations of "original" is "origins," and origins not limited to the European past—Greek, Roman, or Hebrew and Christian traditions. This admonition sets Emerson at a critical distance from Europe, the Old World, with its tired conflicts, castes, creeds—itemized worldviews.

The confluence of European philosophical thinking and the indigenous life and thought of the New World cast up in its turbulence surprising patterns of thinking and living, some of them primal. And some of these patterns found their way to thoughtful persons of European origin.

By the time of Emerson, writing in mid-nineteenth century, Europeans had been settling on the North American continent and interacting with its indigenous peoples for 250 years. Something distinctly Euro-American arose. As we grapple with the bald fact of the near extermination of indigenous peoples worldwide, we try to come to grips with the history of Europe's contact with the rest of the world.

By the mid-nineteenth century, a New World was rapidly forming all over the globe: irruptive mechanical and, more recently, electronic modes of communication and transportation that mixed elements never mixed before, with unpredicted and unpredictable results. In other words, by midpoint of the last century, a way had been opened for remnants at least of primal, hunter-gatherer thinking and being to mix in the stream of world-history at large (at least as Europeans have conceived "world" and "history"). Today we try to figure out what has happened. How else explain various and sundry New Age movements? In the face of incredibly rapid and disruptive change—what some call future shock—are there any basic or primal human needs and human nature, any roots? Can we still smell the vegetation? Do we really need to?

To characterize the classic American thinkers of the nineteenth and earlier twentieth centuries as creative is to use too weak a word. But it's with the most surprising aspect of this creativity that I deal in this book: their dawning realization that proud European Enlightenment and surging "progress" have outrun our life-support system as ancient children of Earth. If the nineteenth century is described as a turbulent river cascading and pooling itself, it is the swirling back-current that intrigues me most—the attempt, as far as possible, to run backward, to reach back to origins, to something like indigenous ways. In other words, to reach back to the primal matrix of Nature in which we—along with our prehuman ancestors—were formed over many, many millennia: to regain a sense of the First Day.[1]

So in the grip of Europe's dogma of inevitable progress have most of us been, we have not seen what our best European-American, our canonical, thinkers have seen prophetically: namely, a convergence with the thought of Black Elk, for example, the Oglala Lakota holy man and thinker. None of them is caught up in modernism's dualisms, its divisions, such as mind versus body, spirit versus matter, scientific or real knowledge of this-here physical world versus superstitious belief in a nonphysical world off-there. All agree that fullness of life cannot derive from what's disclosed by the ever-growing class of scientific experts. For this we must expand our perception and empathy to disclose what is hidden to that class. Hidden, but not out of this world! Hidden but disclosed when the perceptual and empathic field is unpacked, its hidden folds and reaches revealed. The spiritual is not the nonphysical. It is the earth, the sky, our bodily selves in the surprisingly full amplitude of their ensemble. It is the hidden centrality of the earth.

The thinkers with whom I mainly deal were profoundly critical of the very idea of modernism. No one better epitomizes this idea, this program and cause, than René Descartes, seventeenth-century French mechanistic-mathematical physicist, appropriately dubbed father of modern philosophy. We are supposed to be minds attached somehow to mechanical bodies. In contrast, our American-pragmatist philosophical thinkers of the nineteenth and earlier twentieth centuries are organismic to the core: the world is like an organism and we organisms are most mindful and most spiritual when most involved ecstatically in the world-whole. They are pragmatic *and* primal. They begin turning back toward indigenous life.

Cornel West has written *The American Evasion of Philosophy.* He means that the thinkers we focus on did not work their way through Descartes in search of a modernist enlightenment, but detoured completely around him, trying to root themselves in ancient sources. This movement propels them around Descartes and injects new life in the present. Appropriately, West's book features on its cover a marvelous picture of a tree—one reminiscent of the World-Tree, a central mythic symbol of the vital integration of all things. Its roots plunge in the dark and fertile earth, its trunk surges up in the middle world, and its branches reach into the beyond, the sky. Rightly enough, Emerson is shown as the trunk, with thinkers he influenced as the branches. We are left to imagine what lies deep in the roots—as well as in the beyond, the sky.[2]

There is much to be learned from West's audacity. The German G. W. F. Hegel, although critical of Descartes, still could say that with the Cartesian idea of the subjective self the ship of philosophy sailed into port. But the American, Charles Peirce, asserted that the first order of business was to discard Descartes and to start thinking afresh. The idea that thoughts and feelings were in the mind, as if they were elements inside a sealed container, was what Peirce called an egregious error, the source of endless other errors. In one stroke we are cut off from the Earth that formed us and from the animals and plants with whom we evolved in the most intimate, intricate, and reciprocal ways over countless millennia. And we have no idea what is to guide and stabilize us as whole beings in the future.

All the American pragmatists believe that we must begin with where we actually find ourselves, not lost in the abstraction, "the mind," and in paper doubts about the "external world," but enmeshed as organisms in the world, the world of living and nonliving things that has evolved and formed us out of the depths of time. Along with this world, in the most integral relation imaginable, are the funded myths, rituals, origin stories, and common sense that have grown up by entwining with ever-regenerating Earth and its seasons—daily, monthly, yearly, generational. The modernist pretension to throw off the past as superstitious burden is simplistic pride and egregious arrogance.

This is the unmistakable birth in Thoreau and Emerson and their legacy for James, Dewey, and others: a visceral sense of a new lease on life and thought by redefining progress to require return to sources. They connect unmistakably with the orientation of Black Elk. This surprises most people still caught in the spell of modern Europe and the dogma of universal progress.

"Black Elk, Thoreau, Emerson, and Their Aura," the second chapter, takes the point further, and I think deeper into our experience. There are good reasons to abandon the widely held belief that because Black Elk is supposed to have been converted fully and finally to Christianity, he cannot speak for indigenous peoples such as his own Oglala Lakota. I set out the reasons for paying close attention to him.

The third and fourth chapters are "William James, Black Elk, and the Healing Act" and "James: 'Wild Beasts of the Philosophic Desert'" (the phrase is his). At the end of his life, James searched for radically different clues and vistas, and did not expect his academic colleagues to follow him, and they did not. He had so completely broken loose from Descartes' modernism and rationalism, his atomism and mentalism, that he stood on the brink of appropriating the most archaic of all attitudes toward the world: that of the shamanic healer.

James's notion of "pure experience" broached five years before "wild beasts" prepared for them: a primal level of experience, anterior to the distinction between subject and object (and mind and matter), in which the very same, numerically same, beings that move in their histories through the world also move in and through ours. This can happen *if* we dilate to them, if we are not panicked by their presence in us.

Let me reiterate: the numerically identical regenerative animal or plant—a bear, say—the very thing itself, can move into and reanimate our lives. This is a poetic and religious insight that is simultaneously a philosophical and medical one. The world is not "out there," but its presences move through us—constrictedly, or fluently and regeneratively.

Integral to this breakdown of mind/matter dualism is the surprising testimony of twentieth-century field theories in physics: Things are not self-contained within their surfaces, more or less self-sufficient, but are nodes of interfusing fields of energy and radically interpenetrate one another.

James puts us in touch with our immediate involvement with things, before abstraction, routinization, professionalization place things in neat boxes: selves versus others, mind versus matter, practical versus theoretical, and so on. This is the radically prereflective, somewhat trance-like, level of experiencing—the primal level, as on the First Day, its energy always new.

The fifth chapter follows apace, "James on Truth: The Preeminence of Body and World." Most of the many critics of James's theory of truth did not and do not appreciate how completely he bypassed Descartes, and modern mentalism, dualism, technology, and management theory. They are still lost in the spell of Europe and its congealed abstractions and tired methods. They assume that truth is something that occurs "in the mind" (or "in language"). It then, somehow, connects with "the external world." Not fitting into these concepts, James's "mistakes" about truth are caricatured by his critics.

But James has jettisoned all these ossified concepts. There is no "mind," and no "external world." Pure experience in its various articulations *constitutes* the world as we know it. So he must say that truth cannot correspond to something "out there," but is the fruitful leadings and workings of experience within the domain of the experienceable. *Truth is no mere subjective happening in our minds, but is comprised of those fruitful leadings and workings that hold the experienceable world together*—the only world we can know. Nothing less than that!

How can we say that truth is a correspondence between mind and world when the very meaning of "world" must be constituted by what leads us truly—that is, reliably, fruitfully—in forming our experience? James's thought is fresh, before the strictures and constrictions of analytic and scientistic philosophy in our century. It points to the future as well as to the indigenous and primal.

Next comes "John Dewey: Philosopher and Poet of Nature." James helps us grasp this complex and far-ranging thinker: When Dewey speaks of quality or qualia in experience, he is not talking about a sense datum, some sense qualia in some private consciousness—a mental patch of blue or blueness, say. But he means the felt quality of a whole lived situation that organisms can sense, some by human ones alone, but many others by nonhuman ones as well. Discrete sense data "in the mind" are not the primal building blocks of experience, as British empiricists inspired by Descartes had thought, but are the artifacts of an analysis that forgets itself.

Undoubtedly Dewey is one of the great synthesizers: the power of the horizonal, synoptic, and refreshingly connective seems to dwell in his genes. He builds broadly on the work of earlier American philosophers, and on Hegel, Aristotle, and Darwin, and most of the science of his time. Moreover, one of his greatest works is a premier treatise, *Art as Experience.* Although he seldom mentions indigenous thought and ways, he appreciates James's radical notion of prereflective experience, and his idea of "chemical union" with certain environments—ideas that point at least toward indigenous life and shamanic healing. It is tempting to say that if anyone can reassemble and reanimate the scattered members of the irruptive nineteenth and twentieth centuries and guide us in our turbulent New World, it is Dewey.

But great as he is, his vast world-that-is-thought exhibits tremors and strains. He suffers for us in the twentieth century the travail of trying to give birth to a livable world in the midst of cataclysmic encounter and abrupt transition. He would dare to connect science and poetry in a panoramic view of meaning, truth, and reality. That he was only partially successful illuminates better than anything else could just how without polestars and cardinal directions we are today.

He was uneasy about the philosopher-poets, the romantics, who influenced him. How could all this be squared with hard science? And he did not sufficiently acknowledge, I think, the influence of indigenous cultures on his thought. Nor did he adequately appreciate the need for ritual—ritual in concert with Nature—to stabilize and connect us. We delve into his nature poetry, works that he wrote with passion and concentration, and then threw out (to be retrieved by a "Boswellizing librarian" at Columbia University). We probe also into his attempts to reground and re-situate education.

I press on what I think weakest in Dewey: his failure to perceive how deeply huge remnants of mythic or primal consciousness remain with us. I press on this point not because it is weakest, but because primal or mythic consciousness is the chief theme I wish to develop in this book.

Following on this is "Body-Mind and Subconsciousness: Dewey and Tragedy." In some of his greatest thinking, the internal books of *Experience and Nature*, he departs radically from Descartes' equation mind = consciousness—and self-reflexive consciousness at that. For Dewey, mind is the vast and intricate minding that certain organisms do as they adjust to environments. It need not be conscious. Indeed, consciousness arises only with some fairly strong perturbation or glitch in the adjustment.

Dewey illuminates how consciousness, so easily losing itself in abstractions, loses touch with, or badly clutters-up and confuses, the subconscious and organic bases of its own activities. This is the breeding ground for failures and tragedies of countless varieties—dissociations, megalomania, delusions of persecution, and so on, which infest the post-Enlightenment world as much as the pre-. These grim musings sound discordant notes in the general mood still prevailing at the time Dewey writes, that is, the optimistic attitude of Yankee ingenuity, enterprise, the inevitability of scientific and technological progress.

We can hear the somber notes now. Most of Dewey's contemporaries did not or could not, did not dare to.

The book then turns to "Passion for Meaning: William Ernest Hocking's Religious-Philosophical Views." Hocking was a figure well known in his day, but practically forgotten now, and a great deal can be learned from this about the mass turning to "scientific" or "analytic" philosophy in this century (at least in academic philosophy).

Hocking, born in 1873, fourteen years after Dewey, was also a great synoptic thinker. But much more than Dewey, he emphasized poetic and religious insight. Not surprisingly for someone who wrote his dissertation under the author of *The Varieties of Religious Experience*, William James, Hocking's first and perhaps main fame came from his *The Meaning of God in Human Experience* (1912). This is a monumental investigation of the roots of our being, owing much to James and Josiah Royce, and also—not often realized—to one of the most famous exponents of phenomenology, Edmund Husserl. Phenomenology opens up the vastnesses of our immediate involvements in the world. As practiced—particularly by James as we will see—it is a broad pathway into indigenous or primal life.

Hocking's *The Meaning of God* is probably the most important systematic investigation and analysis of religious experience in this century. It is so broadly and generously based, and so intensely human, that it beckons us brightly into indigenous religious experience worldwide.

Nothing philosophical is alien to Hocking, not twentieth-century physics, or international law, or speculations about how the human body might be inserted into alternate systems of space-time and achieve a kind of immortality. Grasping for ways to categorize Hocking, one might call him a Nature mystic, one who could still smell the massive freshness and verdure and shadowed depth of the New World. And who, like Emerson—but much more systematically than that poet-philosopher—believed we can achieve an original relation to the universe.

We then turn to a dissident academic philosopher, deeply at home in immediate experiencing and in wilderness, Henry Bugbee. His *The Inward Morning,* published first in 1958 and for a third time in 1999, became an underground classic. It is a quiet and relentless defiance of the whole drift of scientific, technological, and Enlightenment thought that characterizes our age. He continues Emerson's and Thoreau's search for roots, and connects as well with the existential and phenomenological tradition, as exemplified particularly by Gabriel Marcel. The Hocking-Marcel relationship connects with the later Bugbee-Marcel conversation to pose a distinct alternative to modernism and scientism. It keeps the door open as well to a thoughtful rapprochement of European and indigenous modes of thought and life, a chance to heal the wound that has opened up worldwide between European culture and indigenous life—between entrenched European ways and primal needs, impulses, behaviors. It reminds us that current multiculturalism is not just a New Age fad. What is at stake, I believe, is our sanity.

Between Hocking's birth in 1873 and Richard Rorty's in 1931, a vast shift in philosophy—at least academic philosophy—occurs. It seems to be a part of the inexorable movement of modern science since the philosopher-scientists of the seventeenth century such as Descartes. Hocking in his later years, and Henry Bugbee throughout his life, are dramatic exceptions. The earlier American thinkers I have mentioned felt the pull of Nature throughout their whole selves, detoured around Descartes, and would never have assumed that natural science alone is sufficient to know Nature and to orient ourselves within Her (the capitalized noun and pronoun sound quaint and frivolous today—but, again, I use them because they retain the mythic force I want).[3]

But most academic philosophers today assume that science is sufficient to know Nature. For example, Willard van Orman Quine, an older contemporary of Rorty, whom some regard as the greatest living American philosopher, has sometimes been labeled a pragmatist, thus connecting him with James, Dewey, and others. For example, his important article, "Two Dogmas of Empiricism" (1950).[4] Its gist: when investigators encounter unexpected or anomalous events, Quine writes, they can either alter an empirical or scientific belief on the outer reaches of the field of knowledge, or reorder basic ideas and revise conceptual, analytic, or necessarily true beliefs closer to the center of the field. The criteria for deciding are, he thinks, pragmatic: which move will most fruitfully advance investigation?

But Quine assumes that the field of knowledge of Nature is constituted and exhausted by natural science, and science more or less as we know it. When some, like myself, wanted to run with the ball he seemed to have thrown us in that article, and not limit knowledge to science, he was appalled, and redirected his later work.

Quine's is a fateful departure from the earlier American thinkers of European extraction. They never would have asserted that knowledge is only the scientific sort. His work is part and parcel of the objectivism and fragmenting specialism and corrosive doubt about intuition and values that have characterized twentieth-century American life, ever more urbanized, ever more removed from any philosophy of Nature that could orient, ground, nourish a philosophy of life.

Quine pretty well returns to the seventeenth-century tradition that the thinkers I admire bypassed. His position invites the charge of scientism: Only science can know. But how can science know that *only* science can know? It would have to enter into all other possible ways of knowing Nature and know they get us nowhere—art, say, or everyday intuition, or religious experience. But with this venture science would exceed its competence and evidential base. With this, it becomes ideology—scientism, not science—and cannot know even that it can ask all the important questions.

Enter Richard Rorty into the sequence of thinkers, animated apparently by the age-old philosophic urge to sketch the big picture, supply a map, aid disoriented humankind. He leaves room for "nonscientific" philosophies, "edifying ones." But do they really know anything? That is a subject of debate among Rorty scholars. He has very little patience with anything remotely suggesting philosophy of Nature or romantic or poetic intuition of reality, "wild beasts of the philosophic desert"—what James sought. As true of many of "the enlightened" today, "romantic" and "intuition" become synonymous with the nostalgic, the softheaded, the self-indulgent. But the thinkers I admire were developing in trenchant and mordant fashion what they and we can, with good conscience, call a new realism.

Emerson asked, What is it that Nature would say? Rorty asserts, Only humans speak: he radically limits what "speaking" can mean. Emerson would think that Rorty leaves us bereft of auxiliaries, alone in a shrunken humanity because alienated from our animal and vegetable kin in Nature, lost in the latest verbalisms, uprooted from the earth and oblivious of the sky. That is, Rorty has torn himself loose from the matrix of myth, ritual, common enjoyments, and maturing life as this has been built up by humanity over many, many millennia within the regenerating earth. But Rorty asserts a kind of tragic and noble liberalism, and offers something to people without belief to believe in.

Rorty loves to tweak the noses of analytic and "scientific" philosophers, at least some of them sometimes. He says impish things when questioned about his lack of rigor on traditional issues like truth, such as: Establish a real liberalism, a real democracy, and truth will take care of itself. I mark the gulf that divides Rorty's neopragmatism from the pragmatism of his forebears, and ask if he isn't more under the spell of scientistic and modernist philosophy and its implicit dogmatisms than some like to think.

"Ways of Knowing" begins the last section of the book. It attempts to regain and develop the more balanced view of knowing and meaning that emerged in the earlier pragmatists who had not lost touch with primal experience. They are, as I said, both pragmatic and primal. Special emphasis is given to the cognitive powers of the fine arts, and the humanities—including philosophy—as the logical or natural center for maintaining some contact with Sources, for integrating knowledges and guiding us in living.

After the chapter on Rorty and neopragmatism, "William James's Prophetic Grasp of the Failures of Academic Professionalism" appears. As academic philosophy shrinks in importance nation and culture wide, we should ask ourselves what new forms of inquiry and communication nonanalytic philosophers in universities can discover and use.

The penultimate chapter belongs to Charles Peirce. A scientist, he was also our greatest logician. His greatness as a philosopher, and his profound influence on other philosophers, owes in large part to his seeing the limits of logic and science. Showing the influence of Emerson, Peirce roots again in instinct and in Nature.

The final chapter sounds a personal note—"Shamanism, Love, Regeneration." If thinking philosophically has no value for enduring the shocks of life, it has lost most of its reason for being, as people have commonly regarded this through the ages. I myself want to be both primal and pragmatic. I want to embrace, if I can, what our very ancient forebears discovered as they faced tragedies—particularly, the solacing of a mothering Earth that is always more than the particular times or places that hold us, always more than the chances that befall us. There are strange presences that buoy us and that come and go for no detectable reason.

I have fashioned an introduction, and have done so after writing most of the essays that follow. To think that even now I can exhibit fully the assumptions that drive my writing would be presumptuous. Some assumptions always remain inadequately examined within any project. For the assumptions must guide and limit the examination of the project, including the assumptions themselves.

I continue to study indigenous thought and practice. The assumption that philosophy develops mainly in the European tradition is constricting and misleading. This culminates in distinctly modern science, yes, but there is more to basic thought and life than this. Contemporary malaise is thick around us—addictions, allergies, burnouts, family disasters, alienation, dull or dramatic unhappiness, senseless violence.

As I said, thinkers of European extraction—Thoreau, Emerson, Peirce, James, Dewey, Hocking, Bugbee—had, together with their ancestors, settled into, and interacted with, this continent and its native populations for hundreds of years and are distinctly American. Yet they cannot substitute for harkening to indigenous Americans themselves. These think, act, and direct our attention with an authority that is bracing and surprising.

Getting to know the material broached in these essays, I see, is more than merely grasping how one statement follows from another. It is a matter of centering down into a level of bodily, global, and immediate experiencing that we each already know in a sense, but most of us have not learned to develop. The challenge is to think afresh. And to think yet again afresh, and again, and again—always to the limits of one's abilities. The challenge is to be ever willing to begin again.[5]

And all this is easier written than done! I try to expand my limits, but I am limited by my limited ability to know what my limits are! Oh, you say, but each has an identity; we are conscious, so we must have a basic grasp of our identity. No, if for no other reason than our Euro-culture, with its clinging psycho/physical dualism, has no single self-identical sense of identity. For John Locke, for example, my identity as a subject, mind, or person is given by my ability to remember what *I* did back then (so as a person I wasn't born!?). There's also the identity of my body as an object, what somebody else could identify as the same one. Typical of much European culture, Locke has fallen into the psycho/physical split, this hopelessly limited framing of alternatives. Missing in the account of self is my body as I immediately live it, in all its unencompassable possibilities of meaning-making— which is essential to anyone's sense of who they are. The lived body is neither simple subject nor simple object. Luckily, given the horizons opened up by our American thinkers, the psycho/physical split can be avoided. Whole selves, we can be so open to powerful beings and numinous surrounds that we participate in their being at a level of identity that boggles the conventional mind.

Notes

1. Terms that might retain, even for us, a mythic force I capitalize. I mean a sense of what is unconditioned and unconditionally powerful and valuable. Concerning The First Day, see Robert Lawlor, *Voices of the First Day: Awakening in the Aboriginal Dream Time* (Rochester, Vt.: Inner Traditions, 1991).

2. Concerning the avoidance of Descartes, also see Robert Neville's *The High Road Around Modernism* (Albany: State University of New York Press, 1992).

3. See my *Wild Hunger: The Primal Roots of Modern Addiction* (Lanham, Md., and New York: Rowman & Littlefield, 1998).

4. Quine's article has been reprinted numerous times, for example, in *Classics of Analytic Philosophy,* ed. Robert Ammerman (New York: McGraw-Hill, 1965).

5. See David Ehrenfeld, *Beginning Again: People and Nature in the New Millennium* (New York: Oxford University Press, 1993).

Black Elk, Thoreau, Emerson, and Their Aura

> Birds make their nests in circles, for theirs is the same religion as ours.
> —Black Elk

> All things good are wild and free.
> —Thoreau

> What is it that Nature would say?
> —Emerson

I realize the position I take up in this book is radical. It goes against entrenched invidious distinctions—that set Europe and progress over the indigenous and the primal, for a prime example. In the usual way of presenting pragmatic thought, its emphasis on possibility and futurity is focused. Look from roots to fruits—one of William James's aphorisms. But we will find that there are plenty of roots to be exposed as well. Indeed, we find that exposing roots reveals manifold enlivening possibilities for us today: ancient residua spring to new life. Let us survey the territory with its surprising levels of disclosure and unexpected confluences of traditions, neither bolting into it, nor bolting away from it.

Western science and technology have overrun the globe. Satellites flash Hollywood movies into antenna dishes in Outback Australia. World cultures begin to dissolve in the face of this power, real and illusory. Some will not dissolve easily. Think of tenacious ethnic, religious, national bonds cementing groups of Slavs in the Balkans—groups that attack one another with genocidal fury. Think of Islamic cultures—or at least great nodes within them—or of groups of Aborigines gamely returning to their Sources, their traditional ways of life.

The power of Western science and technology depends on a certain narrowed involvement in Nature. The ability to disclose hidden forces of Nature and to harness them to satisfy immediate aims and desires requires that only one aspect of Nature be considered: what in it is orderable and predictable and quantifiable. We must then appear to ourselves as those who order, predict, quantify, manage, control.

One might think that this scientific venture entails emotional detachment. But this is only half-true (see Chapter 10). For the narrower the involvement the more intense the emotions generated. And effective scientists and technologists counter this emotional involvement with a desire not to be duped which is equally intense and narrow. Western science and technology bore into the world. As Francis Bacon put it famously, we put Nature on the rack and force her to answer our questions.

Previously hidden forces and elements are revealed, and marvelous new powers accrue from harnessing these. But the cost is uprootage from a strangely familiar primal world and the intrinsically valuable skills and experiences through which human body-selves have evaluated themselves—have built themselves, and been built and empowered, for many millennia.

We need a deep level of description and analysis. Before we build ourselves, we are built. Before anything can belong to us, we belong to Nature. Our nervous systems evolved and took shape through adaptation over thousands of millennia in the enwombing pulse of Nature's matter. We know now that evolved in the brain is capacity to produce morphines, natural highs, to induce and reward stress and restoration, and all in synchrony with larger regenerative cycles of Nature, daily, monthly, seasonal, generational.[1]

There is a grain of truth in the view that western science and technology entail emotional detachment: Even when marvelously revealing certain sectors of the universe, science and technology's intercourse with the world is so narrow and self-involved that the full gamut of emotions and instinctual adjustments that enliven indigenous peoples' habitual involvement with the world are masked-out and suppressed. The feeling of belonging to the land and of being cared for by it—cared for if we are sufficiently aware and skilled, reverent, careful, fortunate.

For indigenous populations, feelings of being enlarged, enlivened, and oriented stand and resonate in direct ratio to the breadth and depth of their care and celebration within the sensuously evident world. They feel this power that many of us no longer imagine. If we could, it would drive out mere abstractions, high-flown projects, as well as paper doubts, as Charles Peirce put it—doubts and inhibitions that clutter and trip-up our rampaging modern world.

The North American holy man and thinker Black Elk reported to John G. Neihardt the great vision that came to him as a boy:

> Then I saw ahead the rainbow flaming above the tepee of the Six Grandfathers, built and roofed with cloud and sewed with thongs of lightning; and underneath it were all the wings of the air and under them the animals and the men. All these were rejoicing, and thunder was like happy laughter. . . . [A]nd I saw the Six Grandfathers sitting in a row, with their arms held toward me and their hands palms out, and behind them in the cloud were faces thronging, without number, of the people yet to be.

> "He has triumphed!" cried the six together, making thunder. And as I passed before them there, each gave again the gift that he had given me before—the cup of water and the bow and arrows, the power to make live and to destroy; the white wing of cleansing and the healing herb; the sacred pipe; the flowering stick. And each one spoke in turn from west to south, explaining what he gave as he had done before, and as each one spoke he melted down into the earth and rose again; and as each did this, I felt nearer to the earth.[2]

Any commentary seems impossible, for most very late twentieth-century prose occupies a different realm of being and presencing: it presupposes the "objective realm" as something divided from "the merely subjective"; it takes the division of the physical from the psychical completely for granted. Any attempt to move Black Elk's words into either of these areas will mangle them and make them look absurd. Take the common practice of many North American indigenous peoples to sing the sun up at dawn. European—now North Atlantic—mentality gives this short shrift: "Simply experiment. Refuse to do the ceremony and see if the sun needs our efforts to rise."

But for us the sun now is only a globe of gas, and, of course, as such, it does not need our efforts to rise in the sky. But this patent truth obscures another older, broader one: that our lives, evolved over millions of years in

Nature, have taken shape with the sun, and that if we are to rise with the power of its rising we must celebrate that rising. We must do our part.

Black Elk noted that both his people and birds built their abodes in circles: "Birds make their nests in circles for theirs is the same religion as ours." With this he voiced the paganism or "pantheism" that had so revolted and frightened Christianized Europeans who appeared in numbers on this continent in the sixteenth century [195]. They would think, "Only subhuman beings could believe such a thing, only they so benighted as to know nothing of the metaphysical and moral gulf that divides human beings from the rest of creation, divides the favored few set down on the Sixth Day of Creation from the many and sundry created on the Fifth and preceding."

But not everyone of European ancestry repeated automatically the mind-set of their fellows.

By now Thoreau and Emerson have been pretty well domesticated. So often have their writings been included in textbooks and anthologies, their rebellious reaction against scientific Enlightenment has been sanded down and softened. "Isn't it charming to see them go native." But they foretold the major and perhaps intractable conflicts appearing now at the close of our millennium: the juggernaut of science and technology in service not just of pure knowledge but of money-profit and immediate gratification. How could this juggernaut possibly be coordinated with the full gamut of needs, emotional life, and latent powers of earth and earthlings built up and funded over countless millennia in Nature? It cannot be. The demand for immediate gratification amounts to an addictive and driven mode of life.

Thoreau and Emerson sense that the distance in which Europeans think that they stand from the rest of creation has spawned an alienation and loneliness that will break our hearts even as we expand our apparent power. They endeavor to think and act their way back into an intimacy with the world that Europeans have almost completely forgotten. We must reclaim an original relation to things, Emerson reiterates; each person must write his own Bible. He was deadly serious, not merely spooky or entertaining, when he described the direct impact and providential quality of Nature.

Here lies our attenuated and nearly lost bond with indigenous peoples. In the freshness of truly immediate experience, the line between subject and object is not yet drawn; object is not set over against subject. *I* do not regard the other simply *as* other. Regard floats in the situation: strangely—very strangely—but it can be detected if we are in touch with immediate involvement—each element regards feelingly all the others. Emerson asserts that the woods will be experienced as haunted, as if some activity had been suspended just before we entered, and we are being watched.[3] He resonates to vegetables, plants, and trees: "I have no hostility to nature, but a child's love of it. I expand and live in the warm day like corn and melons" [70]. And again, "The greatest delight which the fields and woods minister is the suggestion of an occult relation between man and the vegetable. I am not alone and unacknowledged. They nod to me, and I to them. The waving of the boughs in the storm is new to me and old. It takes me by surprise, and yet is not unknown. Its effect is like that of a higher thought or better emotion coming over me" [39].

Thoreau likewise reclaims indigenous intimacy and at-one-ness when he describes the way the world lives within him, authorizing him, humanizing him, that is, showing him his vital place within the community of all beings and all materials. "I hear the sound of Heywood's Brook falling into Fair Haven Pond—inexpressibly refreshing to my senses—it seems to flow through my very bones—I hear with insatiable thirst—it allays some sandy heat in me—it affects my circulations—methinks my arteries have sympathy with it. What is it I hear but the pure water falls within me, in the circulation of my blood—the streams that fall into my heart."[4]

But to say, as I just did, that this experience shows him his place within the community of beings is, though well intentioned, somewhat misleading. For it may suggest, again, European-scientific dualism and distantiation, even atomism. As if it were merely nice, or made one feel good, to know one's place in the community of beings! As if the world as one immediately takes it in and resonates in it is not organically fused into one's very being. *That*—or something very like that—is what Thoreau is really saying.

We must try to realize how outrageous all this seemed to very many of Emerson's and Thoreau's contemporaries, and, I think, how outrageous this still is to many of us. But which is so hard for us to acknowledge, given both the domestication of our own "Nature writers," and the degree to which we are inured to European objectification, dualism, distancing—our insulation, shielding, and straitened nurturance taken so completely for granted we are unaware of it.

But we are needy and vulnerable, and we do belong in a vast community even when we forget it, which is why so many secretly exult when a great storm shuts down cities and some of our technological marvels. At last we are where we belong—in community, in interdependency, even when our delight is sheepish and we don't know how to speak our ecstasy.

It may help us to speak it if we go to more recent American philosophers, those able to recontact and articulate in cold prose (for the most part) the assumptions of European science and technology within which we work, but which are too close for most of us to thematize and to reassess. Without these assumptions acknowledged and put in their place and critically reevaluated, we must remain as most of us are: vaguely dissatisfied and alienated. Either vaguely excited by what Black Elk, Emerson, Thoreau, and James say—but not knowing how to weave it into our everyday behavior. Or simply muted and numbed to what needs to be touched and spoken beyond our scientific-technological-commercial assumptions' constrictions, but can't be. Perhaps only a vague restiveness and dissatisfaction are felt.

Feelings unarticulated and suppressed require addictive distractions to keep them anesthetized. They get them. Take the pervasive addiction to noise, to constant background electronic babble or Muzak that partially conceals the emptiness, an emptiness we would not have when silence encompasses us if we were situated vitally within a natural piety and world-story that commanded commitment.

A thinker living within the aura of Thoreau and Emerson—and subliminally perhaps of Black Elk—and peculiarly fit for the task of awakening and reweaving a whole life is the scientist-artist-primitive-sophisticate William James, one of the strangest and most complex human beings. We might think of Socrates, likewise roiled within divergent demands of his humanness, looking both backward and forward in time, trying to make sense of a world caught in transition, but which most of his contemporaries resisted acknowledging, wanting to be comforted in the tried and true.

James is peculiarly fit to speak for us today because he suffered in his own person the diremptions and dislocations that afflict so many now. Trained as a scientist, he could not connect what science told him about who he was with what he needed to think about himself. He needed to believe he was free to choose and to make a difference in his life; science told him he was determined by circumstances and physical makeup. So severe was the tension that he suffered a psychological breakdown after receiving an M.D. degree from Harvard. He had seen a catatonic patient in an asylum, and so identified with him that he wrote, "He sat there like a sort of sculptured Egyptian cat or Peruvian mummy, moving nothing but his black eyes and looking absolutely non-human. . . . *That shape am I*, I felt, potentially. . . . [I]t was if something solid within my breast gave way entirely, and I became a mass of quivering fear."[5]

James was willing to try anything to escape his crippling terror and depression. He began to explore the domain of possibility. He enrolled himself in possibilities. He so challenged himself that after a year he thought himself, tore himself, out of bed.

From this near-death experience emerged, first, a sort of American existentialism before the name. For he concluded that *if* he were free, then, logically speaking, the first act of freedom should be to freely believe in free will![6] To *wait* for evidence of *freedom* is absurd. Since science could not really decide either way, he freely believed in his freedom. He got up. Second, he remained ever open to psychical research and to reports of religious experiences. Third, he spent the rest of his life as philosopher formulating an account of the world that would rally himself and others from stupefying, demoralizing fears of impotence and meaninglessness. Along with Nietzsche and a few others, he foresaw the advent of nihilism and despair, almost as if he and they could foretell the plays of Samuel Beckett in the midst of our century: plays in which characters live capped in ashcans, or buried up to their necks in sand, or paralyzed "Waiting for Godot." In what is most central for us in this book, James uncovered primal resources for living, ways to find or re-find "feelings of excited significance in things," the originals of all value.[7] Because of his powerful abilities to describe our immediate involvements, he can be called an existential phenomenologist.

So my essays on William James—an opening for those of European ancestry to the most ancient shamanic practices. Only such an approach, I am convinced—one that takes the bull by the horns—can properly frame and contextualize his much debated and misunderstood pragmatic theory of truth. Misunderstood because, as I've said in the Introduction, critics assumed that he was writing within the assumptions of "scientifically respectable" dualism and "realism." He was not. He had come up with the truly radical metaphysical view of pure experience, experience pure because not yet sorted into physical or mental compartments. This is a pivotal, world-historical insight, blooming in the aura of the earlier thinkers. If we put a label on it, we should call it direct realism, as has Hilary Putnam.

James had discovered a primal level anterior to the very distinction between subject and object. He is poised to make philosophical sense of ancient shamanic procedures in which the healers open themselves and their clients to powers of paradigmatically regenerative beings. In his last work—*A Pluralistic Universe*—he flirts seriously with Gustav Fechner's hypotheses concerning plant souls, animal souls, even earth soul.

Though published and readily available for ninety years, this material has seemed so strange to most philosophers and philosophical thinkers that it has not been given the attention it greatly deserves. Placing him in a context primed by Thoreau, Emerson, and Black Elk helps direct this attention. Centering and recentering ourselves at this spontaneous and prereflective level, we may gradually feel our way back into our own sources in Nature. For voluntary attention to be sanely directed and maintained, it must be cradled and oriented by what James called the involuntary level. So cradled and nourished, we may create possibility, and create it so that it abides with us and transforms our lives.

John Dewey, like James, has suffered the fate of fame: he is read for what he is famous for, that is, for what conventional others of European ancestry could appreciate in him at the time. These others are still caught in the spell of Europe. They broadcast a gravely limited view of John Dewey (and Dewey's own limits are not clearly seen). For example, his idea of the domain of organism-environment interactivity, which is adaptive and mindful, but not accessible to voluntary turnings of consciousness—that domain has been pretty well ignored by philosophers who wish to develop only what Dewey says about conscious, deliberate intelligence, problem solving, getting ahead. They have not considered his formative work with the psycho-bio-therapist F. M. Alexander, and how we must allow the body to take the lead if we are to form potentially fruitful, transformative hypotheses about body-mind or body-self.[8]

Nor have they considered Dewey's Nature poetry, which gives important clues concerning our engulfment in Nature. Even salient sections of his monumental *Logic: The Theory of Inquiry* (1938) go practically unread. Right off the bat, he writes that without a sense of the pervasive emotional, sensory, and moody quality of the situation within which inquiry originates, searching will have closed-off potential horizons before it begins.

Here he advances his version of what Continental thinkers call the hermeneutical circle. But more to the point, we hear an echo of the epigraph above from Black Elk: Birds build their nests in circles, for theirs is the same religion as ours. That is, for Dewey, human finitude dictates that there is no privileged, self-certifying place to found and to start one's inquiry. All we have is a lived coherence of experience, kinship, existence within which hypotheses emerge that are either fruitful or not. We have to wait and see if a hypothesis pays off, or if perhaps a more fruitful coherence might have taken shape behind our backs and is now available.

For all our distinctive intellectual power as humans, we no more than the other animals can step outside the world to gain a vantage point on the whole. Given surprising breakthroughs of awareness in the past, it is very probably true that more sorts of things are going on in any actual situation now than we can imagine. We might exhibit a conscious piety or trust that we see birds and animals exhibiting unconsciously. Emerson in "The Transcendentalist": "I mean we have yet no man who has leaned entirely on his character . . . who, trusting in his sentiments, found life made of miracles; who, working for universal aims, found himself fed, he knew not how. . . . Only in the instinct of the lower animals we find the suggestion of the methods of it, and something higher than our understanding. The squirrel hoards nuts and the bee gathers honey, without knowing what they do, and they are thus provided for without selfishness or disgrace" [245]. Dewey's natural piety links him, along with Emerson, to indigenous peoples, a linkage seldom or ever appreciated.

In William Ernest Hocking and Henry Bugbee, we still feel the fresh, electric aura of the earlier thinkers, but in Richard Rorty, hardly at all. In my article on our interesting, but I think conflicted and self-interrupted, contemporary, I try to re-collect and reanimate the aura by sketching the limits of scientific investigation as well as of merely verbal exercises. If insights and practices of primal peoples are retrieved to some extent, our ecologies may round themselves out as we live in our environments, and as we ponder the conditions of flourishing life. As long as European psycho/physical dualism reigns supreme, all our interest in "the environment" will never get to the heart of our crisis.

How do we keep reflecting on the prereflective, spontaneous life in which we feel most alive—and do so without withering it? How do we avoid the ruts of habitual life and of prejudices so profound that we don't imagine we are prejudiced? It may help to keep in mind a startling fact: Emerson, for example, and his more immediate ancestors, came to this continent as members of the conquering waves of Europeans. Black Elk speaking to John Neihardt in 1931 speaks out of a broken heart and a broken nation. Obviously, the two thinkers differ in many salient respects. They do, nevertheless, agree on a certain level, and this agreement emphasizes, startlingly, how fundamental that level is. They both believe we live in a broken world. Just what is it that's broken?

Relating finally the great vision he experienced at age nine, Black Elk tells Neihardt, "Then I was standing on the highest mountain, and round about beneath me was the whole hoop of the world. . . . And I saw that the sacred hoop of my people was one of many hoops that made one circle, wide as daylight and as starlight, and in the center grew one mighty flowering tree to shelter all the children of one mother and one father. And I saw that it was holy" [43].

Black Elk's lifetime coincides with the destruction of his people's way of life in Nature. Out of great suffering he declares that his nation's hoop is broken. But Emerson asserts that we all are broken. As indigenous peoples have lost their orientation in Nature through being conquered, so we, in conquering, have further lost ours.[9] As Rousseau had noted before them both, we no longer have fatherlands or motherlands. We no longer relate to the land as ours in the most intimate way, as our home in which we have been born and that has been given us. We are broken and homeless. In one of his first great utterances, Emerson writes in "Nature," "Miller owns this field, Locke that, and Manning the woodland beyond. But none of them owns the landscape. There is a property in the horizon which no man has but he whose eye can integrate all the parts. . . . This is the best part of these men's farms, yet to this their warranty-deeds give no title. . . . To speak truly, few adult persons can see nature. Most do not see the sun" [38].

The horizon is Emerson's version of Black Elk's vision of "the whole hoop of the world," of the cosmos, extending "as far as starlight." For the horizon is double faced: pointing inward toward all we can directly perceive and on its outward face toward *everything* else. If we fail to grasp it, we fail to grasp ourselves and the possibilities that can magnetize us, for the horizon, Emerson says, is "somewhat as beautiful as [our] own nature" [39]. Without Nature we lose the ecstatic amplitude and pulsing heart of our own nature. The horizon, really perceived, draws us out into the more, the not-yet, the unknown. Losing touch with it, we lose touch with ourselves and fall to pieces, obviously or subtly.

Emerson sees beyond the plots of land owned by Miller, Locke, and Manning. He sees what environs and holds it all together: the horizon, the cosmos, that to which their warranty deeds give them no title. This belongs to anyone who can be caught up ecstatically in it, who can see with their hearts as well as their eyes the sun and the stars and the wild places.

But, of course, we don't really own the horizon, make it one of our belongings. It is essential to our ecstatical nature that we belong to it. Emerson: "In the presence of nature a wild delight runs through the man, in spite of real sorrows. Nature says—he is my creature, and maugre all his impertinent griefs, he shall be glad with me" [38]. Emerson is regaining initial contact with our earliest ancestors, the hunter-gatherers who first appeared in prehuman form two and a half million years ago. They belonged to Nature in the most profound of all possible senses. As I've said, our nervous systems, and regenerative and immune systems, were formed by Nature as our ancestors adapted and developed. Our primal needs were formed by Nature, as were our primal means, our skills, to satisfy the needs. We belonged to a vast community of freely roaming, interdependent beings.

With the agricultural revolution ten thousand years ago, human identity-building shifted on its foundations. We settled down on plots of ground and gathered possessions of all sorts to be stored and protected. Instead of identity being predicated on what we belonged to, vast Nature, it shifted toward what belonged to us. Probably, I think, with the loss of hunter-gatherer cultures and competencies a generalized paranoia settled on human life. Yes, life had always been dangerous, but primal needs and skills formed and fostered by and in Nature allowed our earliest forebears to feel gratitude at the mere fact of survival. Given a modicum of good fortune, Mother Nature typically did provide. Life did not depend on protecting goods, we and they sitting ducks for marauders. Though it is extremely difficult for us today to conceive, we may very well have lost with the advent of agriculture a primal sense of mobility, adventure, and competence, a sense of belonging to, and being protected by, Nature. Thus ensued what I take to be the generalized paranoia.

Out of this basal Emersonian insight—so close to the life and ways of indigenous peoples of this and other continents—can be seen to flow some of the most important themes of James, Dewey, Hocking, and Bugbee. Take for now just James: He knew that we belong to Nature in ways that vastly exceed the scope of any actual or possible consciousness. In his *Varieties of Religious Experience,* the section on conversion, he noted that many are dogged by feelings of incompleteness. Lost from consciousness today is even any clear ideal of coherence and unity: we do not know what to strive for or aim at. So what must we do? Relax and trust, and that for us is greatly difficult.

> A man's conscious wit and will, so far as they strain towards the ideal, are aiming at something only dimly and inaccurately imagined. Yet all the while the forces of more organic ripening within him are going on towards their own prefigured result, and his conscious strainings are letting loose subconscious allies behind the scenes, which in their way work towards rearrangement; and the rearrangement towards which all these deeper forces tend is pretty surely definite, and definitely different from what he consciously conceives and determines. It may consequently be actually interfered with (*jammed,* as it were

like the lost word when we seek too energetically to recall it), by his voluntary efforts slanting from the true direction. [172]

With this we witness one of the most spectacular attempts by anyone of European ancestry to grasp the obsessiveness and drivenness of North Atlantic culture, and how they shut us off from the regenerative powers of Nature that formed us in the first place. It helps us grasp how sick we seemed to indigenous peoples.

On the matter of ownership, Emerson and his spiritual progeny sound the abyss that divided insurging Europeans from native Americans. The latter were essentially hunter-gatherers, those who had not changed much since our earliest direct forebears on Earth, hundreds of thousands of years ago in the Paleolithic age. They could not conceive the possibility of owning plots of land. It would be quite literally to cut up the body of their Mother, Mother Earth. To plow would be to rape Her, to harvest grain would be to clip off Her hair and humiliate Her.

Most Europeans, on the other hand, derive unquestioningly from the intervening agricultural, pastoral, or Neolithic age. And as if that were not enough, the industrial age also (we of course now live in the electronic as well). Life becomes basically sedentary. The boundaries of owned and culti- vated land are edges and walls; there are no easeful translations across them into a companionable beyond, no friendly relations with wild Nature. That is only terrifying wilderness, and the only hope—and indeed the tenacious and desperate belief—is that somewhere beyond the horizon a transcendent Deity, friendly to the nation, rules over everything.

Whereas for indigenous Americans the ownership of land was inconceiv- able, for European-Americans nonownership was so. For most indigenous Americans—at least after awhile—Europeans were pale, ill, or crazy; for most Europeans indigenous Americans were from the first benighted primitives, savages. Black Elk spoke of gold, that beautiful mineral, as the metal that drove them crazy. Theodore Roosevelt believed that our great land could not be left as a hunting preserve for savages. At the end of our century, we are trying to think more comprehensively and sanely about our place in the world. But dualistic, mechanistic, grasping, and detaching habits of thought are deeply entrenched, and we are more mired in them than most of us are able to imagine.

Primal experience is very similar from culture to culture, although for Europeans—dividing ourselves ever more from our Paleolithic past—it is generally harder to tap. Drawing directly from Norse legend, Emerson speaks of the World-tree, Yggdrazil. Ygg equals egg, the Source of all things, the Tree that roots in dark Earth, thrusts upward in its trunk, and exfoliates through the heavens.

Pragmatically and primally put, Emerson's horizon and Black Elk's one circle, wide as daylight and as starlight, amount to about the same thing. So does Emerson's Yggdrazil and the indigenous American's great flowering tree at the center that shelters all the children of one mother and one father. And both see that the whole is holy.

As Black Elk laments that his nation's hoop is broken, that the Tree no longer flowers, and that the vision of the encompassing hoop of the cosmos is broken, so perceptive Emerson in "The American Scholar" laments that "[t]he state of society is one in which the members have suffered amputation from the trunk, and strut about so many walking monsters—a good finger, a neck, a stomach, but never a man" [84].

The parallel between this Euro-American and this indigenous American is closer than most have discerned. If we can hold this before our sight and feeling, we may be jolted out of the ruts of everyday life and the compulsions of scientism.

We stand on the brink of a future that entices, beckons, and troubles. Our primal and pragmatic philosophers converge toward indigenous views of cosmic kinship. Not only this. As I mentioned in the first essay, twentieth-century physics can be read as converging toward this, too. Gone are assumptions of seventeenth-century science: matter as inert and always conserved; elements as fundamentally and irreducibly individual, and the whole a mere set of elements; the world as a machine with easily locatable and substitutable parts. Thinking within the successes of relativistic and field theories in physics, and on the verge of the eruptive formulations of quantum theory, A. N. Whitehead speaks of the intertwined fallacies of misplaced concreteness and simple location that dog us from the past.[10] Quantum physicist David Bohm writes that certain entities that have originally been combined show a peculiar nonlocal relationship, "which can best be described as a non-causal connection of things that are far apart."[11]

There are possibilities for convergence and reconciliation that may be more than we dare imagine. Our life seems to be a race against time (yet we must relax, too!). How can we think, feel, and act communally in time to stave off disaster from weapons and other sources of mass destruction? These are held in the hands of individuals and nations still in the grip of paranoid fantasies—largely Neolithic—and ancient grievances concerning encroaching and oppressive others.

How can we, obsessed with management and control, trust the trance-like and visionary level of immediate involvement in interfusing Nature adumbrated by Emerson, Thoreau, William James, and ecstatically recalled by Black Elk? It seems too much to ask.

Black Elk evokes nonlocality in space and in time:

> It was a clear evening with no wind, and it seemed that everything was listening hard to hear something. While I was looking over there I felt that somebody wanted to talk to me. So I stood up and began to sing the first song of my vision.
>
> "Behold! A sacred voice is calling you!
> All over the sky a sacred voice is calling!" [178]

"Something," "somebody," "a sacred voice," "all over the sky," "listening." All this suggests the conversion experience that completes us, according to James. We cease trying to pick out individuals in the focus of consciousness. But rather allow tendrils of tendency in the fringes to reach out beyond ordinary consciousness altogether into a fittingness and feeling of rightness in "the more." Black Elk trusts a strange feeling in his body that comes up from the Earth through his feet and legs. This relaxation lets loose subconscious allies that work behind the scenes to promote a more organic ripening as their own prefigured but inarticulable end. Is the completion of self a return to our belonging in the matrix of Nature that formed us before any human consciousness was possible?

Nonlocality in space and time! Unexpected connections between primal experience and twentieth-century physics. Black Elk speaks:

> And as I looked . . . and wept, a strange light leaped upward from the ground close by—a light of many colors, sparkling, with rays that touched the heavens. Then it was gone, and in the place from whence it sprang an herb was growing and I saw the leaves it had. And as I was looking at the herb so that I might not forget it there was voice that woke me, and it said: "Make haste! Your people need you!". . . Then the daybreak star came slowly, very beautiful and still; and all around it there were clouds of baby faces smiling at me, the faces of the people not yet born. [186–87]

He sees in his vision what he will later find and use "in the real world" to cure the boy, the four-rayed herb for his first healing.

But, of course, what is "the real world"? Independent existences pushing one another causally-mechanically? Or an interfusing universe of cosmic kinship, "Circular power returning into itself," as Emerson has it? [85].

Astonishing in its contemporaneity (or is it ahead of us?) Black Elk speaks of his vision and its reenactment for the people:

> Then the Grandfathers behind me sang another sacred song from my vision.
>
> > "At the center of the earth, behold a four-legged.
> > They have said this to me!"
>
> And as they sang, a strange thing happened. My bay pricked up his ears and raised his tail and pawed the earth, neighing long and loud to where the sun goes down. And the four black horses raised their voices, neighing long and loud, and the whites and the sorrels and the buckskins did the same; and all the other horses in the village neighed, and even those out grazing in the valley and on the hill slopes raised their heads and neighed together. Then suddenly, as I sat there looking at the cloud, I saw my vision yonder once again—the tepee built of cloud and sewed with lightning, the flaming rainbow door and, underneath, the Six Grandfathers sitting, and all the horses thronging in their quarters; and also there was I myself upon my bay before the tepee. I looked about me and could see that what we then were doing was like a shadow cast upon the earth from yonder vision in the heavens, so bright it was and clear. I knew the real was yonder and the darkened dream of it was here. [168–69]

The sacred tepee and their grouping on the ground is paralleled and immensely enhanced in the sky. Lodged within mechanistic, and common-sensical, categories of thought, this will appear to be merely hallucination brought on, probably, by sleep deprivation, hunger, and extreme emotionality. "One thing cannot be in two places at once." But we might dare to imagine other possibilities. Perhaps it is under these extreme conditions that we best see certain features of reality that are usually eclipsed in the deadening glare of routinized, everyday life. Among them: the actual interfusion of things as nodes of interlacing fields of energy, and that one can be so ecstatically at home in the sky that one is as much—or more—*there* as positioned on the earth. We are multiply positioned. This should be related to nonlocality and superposition in quantum physics. And recall Emerson: "In the distant line of the horizon, man beholds somewhat as beautiful as his own nature."[12] We are here *and* there.

Perhaps this is the time for us all to try to achieve what the Western Apaches call "smoothness of mind," and its coordinate traits, "steadiness and resilience."[13] We need steady, resilient, enduring imagination, effort, empathy.

A word about Black Elk and the provenance of his thought and action. It is widely thought that by the time of his 1931 interviews with John Neihardt he had been so long converted to Christianity that his is not a reliable account of his people's ways. It is true that he had been for some years a Catholic catechist among his own people. We can only suppose that he was sincere (trusting our own sense of "sincerity" to reveal reality).

Raymond J. DeMallie has thrown light on this complex and hitherto obscure situation.[14] He has published the complete transcript of the interviews, situating them in their cultural setting, and provides a lengthy, generally orienting, and highly judicious introduction. It seems that Black Elk believed that the only possible hope for his people's survival was to go along with the Christianizing invaders.

But an amazing thing happened when Black Elk, already in his sixties, met the poet John Neihardt. A great affinity abruptly formed between the two men, a strange chemistry. Black Elk realized that this might be his last chance to communicate his great vision and earlier practice to the world. He had felt burdened for decades by the undelivered message.

To the appalled regard of the Christian authorities of that locale, Black Elk "reverted"—at least for the time it took him to tell his story. A surge of energy connected him with his earlier life. When, for example, comparing his people's round dwellings with birds' nests, he said, and it bears repeating, "Birds build their nests in circles, for theirs is the same religion as ours" [195], he was uttering a way of being in the world that cannot be found in the whole Jewish-Greco-Christian tradition. (Though vague hints of this survive in a few of Jesus's parables and in some pre-Socratic Greek thinkers.)

But what about portions of the original transcripts omitted by Neihardt? These can be found in DeMallie's patient reconstructions, and they are not unimportant. Take for example, "the blue man." Like most shamans, Black Elk "extracted" disease entities from patients by drawing or sucking them out of the body. When he did so, he sometimes saw the small "blue man" swimming in a cup into which he expectorated.

But Neidhardt is true to his purpose: to help Black Elk communicate himself to the vast world. That is, the average North Atlantic reader can only conclude that the shaman practices trickery: "he brings something hidden in his mouth to the 'cure' and then produces it, claiming to have extracted it from the sick person's body." Such an impoverished and abstract conception of symbols the European or average white American brings with himself!

Neihardt is a canny reporter, and I take his *Black Elk Speaks* very seriously.[15]

If we allow ourselves to be interrupted, to be slowed down or blocked unexpectedly, perhaps we can begin afresh—ever awaken to the magnitude of Earth and our dull burrowing and hiding places within it—as well as possible points of vantage, releasement, wakefulness? Let us hope.

Notes

1. See my *Wild Hunger: The Primal Roots of Modern Addiction* (Lanham, Md., and New York: Rowman & Littlefield, 1998).

2. John G. Neihardt, *Black Elk Speaks* (Lincoln: University of Nebraska Press, 1979 [1932]), 44–45. *Subsequent references to Black Elk refer to this book, with pages marked in brackets.*

3. "History," in *Ralph Waldo Emerson: Selected Essays*, ed. Larzar Ziff (New York: Penguin Books, 1982), 158–59. *Subsequent references to Emerson are to this book, with pages marked in brackets.* For Emerson's influence on C. S. Peirce, see Chapter 13.

4. His journal, July 11, 1851 [6:562], quoted in Sharon Cameron, *Writing Nature: Henry Thoreau's Journal* (Chicago: University of Chicago Press, 1985), 31–32.

5. *The Varieties of Religious Experience*, Lectures VI and VII. In this case, I use the critical edition: William James, *The Varieties of Religious Experience: A Study in Human Nature*, *The Works of William James* (Cambridge, Mass.: Harvard University Press, 1985 [1902]), 134. *In cases in which I use another, older, more widely available edition of a William James work, I nevertheless cite the critical edition at the close of the note.* The passages from *Varieties* used in this essay are also excerpted and pointed up in my anthology, *The Essential Writings of William James* (Albany: State University of New York Press, 1984), 232–33. *When a first-cited edition is cited again, page references to that edition are inserted in brackets in my text.*

6. From *Talks to Teachers on Psychology and to Students on Some of Life's Ideals* (New York: Henry Holt & Co., 1915 [1899]), the section "The Will," 83 ff. Also excerpted in my anthology, *The Essential Writings of William James*, 42–43. William James, *Talks to Teachers on Psychology—and to Students on Some of Life's Ideals*, *The Works of William James* (Cambridge, Mass.: Harvard University Press, 1983 [1899]) (hereafter cited as "critical edition"), 101 ff.

7. "On a Certain Blindness in Human Beings," in *Talks to Teachers on Psychology and to Students on Some of Life's Ideals*, 229 ff., and excerpted in my anthology, 332–33. Critical edition, 132 ff.

8. See my account in *Wild Hunger*, 157.

9. Australian Hannah R. Bell documents how destruction of Aboriginal cultures destroys the environment in which we all must live—it is self-destructive. *Men's Business/Women's Business* (Rochester, Vt.: Inner Traditions, 1998), 160–61, 171–72. Concerning the theme that in conquering we are conquered, see Marc H. Ellis, *Unholy Alliance: Religion and Atrocity in Our Time* (Minneapolis: Fortress Press, 1997), xvi–xvii: "Some indigenous aspects of Judaism and Christianity have been covered over and transformed, just as Jewish and Christian understandings and images intermingle. It should not surprise us then that, even though conquered by Judaism and Christianity, indigenous religiosity retains aspects of its own life that may ultimately reorder both religions." This reordering is occurring, I believe.

10. See Victor Lowe, *Understanding Whitehead* (Baltimore: Johns Hopkins University Press, 1962), 190–91.

11. *Wholeness and the Implicate Order* (London: Routledge & Kegan Paul, 1980), 175.

12. In *Ralph Waldo Emerson*, ed. Larzar Ziff, 39. In 1994, the distinguished physicist Roger Penrose published *Shadows of the Mind* (New York: Oxford University Press, 1994). He speculates that to understand the noncomputational and immediate quality-feeling powers of mind we need a new quantum physics of the brain that would grasp how neurons' microtubules generate quantum fields of interactivity. Nonlocal phenomena may occur in the brain as it connects in regenerative loops with the rest of the world, and visions such as Black Elk's may be a vivid display of our powers, our full exercise. When Black Elk's perception is especially excited and he is ecstatically dilated, the earth around him is experienced to be also in the sky. As the universe pours through that node of itself that is his organism, why shouldn't there be this mixing of the perceived earth and sky? One element or event may be superpositioned onto another.

13. Keith H. Basso, *Wisdom Sits in Places: Landscape and Language Among the Western Apache* (Albuquerque: University of New Mexico Press, 1996), 126, 139.

14. *The Sixth Grandfather: Black Elk's Teachings Given to John G. Neihardt* (Lincoln: University of Nebraska Press, 1984).

15. Concerning Black Elk's authority, and the Indian Reorganization Act of 1934, Vine Deloria Jr. writes, "Traditional Indians could no longer be placed in prison for practicing old tribal ways. Ceremonies began to be practiced openly, and there were still enough older Indians alive that a great deal of tribal religious traditions were regained. The Great Black Elk, today perhaps the best remembered of the Sioux holy men, was still alive in 1934. It is said that he had frequent conferences with the holy men from other parts of the tribe living on different reservations." *God Is Red: A Native View of Religion—The Classic Work Updated* (Golden, Colo.: Fulcrum Publishing Co., 1994), 240. Note also a fundamental point made by Deloria: the communal or tribal nature of religious experience for traditional Indians. Only by knowing this, can we explain how Black Elk's personal vision was not fully real (!) until he had enacted it for his people. "There is no demand for a personal relationship to a personal savior. Cultural heroes are representative of community experience. They stand as classic figures such as Deganiwidah, Sweet Medicine, Black Elk, Smohalla . . . ; but they never become the object of individual attention as to the efficacy in either the facts of their existence or present supratemporal ability to affect events. The revelation that establishes the tribal community of beings . . . is a communal affair in which the community participates but in which no individual claims exclusive franchise" (195).

3

William James, Black Elk, and the Healing Act

We need to witness our own limits transgressed, some life pasturing freely where we never wander.

—Thoreau

These are tumultuous times for the institution of medicine. Natural sciences make spectacular strides that impact our deepest conceptions of self, body, health—discoveries in genetics and in the neurotransmitters of the brain, to take two examples. At the same time, the wildest-seeming nostrums from the New Age begin to invade the medical establishment, sometimes backed by M.D.s themselves—I mean prayer therapy or the use of visual imagery in combating cancer, to take but two examples.

As long as we stay ensnared in hoary dualistic conceptions that oppose mind or spirit to body, there is no hope for a unified view or for a unified approach to therapy. The medical establishment will insist that only science can know. But that is not a view supportable by science; it is not a scientific view; it is an ideology. New Age will insist that scientific methods and categories are too crude and materialistically biased to either confirm or disconfirm nontraditional cures. But that supposes that science cannot expand and grow more flexible, which cannot be proved, so that is an ideology.

The prognosis for the two ideologies going at each other head to head is poor. Only reconstruction of concepts at the most basic level imaginable holds any hope for the insights of practitioners coming from different quarters to complement one another. The dualism of mind over against body has to go. Easier said than done, but I think William James's thought can be freshly appropriated, so that Western science can finally join hands with indigenous American healing traditions.

William James's only degree was M.D., and he spent at least fourteen years of his life trying to construct a psychology he called natural scientific. He wanted to discover laws of functional covariation that linked mental states and brain states. There are thoughts and there are things—for him initially that's the unquestionable premise. It is an irreducible mind/body dualism. His attempt finally comes to grief, but in a way that suggests James Joyce's aphorism that the mistakes of genius are the portals of discovery.

Very briefly—I will expand on this in the next essay—he finds he cannot specify mental states without specifying what they are of or about. And what they are of or about is not just the particular thing that interests him, but the whole experienced context that holds that thing and gives it meaning. But there must be a thinking of all this that is thought-about! Yes, but all he can pin down about that thinking is something his body is doing, particularly something happening in his head and throat and behind his eyes, which appears fleetingly on the margins of the field of what is thought-about. And all he can pin down about his very self is his own experiencing-experienced body in the world as he immediately lives it all.

James had thought that natural science could avoid philosophical questions like, How do things get known into thoughts? However, if we do know them, we pick them out of *the world*. So we must mean "world." And natural science cannot explain how we mean this. James finds he must go beyond natural science if he would know how natural science is possible.

At the close of fourteen years' efforts to produce a natural scientific psychology, he writes that the waters of metaphysical criticism leak into his project at every joint.[1] There are no purely mental data, thoughts in themselves, a barrier that separates us from the world. Thinking is passing states of this body as it interweaves productively or nonproductively with world thought about. Thinking is just a distinctive arrangement of the very same "specific natures" or "pure experiences" that constitute the world at large. The very hardness of a stone, say, that characterizes its history in the world at large, that very hardness also figures in the ongoing history of the knowers, ourselves; we call a stretch of this history our perceiving the stone. It is hardness "thought of in a perceiving" only because it is not stubbornly located in the world after the immediate perceiving of it; that is, it might be remembered in conjunction with other properties; or it might be entertained fancifully: Imagine pinching it into powder with your fingers.

But regardless of these "powers of mind," we are not merely *in* the world, we are *of* it—constituted of its very stuff. To take the simplest example, when we run into stones their specific nature, their hardness, reverberates through our body-selves. James is coming up with his own version of so-called identity-philosophy, the identity of subject and object. We are radically worldly beings, open, porous, participatory.

The very thing known that lives its history in the world also figures in the history of ourselves, the knowers, that is, the *numerically identical* thing. Things are not out there, sealed off from us. They irradiate, interfuse, permeate us, to one degree or another. If the thing known is an animal believed to possess regenerative powers, such as a snake or a bear, this power itself possesses us—if we let it. We are caught up in its exfoliating shells of energy.

At this point, James's fingertips and Black Elk's can touch. In precious interviews granted to John Neihardt, Black Elk relates how his cousin, Crazy Horse, got his name.[2] As he was seeing his horse in a sacred manner, it shimmered crazily. People schooled in the field theories of twentieth-century physics, schooled that things are nodes of energy exchange in a sea of circulating energies, should not find this inscrutable. The nodes overlap and interfuse; they are not sealed off from one another. Crazy Horse is not crazy. Thinking that things are sealed off outside us—that is crazy.

There is intimate communion and engulfment with the rest of the world before we have had the chance to reflect and neatly contrast the context of pure experiences that is our perceiving and thinking selves with the context that is the rest of the world, the world at large perceived or thought about. It is easy to skip out of this moment before we grasp it. This is the moment of "sciousness," as James ingeniously calls it, utterly prereflective awareness, not awareness of awareness, not *con*sciousness.

Almost inevitably we slip into dualistic, mentalistic, and atomistic assumptions embedded in our grammar. We say, "I regard it"—and we think of ourselves as a subject over against an object. But thereby we miss the immediate experience of excited interfusion with regenerative things in the world, which a healer such as Black Elk taps when his cure works.

Emerson before James had already seen much of this. We cannot be in the world without sensing, however dimly, a horizon that divides what is more or less accessible to us from what lies beyond the horizon, *everything else.* The immediate impact of this vast unknown destabilizes us: we do not neatly separate ourselves as subjects over against a world of objects. For example, to ride into a forest is to feel that one has disturbed something that had already been going on, and that one is being watched.[3] This is the trance-like primal level in which the distinction between self and other is suspended. It's misleading to say I regard the other, or even it regards me. Perceived in its immediacy, regard or regarding floats between things, permeating the world-experienced. Uncannily, things feel regarded. Traditional dualisms such as agent/patient, active/passive, subject/object—along with mind/matter, self/other—collapse, and something else entrancedly replaces them.

At age nine, the Oglala Lakota, Black Elk, experienced what he called his Great Vision.[4] Ill, lying for days in a kind of coma, he experienced the cosmos spread around him in the most personal way, though of course in his people's terms as well. With a sensuous vividness and meaning that, he says, defies words to tell completely, he experienced himself oriented, aligned, authorized, and empowered by the six cardinal directions, as they appeared to him in the form of the Six Grandfathers: The Powers of north, east, south, west, and of the upper and lower worlds. At the center of the vision was the World Tree, pulling all the Powers within itself and emitting them again amplified in its blooms.

The World Tree is a kind of consummating center, or seventh dimension, with which we living beings can immediately and intimately identify, and be refreshed, enlightened, empowered. We are refreshed because regarded, fed from every quarter.

Enclosing this vast scene, extending as far as sunlight and starlight, was the Hoop of the World, with the Hoop of his own people enlaced in it. Within this nest, Wakan Tanka had intended the Lakota to brood and to raise their children in integrity with the Whole. (Wakan Tanka—commonly rendered in English as Great Spirit—should probably be rendered as Great Mystery, for "spirit" carries dualistic overtones, suggesting something above and beyond "mere matter.")

Of course, Black Elk's own account must be read. Yet I must employ enough of the detail in this essay to connect it to William James's theoretical account of pure or neutral experience, what James called "the mysterious sensorial life."[5] Without the concrete detail, we slip out of the primal and immediate level of experience and lose ourselves in airy abstractions like Mind, Spirit (or Great Spirit). Lost in Western dualisms, we miss the actual visceral and total involvement that constitutes shamanic healing experience.

For example, when Black Elk's words are translated as "the Other World behind this one," did he mean something like "non-natural" or "supernatural" in the typical dualistic, mind-against-matter Western sense?

The whole context of his words indicates that he did not, that he meant an interlacing of the worlds much more intimate and sensuous than Europeans typically imagine. Why think that Crazy Horse thought his horse was nonphysical? It rather suggests—following James—that the horse itself was being seen in a more dilated and revealing way—seen as the exfoliating node of energies that *is* the horse. It does interact and interfuse with us and the rest of the surroundings. It must interact and interfuse to *be*—it must figure as a movable node and field of energy—and, again, twentieth-century physics can help us understand this.

A few more of the concrete details that must at least be mentioned if we are to have any chance to grasp what actually went on in Black Elk's first healing: the appearance of the Sacred Pipe in his vision, the smoking of which bonds participants with the Powers of the world; the appearance of Virgins in one or other of the Four Quarters, which connotes, I think, the power of new or fresh life in its very possibility; the need to finally enact (if that is a tolerable word) portions of his Vision for the people to witness— an enactment necessary for the very reality of the Vision and its efficacy, its consensual being, or its "objectivity" (to use a very European-parochial and dualizing word). He fears death if he does not do it.

When the nine-year-old recovers from his coma-vision, people realize that he is changed, but he is reluctant to disclose the reason. In fact, over fifty years later Black Elk tells Neihardt that he is telling it all—or "all that can be told"—for the first time. But given the desperate plight of his people following their Pyrrhic victory over Custer in 1876, and ten years after the Vision, Black Elk feels compelled to heal if he can. Following fasting and immersion in a sweat lodge for several days, then lamenting on the plains during a cold and stormy night, Black Elk experiences a kind of replay of the Vision, or portions of it. The next day, in a more or less wakeful state, and in the company of a trusted friend, he seeks in the area items that had appeared to him in the replay of the Vision. In this he had, for example, seen a four-rayed-star herb on the side of a gully. He and his companion now go there in the full light of day—to use the stereotyped phrase—and dig it out. He tells Neihardt that, for some reason he did not know at the time, he knew he would have need of it. And lo, later that very day, his fellow Oglala, Cuts-to-Pieces, father of a young boy, informs Black Elk that this son is very sick, and requests him to go to minister to him.

Before we sketch his first cure, let us ruminate further on two matters. Given ingrained ancestral dualisms, Europeans tend to think of visions or trance states (if they take them seriously at all) as experiences of a transcendent domain, something outside the "merely" natural or physical. This view completely misleads about the power and scope of shamanic trance and vision. I think these apparently strange modes of perceiving keep us housed where we should be: in what James calls the instant field of the present, the immediate encounter and actual interfusion with things. Before, that is, reflection and abstraction have had a chance to neatly divide self from other, subject from object, and we have had time to forget the interfusion, the exchange of energies between things themselves. Studies of shamanic healings can give new life to Husserl's rallying cry, inspired in great part by James: To the things themselves!

The second matter: shamans, it is said, have the power to heal only because they themselves have passed through a death or near-death experience, have themselves been reborn or regenerated. Clearly this is true of Black Elk. I imagine that it applies to some extent to William James. As I have noted, he endured a nervous collapse after receiving an M.D. from Harvard; apparently he was institutionalized for some of this time (the hospital records are still sealed, a colleague informs me). More, the limits into which he ran developing his natural scientific psychology stymied and shocked him for several years. Then he suffered heart trouble in the last years of the last century, and wrote much of his monumental *Varieties of Religious Experience* (published in 1902) while in bed ("even sick rooms have their special revelations").

Now let us grasp as best we can Black Elk's first cure. Each concrete detail and their sequence is significant, but I can recount only some of them. The sick boy lies in the northeast sector of the tepee. Black Elk proceeds into the space through the entrance, which faces south—the south, believed to be, lived as, the source of heat and life. Four virginal young women accompany him, as does a male colleague who carries the sacred pipe and the four-rayed herb. He first offers the pipe to the Six Powers, then passes it, and all who accompany him smoke. Someone beats a drum as another offering to Wakan Tanka ("Its sound arouses the mind," Black Elk says, "and makes men feel the mystery and power of things"). The young healer carries a wooden cup full of water and a few flakes of red willow bark, and proceeds on the outer perimeter of the inner space until he faces west—the west where the sun sets each day and dies, as each of us must do some day. (In this he acknowledges his own mortal reality, and probably his own near-death experience at nine.) He addresses the Grandfather of the West with the sacred pipe. He then proceeds to the north, "where the white hairs are," where the cleansing cold wind of the north teaches endurance, and addresses the Grandfather there. He participates ecstatically in this Power of the north.

At about this point, the sick boy smiles at him, and immediately Black Elk, who had been unsure of himself, feels power come up through the Earth, the lower world, and through his body—"I could feel something queer all through my body, something that made me want to cry for all unhappy things, and there were tears on my face" [200–201]. Black Elk and the boy inflame each other with possibility. (One can only think of James's idea of the will to believe. Why is it a fault to believe before evidence comes in, as some Western intellectuals think, when with regard to certain crucial matters of living, the belief that one holds generates the evidence that supports it?)

He drinks from the cup with the red willow bark and instructs one of the virgins to give it to the boy for him to drink also. He proceeds to where the boy lies and stamps his foot on the floor of the tepee four times. After some incantations in pulses of four, he puts his mouth on the pit of the boy's stomach and sucks the cleansing wind of the north through his body—the wind that teaches endurance.

He arises and proceeds to address the east and the Grandfather there—the east, the source of new light and understanding each day. He then instructs one of the virgins to go to the boy and to assist his rising and walking. This the boy does, with great difficulty. Black Elk then exits to the south where he first entered, having completed the cycle through the Four Directions and the Six Powers, and not waiting to monitor any further progress by the boy.

The next day, Cuts-to-Pieces tells him that his boy is much improved.

The elderly Black Elk told Neihardt that the boy lived until thirty.

At this point, most persons of European ancestry will—if they give this procedure any credence at all—speak almost automatically of the power of positive thinking. Or an ostensibly more sophisticated response would be, the power of the symbolical. Perhaps it would go something like this: "After all, the boy is dreadfully sick, his life cycle is about to abort. Black Elk's circulating around the floor of the tepee symbolizes vividly a completed life cycle, and this inspires the boy to make great efforts to regain his threatened life cycle. The boy succeeds."

Such responses are well intentioned and not simply false. But they block any real understanding of the healing transaction, for what does "the power of positive thinking" mean concretely? The phrase is an airy abstraction. In giving the impression that an explanation is provided, it blocks further inquiry; it is worse than if nothing had been said. The same applies to the ostensibly more sophisticated talk. Symbols are typically understood dualistically as mental or spiritual, and we are left with the problem insurmountable by dualism: how can such mental or spiritual activity possibly influence the body?

Only James's antidualistic approach brings us to the threshold of what is actually happening. Despite the apparent celebration of mind in dualism, this placing it isolated on a pedestal, it grows increasingly pale and impotent in the face of hard science's ever-deeper exposure of the powers of the physical, such as gains in genetics and brain science. Increasingly in ever-spreading North Atlantic civilization it is assumed that the real world is the "external" world, the world minus our full, minding selves. But we *are* our bodies, I believe, and our bodies include, of course, our massive functioning brains embedded electrochemically in the rest of the body, as the body itself is embedded in the ongoing interfusing world beneath, around, above, and through us.

To speak of the "external world"—*that's* an abstraction, a partial account. As Black Elk lives ecstatically in the far reaches of the four cardinal directions, and of the upper and lower worlds, these Powers are not merely conceived "in the mind," but in the moment's interfusion of energies, he is *identical* with them. His career and theirs intersect and are one. And as the sick boy participates believingly, ecstatically in Black Elk, the Powers become his ecstatically.

The symbolic approach is particularly inadequate to grasp any healing transaction, particularly the climactic moment in which Black Elk draws the North Wind through the boy's body by sucking it through his abdomen. We might say, "The sucking doesn't really do this, but only symbolizes it." But this again repeats the dualistic abstraction: "the north wind is really only what it is minus our mindful participation in it." No, it is more plausible to say that Black Elk draws the North Wind through the boy's body: the wind now understood in its full amplitude as including how it figures in the human nervous system, what it means to us in the interfusing moment *and* over time. As the North Wind works on, in, and through directly perceiving and then memorializing humans, it leaves a potent residue in the body that communicates and radiates directly from body into body in the ritualized situation.[6]

When the healing works, it must be that the world's energies radically augment the boy's immunological or regenerative powers. The engaged energies realign him in what Emerson calls Circular power returning into itself, the regenerative universe. James is less sweeping, but he escorts us methodically to a commanding viewpoint for surveying the surprising ramifications of sticking close to pure experience, to what he calls the immediate, naive, pragmatic. What he helps us finally to grasp is primal *and* pragmatic.

The atomistic idea that a thing's reality is contained within the envelope of its surfaces is deeply ingrained in European and now North Atlantic thought. It is great for analyzing the world into bits technological, manipulable, and calculable. But it totally occludes our own nature as ecstatically involved field-beings. James should be seen as running counter to this deeply ingrained atomistic tendency: his relational philosophy aims to "thicken up" the world-experienced.

Thoreau's, Emerson's, and James's work should be seen as converging with deep patterns of indigenous thought and action. It is difficult for this to happen, for segmenting the world-experienced is built into our Western languages. We try to counteract segmentation with a statement like this: Our being, our identity, partakes of the things and events in which we participate. Now, this is true, but deplorably thin and abstract.

We must allow indigenous expression to help us. Maureen T. Schwarz in her *Molded in the Image of Changing Woman: Navajo Views on the Human Body and Personhood* shares the fruits of her apprenticeship to Navajo ways. She sees how Navajo thought connects with indigenous thought worldwide: "In some Melanesian societies, the body is revealed as a collection of 'substances and flows from a number of sources momentarily come together.' Contrary to the complete body posited by Western biomedicine, this type of Melanesian body, like the Navajo one, is subject to fundamental alteration during the life cycle."[7]

She emphasizes the caressing and molding of the infant's body by parents right after birth and then through the early years. The idea that we are atoms, and that the function of the envelope of the skin is chiefly to keep out disease entities, is revealed as the ghastly abstraction that it is. The incidence in "advanced" cultures of loneliness, despair, addictions of countless sorts should spur us to ever-renewed attempts to interweave Western and indigenous ways.

Postscript concerning the limits of James's approach for grasping indigenous thought: In groping to delineate mental phenomena within his radical empiricism, James writes in one place that mental fires don't burn mental sticks. He should have said, I think, that mental fires don't *necessarily* burn mental sticks; that is, one of our mental powers, is to fancy that they don't. But in the actual perceiving, the immediate minding, of an actual fire burning actual sticks, we *must* perceive it as burning them. And in fact, in the original experience at close quarters the *perceiving itself* is hot; and even remembering this experience, *that perceiving* is not reduced to a mere "mental image" in the traditional dualist-mentalist sense, but excites reflexes, quickens the pulse, and leaves a residuum of this in the neural pathways of the body.

At least equally important for understanding the limits of James's great abilities for grasping shamanic healing: his grasp of what might be called the mythic mode of experience never quite jells, I believe. That is, it needn't be merely *fancying* that mental fires don't burn mental sticks. When Moses heard God's voice speaking from the burning bush—burning without being consumed—this was not a fancying, but an overwhelming experience that stretched beyond ordinary modes of awareness, and touched without grasping a reality beyond everyday distinctions and limitations, something like the Eternal. The story goes like this: "And when Aaron and all the children of Israel saw Moses, behold, the skin of his face shone; and they were afraid to come nigh unto him."[8]

Notes

1. *Psychology: Briefer Course* (New York: Henry Holt & Co., 1910 [1892]), Epilogue. William James, *Psychology: Briefer Course, The Works of William James* (Cambridge, Mass.: Harvard University Press, 1984) (hereafter cited as "critical edition"), Epilogue—it is crucial.

2. Crazy Horse's father also bore that name. In the experience of being named I am about to relate, it is not clear which man first gained that name. See Mari Sandoz, *Crazy Horse: The Strange Man of the Oglalas* (Lincoln: University of Nebraska Press, 1992 [1942]).

3. "History," for instance, in *Ralph Waldo Emerson: Selected Essays,* ed Larzar Ziff (New York: Penguin Books, 1982), 158–59.

4. John G. Neihardt, *Black Elk Speaks* (Lincoln: University of Nebraska Press, 1979), "The First Cure."

5. The very close of "On a Certain Blindness in Human Beings," in William James, *Talks to Teachers on Psychology,* critical edition, and also in my *The Essential Writings of William James* (Albany: State University of New York Press, 1984).

6. Here James should be augmented by what Emerson and Charles Peirce write about universals. Early in "The American Scholar," Emerson laments the loss of the "original unit"—the whole of humanity, the universal Man—"the fountain of power" that "has been so . . . spilled into drops" that it "cannot be gathered." So *individuals* can no longer possess themselves! In viable indigenous societies, this is not the case. Also see Charles Peirce, particularly "The Law of Mind" (in, for example, Justus Buchler, *Philosophical Writings of Peirce* [New York: Dover Books, 1955]). Ideas are not discrete entities inside individual mind containers, but are feelings (Peirce wants this term to be used in a sense neutral between mental and physical)

that generalize themselves over time and space and between things and persons and are real and potent. So North Wind is not merely a compendious name for individual gusts of wind coming from the north—gusts that might be measured by a meteorologist's instruments. There may be no such gusts in the tepee at the moment Black Elk draws the North Wind through the boy's body and out his abdomen. But finally and properly understood as a universal instantiating itself, it is true that he does so. There is more to reality than times, places, persons, animals in their brute particularity. No set of particulars, no matter how large, can constitute a universal. A universal is a pattern of interfusion or interaction that is indefinitely instantiable, a habit of the universe, the most concrete reality. The universal *north wind* may instantiate itself in any number of motions of wind from the north, but also, I believe, in the nervous systems of human beings who are acquainted with winds from the north and with the meanings habitually associated with them. Indeed, it is "brute particularity" that is the abstraction posing as the concrete. The question of the reality of universals is very much alive.

I am critical of the symbolic approach to healing only because today it is saturated in nominalism, reductionism, dualism. Symbols are *mere* symbols. In indigenous cultures, and in not-so-distant sectors of European culture, this is not so. Symbolization involves the habitual, perceiving body-self and structures the world-perceived: it is not "secondary elaboration" or "a general and abstract notion in the mind." Thus when Jesus during the last supper tells his disciples, as he breaks bread, "Take, eat, this is my body given to you . . . ," the bread is a potent, perhaps life-changing symbol. Symbols, so understood, cannot be ordered up on demand! This one grew up out of countless generations in which bread was perceived as the essence of survival and of life itself. (My grandmother spoke of it as the staff of life, and in a ceremonial manner at each meal spread a small bit of butter over a piece of bread and cut it precisely in half.) Now when most of us take food for granted, and when the numinous presence of healing persons is seldom felt, the symbol—and the world perceived in and through it—dwindles away. When the verb of being—the "is" and the "am"—of symbol establishment ("I am the bread of life") is missing, it cannot be fabricated for love or money.

7. Schwarz (Tucson: University of Arizona Press, 1997). She quotes Michael O'Hanlon, "Unstable Images and Second Skins: Artefacts, Exegesis, and Assessments in the New Guinea Highlands," *Man* 27, 3 (1992): 587–608.

8. Exodus 34.30, King James translation. Did Moses believe he was communicating with a Person who spoke through the burning bush? It is commonly thought that Judeo-Christian thought holds that God is a Person (despite simultaneously believing that God is mysterious and cannot be depicted). Holding to this common view, the danger is to project it onto native Americans' experience. The whole world can be lit up, I think, and one's face shine, without believing that one has encountered a Person. Vine Deloria Jr. writes, "Something more needs to be said about anthropomorphic images. Medicine men report the existence of spiritual beings that have or take on human forms. Thus Black Elk and other Sioux mystics report that they have sat with the Six Grandfathers and counseled with them. Much more thought needs to be given to the question of whether the Indians had 'gods' in the same sense as Near Eastern peoples. Was the mysterious power—*wakan tanka* in the Dakota language—the same as the spiritual power that provided life and was superior to any specific personifications of itself? If so, the ultimate representation of this sacred universe—and other sacred Indian universes—was without a deity in the Near Eastern sense." *God Is Red* (Golden, Colo.: Fulcrum Publishing Co., 1994), 95, n. 1.

Currently there is revival, on many fronts, of indigenous American ways of life and thought. It couldn't have come at a more propitious moment in the planet's history. The European notion of God as a Transcendent Spirit or Person models a pervasive attitude that demeans and exploits the earth and our bodies, "lowly, mere matter." (God speaks out of the burning bush, but we learn nothing about God from the bush.) This has enormous religious, and—as many are now seeing—ecological, economic, indeed, survival meaning. Will we denude and poison the earth? One of the very best ways of learning the world-historical role that native Americans are now playing is through novels, the first of which leaps to our attention: the winner of the Pulitzer Prize, N. Scott Momaday's *House Made of Dawn* (New York: Signet Books, New American Library, 1969 [1966]). This book imparts the lived quality—the phenomenology if you will—of a native American struggling to root himself again in the Earth-and-sky and in his people's life in, by, and from the Earth-and-sky. It is this lived quality that draws in readers and imparts reality to what we call the environmental crisis—yet another wispy abstraction, another transcendence! Also see a fine book along similar lines: Leslie Marmon Silko's *Ceremony* (New York: Duality Paperback Book Club, 1994 [1978]).

One more word concerning the crucial matter of how to interpret Black Elk, for example, when he is reported talking of the "world beyond this one." No doubt he is referring to a domain of reality hidden from prosaic, everyday consciousness. But to think it is nonphysical, or that it so transcends the physical that it could exist independent of the physical, is unjustified, parochial, projected from our dualistic standpoint, I believe. Note Roy Rappaport's excellent, posthumous, *Ritual and Religion in the Making of Humanity* (Cambridge and New York: Cambridge University Press, 1999), 48, where he refers to Meyer Fortes: "But Fortes . . . objected that the term 'supernatural' is an artifact of literate cultures, and claimed that the actor, in tribal societies at least, sees the world as composed of the patent and the hidden . . . which present themselves in mixed sequences and which are interwoven into a unified reality. He took this distinction to be wide-spread or even universal." See Fortes's "Religious Premises and Logical Technique in Divinatory Ritual," in J. Huxley, convener, *A Discussion of Ritualization of Behavior in Animals and Man, Philosophical Transactions of the Royal Society of London,* Series B, Biological Sciences 251, 772 (London: Royal Society, 1966).

James

"Wild Beasts of the Philosophic Desert"

Between the burgeoning of Emerson's writings in the 1830s to the 1850s and William James's in the period 1890–1910, there stands a world-historical divide: Darwin's and Wallace's theories of evolution and the evidence for them. Nature comes to be conceptualized in its scientifically focusable aspects, and its earlier "romantic" construal tends to be dismissed.

James's only degree was M.D., his first teaching position instructor in Physiology, and he went as a young man with Louis Agassiz to study the biology of the Amazon. He planned his massive *The Principles of Psychology* to be a scientific study. Perhaps the greatest lesson his authorship teaches is that science alone cannot address our hunger to find meaning in our lives. It cannot because science must objectify and quantify everything it studies. However, as we live caught up immediately in the world around us, we are not objects for ourselves, nor can the lived quality of our lives be grasped adequately through any observer's objectifications and measurements. Without grasping the lived quality of my life just as I live it each moment, the account of my life cannot be complete.

By the end of James's career in 1910, he has returned by a circuitous route to leading themes in Black Elk, Thoreau, and Emerson: What incentive, purpose, eagerness to live can we find as whole beings in whole Nature? How far do scientific inquiries carry us? Where must we take up other methods if we would satisfy our need for meaning? What sense can we make of the circumpressure of the world day by day, as artists, religious thinkers, ordinary folk have all along tried to discern? James clears the way for those of European origin to reappraise the most ancient human form of healing: shamanism. As I've noted, he did not expect his academic colleagues to join his quest for wild beasts of the philosophic desert—"beasts" accessible only to persons personally. Most of his colleagues certainly did not follow him. It would lead to thought "too spook haunted" for them.

The elderly James is the pivotal figure in this second stage of homing movement to primal sources that began in Thoreau and Emerson, the stage that assimilated the Darwinian revolution but was not carried away in it. John Dewey was ambivalent toward this return. W. E. Hocking's epochal *The Meaning of God in Human Experience*—and his later work—is an attempt to systematize the return, to consolidate it without losing the impact of twentieth-century science. Henry Bugbee returns to it in his uniquely passionate yet circumspect way.

Many in our century dismiss this return out of hand, dismiss it as a "romantic" nostrum for saving ourselves through sentiment and nostalgia, an escapist ploy. But the thinkers I am mainly writing about turn the tables: they claim these antiromantics still cling to tacit salvific claims of ever-objectifying and measuring science and technology; they are closet sentimentalists and dogmatists. This homing move helps us to grasp the gallant and somewhat despairing contemporary work of Richard Rorty who scrapes up some bits of moral and emotional nourishment to keep us going.

We must focus in much greater detail the pivotal moment in which James's program for a natural scientific psychology broke down. Much hinges upon this for understanding our situation today. Though brain science has greatly advanced from what James knew, it faces many of the same conceptual problems he confronted over one hundred years ago.

Let's retrace James's odyssey very thoroughly this time. From 1878 to 1892, he worked on a psychology that aimed to avoid the metaphysical assumptions and presumptions of nearly all earlier psychologies. It would be natural-scientific. He was not just another positivist, however. He knew very well that there were legitimate problems of knowledge and of reality that were philosophical: that is, not addressable within empirical inquiry, because that simply presupposes some view or other of knowledge and reality. But he did believe that as a natural scientist with limited aims he could get by with a commonsensical view, a dualism: there are thoughts, on the one hand, and things "out there," on the other. After fourteen years of concerted exertion, he found he could not.

He begins *The Principles of Psychology* with extensive chapters of what he calls physiological preliminaries. Yet he makes room for a criterion of mental activity: the adoption of ends and the choice of means for achieving them. If, for example, a bit of acid is placed on a headless frog's right thigh, its left leg will move to wipe it off. If that leg is amputated, the right foot will try to wipe it off.

But, of course, how do we know the frog exhibits any thought or mental activity? James knows he must elaborate his criterion of mental activity. But he still thinks he can avoid the heavy philosophical problems of the nature of thought, and of how external reality gets "known into" some thoughts. His own thoughts are ready to hand. Who else's are, just as they are thought? After nearly two hundred pages, he abandons the stance of detached observer, which had characterized the physiological preliminaries. He tries to examine his own immediate experiencing: he becomes his own psychologist.

Nevertheless he still pursues what he calls a natural-scientific psychology. He sets up an analytic framework, dividing the "irreducible data of psychology" into four "water-tight" compartments:[1]

The Psychologist	The Thought Studied	The Thought's Object	The Psychologist's Reality
1.	2.	3.	4.

The ultimate objective of the scientist-psychologist—compartment #1—is to establish laws of functional co-variation (causal connection?—it's not completely clear) between The thought or mental state—compartment #2—and The brain state—#4. For this to be a genuinely empirical discovery, the sheer concept of one can't involve the sheer concept of the other.

To specify the mental state, James finds he cannot avoid specifying it in terms of what it is *of,* thought's object, compartment #3. But this is no particular thing—actual or not—denuded of relational matrix. It is "all that thought thinks just as thought thinks it." To convey this, he capitalizes "object" with an "O"—Object.

An example is hearing thunder. We do not perceive thunder pure and simple, but "thunder-breaking-in-on-silence-and-contrasting-to-it." To specify the mental state, we must do so in terms of this whole Object that it is of or about. The *particular* object the thought is of—the clap of thunder itself (presumably a #4)—is only the "topic" of the total Object and must be picked out from within it.

But the same is also true of specifying any brain state, a #4. Though a brain state is not *of* or about any total Object, #3, nevertheless it too must be picked out as a topic within a total Object of thought: the psychologist's as he surveys the brain in the living body. Specification or individuation of both mental states and brain states involves the problem of picking out and demarcating events within total Objects of thought or contexts.

Here is what's happening: Thought's Object, #3, described phenomenologically, engorges both the mental state, #2, and the brain state, #4. Neither can be specified independently of #3. But this turns out to be the full sweep of the experienced or experienceable world! When we somehow observe and demarcate the brain state occurring simultaneously with the subject's reported mental state, we *must* suppose that the subjective report and the observation are tightly correlated. We face the possibility that #2 and #4, a thought and a brain state, are connected in our concepts of them. If so, the discovery of their causal or functional co-variations is not purely a matter of empirical science.

James, of course, over one hundred years ago, was without our positronemission tomography (PET) scans that apparently identify brain states precisely: mildly radioactive substances are consumed by persons, and, as they engage in thinking, the corresponding portions of the brain light up. But even today questions should arise: For instance, is our PET technology sufficiently sensitive to pick up all the brain activity, all the brain state, involved?

But James is most concerned about the difficulties in specifying mental states. He is unable to detect thoughts themselves, #2. As he observes himself thinking, he detects first and foremost, of course, what thought is of or about, but trying to pin down the thought itself yields only an ongoing process of various postures, activities, and sensations felt to be within the body. Particularly vivid are sensations felt behind the eyes and in the neck and glottis.

He cannot detect any members for his analytic compartment #2! All he gets is yet more content in compartment #3, the Object, particularly in the fleeting margins or fringes of Object in which the body's passing states are felt. Thinking is something the body is doing in the world. Consciousness "itself"—if this makes any sense at all—is just a "nothingness," to put it as Jean-Paul Sartre did in our own day.

James is on his way to rediscovering the medieval idea of the intentionality of thought, *obiect specificat actum.* The "act" of thinking must be specified first and foremost in terms of what the thinking is of or about, the intentional object thought-about, whether this object is an actual constituent of the world or merely fancied or conjectured.

But he is rediscovering this in his own peculiar way. He cannot neatly frame or demarcate the intentional object: it balloons into Object, and this ramifies through its fringes and horizons into a whole lived world. All he can find in the way of the act of thinking itself are various felt conditions of the body typically presented on the peculiarly intimate, abiding, "warm" fringes of Object. In perceiv*ing*, the body is immediately presented as engaged in the world perceiv*ed* as present and actual. In remembering, the body is presented as partially disengaged from the present and actual world—likewise in anticipating. The difference between anticipating and remembering is that body-self is directed forward in time in the one case, and backward in the other.

"Thought" and "experience" should really be "double-barreled terms," James concludes: experienc*ing* and experienc*ed*, thinking and thought about, perceiving and perceived, and so on. All modes of experienc*ing* are activities directed upon, and essentially connected with, something experienc*ed* in a certain way. Thoughts or feelings are not discreet mental entities. Thinking and feeling do go on, of course—and he speaks famously of a stream of them—and perceiving, say, must be distinguished from remembering. But they are distinguished only in terms of the whole world experienced. A necessary condition for distinguishing perceiv*ing* X from remember*ing* X is that the very same thing (or topic) perceiv*ed* must also be the thing remember*ed*. We are locked into a conceptual necessity—a direct realism for concepts, as I will put it in the next essay.

"Thought itself" or "mental state" #2 is caught up in total Object #3, and the detective work of precisely specifying thinking and experiencing is intriguing and exacting. For different modalities of experienc*ing*—perceiving, say, and remembering—are tied inexorably to what is experienc*ed*. Yet, experienc*ing* in *any* modality must also be distinguished from what is experienc*ed* in that modality. The experiencing is always the immediate and warm feeling of the body on the fringes of consciousness flowing through time. This is closer and warmer and more habitually in the fringe than anything else could be. And yet it too is given as something happening in the world—as given, that is, in thought's *Object*.

But doesn't the natural scientific psychologist (compartment #1) stand off from all this, a kind of self-constituting, self-reflecting consciousness that inventories its own mental contents? No. James realizes that to really study mental activity the psychologist must intensely scrutinize his own thinking, and that the thinking psychologist is in the world along with everything else. That is, the psychologist's thinking and experiencing occurs within a dimension of thought's Object. Again!

The psychologist is on all fours with the subjects studied. All have what some have called privileged access to their own stream of consciousness or stream of experiencing. And each suffers the same liabilities of this alleged access: ever-present possibilities of self-deception, selective attention and inattention, denial and evasion.

And in general, for any of us, each sort of thing experienced requires its own mode of experiencing. Even in a single modality, the visual, say, the experiencing of a map of a mountain range, for example, is different from the experiencing of the mountain range itself directly in front of one.

Now, what mode of experiencing is needed to grasp the general structures of the stream of experiencing itself? As we saw, this must include the grasp of the whole Object of thought, just as it is thought in all of its regions and levels. This meta-mode of experiencing turns out to be the discipline of phenomenology. James finds he cannot avoid phenomenology, and in grappling with its difficulties greatly influences the founder of twentieth-century phenomenology, Edmund Husserl.

The clues and findings accruing to James's ever-increasing deployment of phenomenological descriptions intrigue and disturb him. He launches into what he later calls, somewhat defensively, an excursus—a description of the full context of the passing thought. Now, where is he the thinker in all this? Trying to find himself, all he can find is thinking. "The passing thought is the thinker," he tentatively concludes.[2] For after all, what of the self beyond this thinking can really be made evident? How much about the self is ingrained supposition, and how much can be made evident—evident to phenomenological scrutiny?

But we have already seen that the "passing thought" #2 can be specified only in terms of #3, the total Object. The Psychologist #1 is also absorbed into the vast and often occluded region of #3! Finally conducted out of the maze of Cartesian and "natural scientific" dualism, this at last comes home to us, and we must reiterate the point: The psychologist cannot stand outside the phenomena to be described, indeed, outside a world to be described phenomenologically. Psychologists cannot exist in grand isolation, their thoughts and their methods specifiable independently of a world thought about—including their brains thought about when they think about those. Empirical investigation must occur within conceptual constraints and difficulties it had not initially envisaged.

It is not enough to champion commonsense dualism as James had initially tried to do, and to say simply, there are thoughts, on the one hand, and there are things, on the other. Thinker, thinking, and thought-about are entwined in the most intimate way. Indeed, they share something *numerically identical.* He finds us engulfed in the world experienced. In fact, we are utterly integral to it, grafted into it, growing or struggling—or whatever—not only within it *but of it.*

"Of" turns out to be crucially ambiguous. Yes, to specify ourselves as thinkers in our thinking we must specify what the thinking is about—*of* in that sense (the example used was a perceiving of thunder-breaking-in-upon silence-and-contrasting-to-it). But this leads us into the fringes and margins of the total Object, and there in the semi-lit vastness we discover the other sense of *of:* our self and our thinking are *of* the world in the sense that they spring out *of* and are rooted in the world—including our brains, of course. This rootedness we cannot immediately penetrate and trace. Many thoughts emerge from we know not where. This recalls Emerson's observation that each of us is a stream whose source is hidden.

Armed with this cautionary and awesome insight today, we can critically address our PET scans. Are they revealing all of the brain activity involved in even our simplest thinking? They reveal vividly something interesting, but how thorough is the disclosure? Beyond this, we are led to ask, Perhaps the brain is a function of the whole behavioral and environmental situation of which consciousness is also a function? It is tempting to think that we only need to study the brain by itself, for, after all, this must be the immediate or proximate cause of consciousness. But if the brain is integrally involved in the environment, a function of it, we must study the whole brain-body-environment feedback-feed-out loop of energies (an insight already greatly developed by John Dewey and beginning to grow in some sectors of cognitive science).[3]

To keep his mammoth natural-scientific project going, James keeps postponing admitting grave philosophical complications. When all he can pin down of his passing thinking is fleeting sensations behind his eyes and in his head and throat, he says he has digressed, and returns to the common-sensical dualistic view that, on the one hand, there are thoughts. On the other hand, there is the world "out there," and some of it somehow gets known into some of the thoughts. Of course, given his own view of the omnivorous total Object, these thoughts aren't just demarcatable entities or sensations pure and simple, but are felt on the fringes to occur within bodily activity directed in some way toward the rest of the world. Thinking occurs only relative to distinctive modes of bodily activity oriented within the world.

Though temporarily halted, his phenomenological exploration is taking him inexorably toward the main channel of his later antidualist thinking: a kind of identity-philosophy—a metaphysics—in which, as I say, thinker, thinking, and thought-about are, in a key respect, identical. In the end, he cannot return to common sense.

James admits this only after fourteen years of gestation and struggle—in the *Abridgement* of *The Principles*, 1892. With stunning candor, he writes in its last pages that the waters of metaphysical criticism leak into every joint of his four-part analytic framework for a natural scientific, as well as dualistic, psychology.

And he unmistakably prefigures his metaphysics of "pure or neutral" experience in a brief but memorable phenomenological description of look-ing into the blue sky. As immediately seen and lived, the blue is "pure or neutral": it is not confined in either a subjective (mental) or an objective (physical) "compartment." The very same, numerically identical, blue that figures in his "inner" ongoing experiencing of it figures as well in the total context of the experienced world at large: as one might say, "The sky is blue on this beautiful day in July on the east coast of the U.S., and is so whether I am experiencing it or not." Only in retrospection—however rapid—is the pure or neutral experience of blue sorted into the different histories: that of myself and that of the world at large. In breathtaking immediacy and intimacy, experiencers belong to the world experienced. It grasps at that part of it that is we-ourselves and pulls us deeper into itself. Sky-i-fied at that moment I am turned up into the blue. Literally, it takes my breath away.

No longer can the identity-philosophy (identity of subject and object, mind and matter) of the postromantic philosophers Schelling and Hegel be dismissed as metaphysical maunderings. Nor can the romanticism of the poets be relegated to a mere term of reproach. For their essential point about the ecstatically "fused" human situation breaks out as an essential difficulty in a natural scientific approach to human nature. James's greatly creative appropriation of all these resources demands our attention.

Even today ninety years after James's death, and following the trailblazer himself, it is all too easy to miss the way and to fall back into Cartesian and commonsensical dualism; if this happens, the spiritual resources of a fuller life are forfeited. For the dualist will say, "The blue of the sky is not really out there in Nature itself, but is only a subjective experience inside our own minds. Dualism is retained."

But James's breakthrough insight is not so easily dismissed. Forget for a moment the example of blue or blueness. Take the property of hardness instead. The Cartesian will say that we have an idea or sensation in the mind of hardness, but hardness itself is not there. But this begs the question in favor of mind/matter dualism. It simply assumes that there is a domain of mind—extensionless, massless, weightless, completely permeable, without physical shape and force, a realm of ideas and sensations only.

James will not buy this. It depends upon reifying abstractions—like "the mind"—and upon separating out modalities of the one experiencing process as if they were independent realities. Particularly is vision favored and elevated in Cartesianism, taken to be the model way of knowing. But vision is the distancing and separating sense par excellence, and taken as the model badly restricts and misleads inquiry.

As a matter of experiential fact, the very hardness of that stone wall that I stumble against reverberates through my whole perceiving body-self. I come shuddering to a stop. I quiver with *that* hardness. The very hardness of the stone wall that goes to constitute the wall itself through time goes also to constitute my career as a perceiving being in the world—I who bear a bruise.

What makes the hardness occur in *my minding of it* is no quality of "mind itself," but the fact that the hardness is no longer stubbornly located relative to other properties of the wall, such as its location and shape standing there on the ground. Rather, figuring in my minding of it, the hardness can be displaced: remembered or anticipated when I am no longer in the wall's immediate presence, or fancied or imagined. That is, as I earlier put it, I might imagine pinching it into powder with my fingers.

All the sense modalities function in ensemble as the modalities of one minding body-self moving about in the world. Seeing requires concomitant kinesthesis and motility. Seeing something there involves anticipatory or possible approach and touch and handling, in some cases ingestion. A number of researchers have noted that people congenitally blind but abruptly given sight must learn to see. Without a great deal of trouble, they can learn to see things they have earlier learned to perceive through touching, hearing, embracing, or ingesting them. But seeing the Moon is terribly difficult. Which goes against commonsense dualism: "The full Moon on a clear night must be easily seen." In fact, it is not.

On James's emerging view, his radical empiricism, there are no completely independent existences. Relations of things are equiprimordial with the things related. On this view, all properties are relational. The hardness of something is relative: diamonds are hard relative to steel or stone; impermeable things are only relatively so, relative to most things, but not to neutrinos; weight is relative to gravitational fields; even mass and kinetic energy are relative to the basic structure and functioning of the universe. From the fact that a quality like blue or blueness is relative to sentient organisms with color-vision capabilities, we cannot infer that we are bottled up in our mental container, or that a blue-producing world does not really exist.

James's technical philosophizing is returning us to the sensorial and spiritual richness of the world—the very world that "the romantics" and Thoreau and Emerson were trying to preserve. And they all are converging to what primordial peoples such as the Oglala Lakota knew before contact with Europeans began to shred it. That is, a world of kinship, of spiritual sharpness and keenness, in which the very substance, the energic reality, of things permeate and become a part of our lives. When these things are living things with markedly regenerative properties—such as bears or snakes or certain birds—their regenerative power can get into us. Can if we let it, if we don't close off in panic.

To say that James spent the rest of his life trying to reconstruct after the collapse of his natural-scientific framework would be only mild exaggeration. His regenerative capacity—his ability to start over again at fifty—is astonishing and reassuring.

Psychophysical dualism is finished. There is no domain or substance called the mind. There is no veil of mental entities—sense-data or psychic images—that separates us from the rest of the world. There is the breathing, moving, hungering human organism caught up in the world in ways that can sometimes be called thinking or experiencing. That is, the body is squeezed and/or enticed, lured, gets projected expectantly, expects things to happen—and may be soothed when they do happen—without necessarily being able to acknowledge that all this happens. As I noted in the preceding essay, primal thinking is immediate involvement in the world, "sciousness," not "consciousness" with its connotation of reflective awareness of awareness itself. There is no mirror-lined mental domain in which we can sequester ourselves.

The world is meaningful only to the extent that those parts of it that are our organisms find it expectable. What is not expectable in any way must be experienced as mysterious—or not experienced consciously at all. When we are caught up in the world in ways that expectations are fulfilled, we can only think that this is truth, for truth is just the way the world is held together and becomes meaningful as *world* within ongoing experience. As we will see in the next essay, James is not confusing confirmation of truth with truth—despite his many critics—for whenever truth happens it must be *of* a world that we *must* mean to have existed and to have held us before we confirmed anything about it. When he speaks of truth as useful, his idea of useful is fundamental in a way that his critics cannot imagine, for they have smuggled into their account some notion of a world already constituted in its meaning as "out there." This is a constitution of meaning they cannot account for, an assumption they beg. Under whatever dress of logical sophistication they present themselves, they are the sort of commonsensical dualist that James earlier tried to be but couldn't.

Only seemingly paradoxically, the richness of James's thought stems from the acuity with which he sees what's actually given to be thought, the limited resources of thought in the actual time of our lives. To limn our embeddedness in a world most of which is opaque, to trace our contours and limits, is to trace our identity as actual, situated beings. The richness of his account stems from his unnamed but beautifully used phenomenology that grounds our knowledge by discovering the limits of what can be experienced in the world. The limits of our experiencing give us "the shape" that what is experienced must take. For example, something can be experienced and known to be a real thing, in contrast to a fictional one, only because it is experienced as overflowing all that we could possibly specify and know about it. Our thinking selves are "thick," the workings of a body embedded in the pulsing of matter and energy that *is* the never completely plumbable—that is, the real—world.

Essential to his phenomenological abilities are his artistic. If asked whether things have determinate structures—molecular or atomic, say—we will reflect and affirm they do. But what's actually experienced immediately may be no definite "what" but only a "that" ("though ready to become all kinds of 'whats'"—it throbs with possibility[4]). Probably influenced by

James, Edmund Husserl supplies a good example: Reading absentmindedly at dinner, we reach for what we take to be water. It is really milk. At the instant the liquid meets the tongue, it tastes like neither milk nor water. It is mere "sensuous matter"—a brute *that*. No wonder we recoil in disgust and may spit it out. Our expectations shattered, it takes a moment to regain poise, rearrange expectations and sensed possibilities, and recognize what has happened. We are delicately poised and incredibly vulnerable beings.

Not only are there "thats" that are not yet "whats," "though ready to become all sorts of whats"—suggesting a radical creativity possible for us. There are also floating "whats," those not yet attached to particular things. James cites watching clouds and the moon, the wind blowing one night.[5] In the instant we are not sure if it is the clouds, we, or the moon that moves, or perhaps all three. But since he implies we *are* bodies, and cannot at that moment set ourselves off from the rest of the world, our own identity blurs uncannily. Radical possibilities of being and knowing suggest themselves.

Only by setting up tests, however rapidly, noting expectations that are either fulfilled or not, do we even know what we mean, and where and who we are. The constitution of the meaning of the world is a precariously balanced and evolving experimental activity, always open ended on some parameters, in which the meaning of things gets established in terms of their experienceability. (Though James never clearly enough distinguishes experienceability from experienced or experiencing; we will trace this unclarity further in the next essay.)

These are not merely psychological matters, or even merely epistemological. They are ontological or metaphysical: issues of what things *are*. Particularly open ended and intriguing is Who are we? We body-selves? Meaning must be constituted within the sometimes very disturbing flux and shock of experience. There is no showcase of finished forms, essences, concepts; and the rest of the world imposes limits to conceptualization that we may discover rudely or happily—or that, in our defensive smugness, we may never imagine.

James acknowledges that concepts form a coordinate realm of reality, and that whenever a "what" and not just a "that" appears at the intersection of personal and world histories, conceptualization is at work within perceptual experience (and extending our reach when perception encounters its limits). But we must forever return to the shimmering "perceptual much at once"— fading out on its margins—to replenish, modify, and augment our stores of meaning, which includes conceptualization itself. For concepts he calls "teleological instruments," ways of setting up expectations and activities that will sort out the experienceable world in the light of our evolving purposes, needs, whims, interests, conjectures (though, when our purposes dictate, we keep the meanings or definitions of concepts constant).

James does not beg questions. He genuinely asks, Who are we? What is the world? He philosophizes with a world-intended or meant truly open ended on its horizons. It is tempting to dismiss as polemical his lines at the end of the radical empiricist essay "Does Consciousness Exist?": "The 'I think' which Kant said must be able to accompany all my objects, is the 'I breathe' which actually does accompany them." But James really thinks our breathing is essential to both our being and our thinking (when we do think). Try, for example, to deny something's existence and to inhale. The full meaning of denial is to exclude something from the world, particularly from that part of it that is one's own vulnerable body-self and its internal fluids, processes, cavities.

Perhaps he was half-aware in 1892 that all he could tolerate of "metaphysics" was his initial example of pure experience—experience neutral, not yet sorted into self and other or subject and object—his example of the blue of the sky directly experienced. As I said, vision is the distancing and detaching sense par excellence: his example buffers somewhat the shock of intimacy and vulnerability that emerges in his new metaphysics. He cannot continue to limit himself. For what he is opening up leads to insights that resemble one of Willa Cather's, writing in *The Professor's House,* the section in which his student recounts discovering an ancient indigenous civilization in the Southwest: "Once again I had . . . that feeling of being *on the mesa . . .*—it was like breathing the sun, breathing the colour of the sky."

As James opens up the breathing body-self he simultaneously opens the most ancient bodily-spiritual disciplines of regeneration and healing, shamanic practices, wild beasts of the philosophic desert. For it is not just the very same, numerically same, blue of the sky that animates and possesses our personal life and history. How about animals such as snakes or bears, from prehistoric times experienced as paradigmatically regenerative? What if we no longer narrowly objectify them, but dilate to them, let their full relational amplitude in its immediacy into our being? What if the gasp of awe, this sudden intake of air, lets them into our being to do their regenerative work there? We are selves that are bodies.

But how do we get to the point where we are willing to do this, willing to abandon the juggernaut of scientific and analytic objectification, detachment—perhaps mentalism of a sort—and the pride of those who control? This point came for James through what he called an inner catastrophe, a second one: the breakdown in his later years of all his rationalistic and scientific pretensions. The very taproot of traditional western rationality, the law of identity, "a thing is itself and not another thing," must be seen to have limited validity and utility. Insight into what we are requires we immediately and viscerally experience that things merge to various degrees into what intellectualistic logic says they are not, that things get translated through one another, suffuse one another, get telescoped into one another. For William James, Professor of Philosophy, this realization shatters his comfortable assumption of an autonomous, commanding, insulated, intelligent self. It strongly resembles what is traditionally called the shaman's death experience, but without which she or he cannot heal.[6] With a year to live James says, "There are resources in us that naturalism with its literal and legal virtues never recks of, possibilities that take our breath away, of another kind of happiness and power, based on giving up our own will. . . . Here is a world in which all is well, in *spite* of certain forms of death, indeed *because* of certain forms of death—death of hope, death of strength, death of . . . competency and desert."[7]

James's metaphysics opens horizons that—dare we hope?—are sufficiently commodious and orienting to allow a truly adequate ecology to form. I mean one that gets beyond the cultural debris left by psycho/physical dualism, that is more than a mere cobbling together of natural sciences, on the one hand, or, on the other, a rhapsodizing in a New Age way that "would lift us above the earth and our dark interior bodies and into the light," and so on. James is trying to discover his own dark interior body and how it merges with other things, for better or for worse. This is the only key to real spirituality that he can find.

Note how James's worldview adds credence, shape, and substance (what Justus Buchler calls contours) to a contemporary's arresting shamanic-like experience. Conger Beaseley recounts accompanying an official of the Alaska Department of Fish and Game. The goal was to shoot four seals so that biologists could analyze blood and tissue samples for toxins, trace minerals, and parasites. Revolted, Beaseley gropes for some redeeming qualities in the experience. After a seal is shot, its blood boils up around it in the icy water. The redeeming feature is there: for the first time he realizes viscerally his consanguinity with seals. He is bonded to a fellow mammal. As they open up the seal's abdomen and extirpate its vital organs, Beaseley notes, "I developed an identification with the animal that carried far beyond mere scientific inquiry . . . the abdomen of an adult harbor seal is approximately the size of an adult human male's. Each time I reached into the tangled viscera, I felt as if I were reaching for something deep inside myself. As I picked through the sticky folds of the seal's heart collecting worms, I felt my own heart sputter and knock."[8] As they extirpate the seal's vital organs, Beaseley realizes—viscerally—that "the physical body contains functional properties, the proper acknowledgement of which transforms them into a fresh order of sacraments." Coiled intestines intertwine and resonate with coiled intestines of all animate things. In the recoiling intake of air, in the gasp of awe induced involuntarily in our bodies, we pay tribute to the wilderness mana energies we share with all animals. In the intake of breath, we let them into our being. The sacrament is the involuntary acknowledgment of our kinship and common preciousness—one that resonates, nevertheless, through our voluntary consciousness and career. It is sacrifice of ego: the acknowledgment of all that we do not know and cannot control, and upon which we depend. It names the sacred.

James's evolved ontological framework might help the science/art of medicine to correct for its eccentric current emphasis on hard science at the expense of a whole view of the whole person. His framework can help alternative physicians and various exploratory neurobiologists to come up with a strong conceptual model of what they are trying to do.[9] For example, Candace Pert, former chief brain biochemist, National Institute of Mental Health, writes, "Consciousness isn't just in the head. Nor is it a question of mind over body. If one takes into account the DNA directing the dance of the peptides, [the] body is the outward manifestation of the mind."[10] James helps us make human sense of the science she synopsizes. Helps us see that there is no mind-stuff inside that gets manifested sometimes, but that what we call mind and body are but two aspects of one dynamical system neutral between subject and object, and mind and matter. Mind—better, various levels of minding—may not be precisely localizable, as bodily processes are, but nonetheless minding is something that the world does through systems such as our organisms.

Moreover, James extends a hand as well to indigenous peoples and their time-tested ways of healing. In fact, his work serves as a bridge between scientific medicine, alternative medicine, and indigenous traditions.

James's last creative efforts appear in *A Pluralistic Universe* (1909) and *Some Problems of Philosophy: A Beginning of an Introduction to Philosophy* (unfinished) (1910). His grand ontological and ecological vision is developed along some dimensions, but retreats along others, the shrinkage resulting probably from flagging energies and deteriorating health. I sketch first the expansion.

James remains painfully conscious of the rootlessness, loneliness, and fragmentation of modern life. He thinks the Absolute idealists' proffered cure for this is as bad as the disease: their attempt to show that the fragmentation of the sensuous and natural-scientific life is knit up in an Absolute Mind that subsumes all finite points of view and connects all things in its battery of universal ideas. For James this is a monstrous abstraction that conceals the wound it cannot heal.

Nevertheless, James feels intensely the disease of alienation and world-loss, and our yearning, "our persistent inner turning toward divine companionship."[11] A hopeful remedy he finds in the panpsychic world vision of the German polymath, Gustav Fechner. If Absolute idealism is egregiously thin, Fechner's view is very very thick. Fechner writes of plant-souls, animal-souls, indeed, Earth-soul.

Now what on earth are scientists like James and Fechner doing speaking this way? Because they are also philosophical, and they realize that stock scientific materialism cheats at the start: supposes that Earth and its members are discrete, inert, or mechanical bodies "out there." Such objectification emerges from, abstracts from, a primal involvement with things: a being-along-with-fellow-members of the earth, and it forgets its abstraction and what it abstracts from.

James and Fechner will not forget. They develop a clue in Aristotle—and in much indigenous and aboriginal thought as well: human soul is not some nonmaterial entity or spiritual force, but is just all that the body does. The body not only eats, excretes, copulates, but it breathes as well, and this breathing is a bridging into the thinking and feeling that it also does. The Aristotelian formula is: Soul is to body as sight is to the eye.

And there are bodies other than human ones; in fact, Earth itself is a body. Why suppose that only human bodies think and feel, or that our thinking and feeling is the only sort that might be? On the primal level of pre-objectifying involvement, we feel not only present to things, but feel them present to us. We feel them as companions. Indeed, like native Americans, say, we may pray to the earth. Or, truer to the phenomenon, and as Richard Jeffries put it in words excerpted by James, we pray *with* the earth, the clouds, the singing river, the breathing sea, the fish, the beasts.[12]

James enthusedly comments on Fechner: "The vaster orders of mind go with the vaster orders of body. The entire earth on which we live must have . . . its own collective consciousness. So must each sun, moon, and planet; so must the whole solar system have its own wider consciousness, in which the consciousness of our earth plays one part. . . . The earth-soul [Fechner] passionately believes in, he treats the earth as our special . . . guardian angel."[13]

Almost one hundred years after Fechner's speculations, James Lovelock advanced the Gaia hypothesis at the midpoint of the twentieth century: Earth is very like an organism, maintaining regenerative forces in equilibrium—or creative near-equilibrium—regulating its own temperature like a mammal (though the sun shines now about twenty degrees hotter on its surface). James in 1909 continues his enthused commentary on Fechner:

> Long ago the earth was called an animal; but a planet is a higher class of being than either man or animal; not only quantitatively greater, like a vaster and more awkward whale or elephant, but a being whose enormous size requires an altogether different plan of life. Our animal organization comes from our inferiority. Our need of moving to and fro, of stretching our limbs and bending our bodies, shows only our defect. What are our legs but crutches, by means of which, with restless efforts, we go hunting after the things we have not inside of ourselves. But the earth is no such cripple; why should she who already possesses within herself, the things we so painfully pursue, have limbs analogous to ours? Shall she mimic a small part of herself? What need has she of arms, with nothing to reach for? of a neck, with no head to carry, of eyes or nose when she finds her way through space without either, and has the millions of eyes of all her animals to guide their movements on her surface, all their noses to smell the flowers that grow? For, as we are ourselves a part of the earth, so our organs are her organs. She is, as it were, eye and ear over her whole extent—all that we see and hear in separation she sees and hears at once. She brings forth living beings of countless kinds upon her surface, and their multitudinous conscious relations with each other she takes up into her higher and more general conscious life.[14]

The contemporary Cambridge biologist Rupert Sheldrake suggests that science itself requires such fantastic visions if it would imagine hypotheses sufficiently radical to account for certain prescient and paranormal behaviors of living things such as possessed by dogs, homing pigeons, and prophetic human beings.[15] Sheldrake proposes "morphic fields" of attraction, interfusion, mimetic engulfment between beings, fields that may be analogous in some ways to electromagnetic or gravitational fields, but have not yet been imagined by anybody—probably, I think, because our ability to conceive minding is still stuck in the residuum of dualism that divides scintillating mind from slogging body, thinks of body and energy far too crudely. To be noted is that these are scientists advancing views that set the average academic humanist's teeth on edge.

James goes on to show how Fechner anticipates what we know today as Carl Jung's theory of racial consciousness and subconsciousness: "Fechner's conception of a great reservoir in which the memories of earth's inhabitants are pooled and preserved, and from which, when the threshold lowers or the valve opens, information ordinarily shut out leaks into the minds of exceptional individuals among us. But these regions are perhaps too spook-haunted to interest an academic audience."[16]

James searches for cosmic community. As in each of us our distinct sensory modalities are compounded in one consciousness, why not suppose that each of our consciousnesses might be compounded in an Earth-mind? Why should a central nervous system like ours be the only physiologically discernible correlate of some kind or degree of awareness?

James ailing and dying, his ardent departure from the beauteous earth sounds in these pages of *Pluralistic Universe* somewhat like Gustav Mahler's at exactly this time in his own last works. James's vision is of reconciliation and universal communion, and is reminiscent of Mahler's *Song of the Earth* and his unfinished Tenth Symphony. James:

> Not only the absolute is its own other, but the simplest bits of imme-diate experience are their own others, if that Hegelian phrase be once for all allowed. The concrete pulses of experience appear pent in by no such definite limits as our conceptual substitutes for them are confined by. They run into one another continuously and seem to interpenetrate. . . . My present field of consciousness is a centre surrounded by a fringe that shades insensibly into a subconscious more. I use three separate terms here to describe this fact; but I might as well use three hundred, for the fact is all shades and no boundaries. Which part of it properly is in my consciousness, which out? If I name what is out, it already has come in. The centre works in one way while the margins work in another, and presently overpower the centre and are central themselves. What we conceptually identify ourselves with and say we are thinking of at any time is the centre;

but our *full* self is the whole field, with all those indefinitely radiating subconscious possibilities of increase that we can only feel without conceiving, and can hardly begin to analyze.[17]

If we recall Black Elk's vision and its enactment for the people, we see immediately that the warrior-healer's communion with Wakan Tanka and James's last insights bear a deep affinity.

James's peroration in *Pluralistic Universe* is magnificent. It could be even ampler and deeper if he had kept his grip on certain insights in his *Essays in Radical Empiricism* five years earlier. As he himself would probably have agreed, to explore most acutely and revealingly the notion of plant, animal, and earth souls, we should not speak of *consciousness*, with its suggestion of a reflexive awareness of awareness, but of primal prereflexive sciousness. This would entail a gritty and imaginative development of body's minding, its being caught up in an evolving and interdependent organismic world, in which there is much more to minding than what we call consciousness. Indeed, consciousness arises only with some glitch, however momentary, in the interfusing, interdepending, interadapting flow and pull of the world that is unconscious minding (as we will soon see, John Dewey develops the distinction between mind and consciousness in the internal chapters of *Experience and Nature*).

Most of all, James's own notion of floating pure experiences—fundaments and raw materials of thought—can expand and deepen his last vision. Note again floating regard: when, on the primal or aboriginal level of experience it is not clear that *I* regard the *other*. The distinction between subject and object greatly blurs or no longer holds. With the suspension of the distinction, *we* are in suspense. We listen hard, as Black Elk puts it, and look passionately, and the plant, the mountain, the earth listens and looks back. The world takes our breath away. Then in our intake, in our gasp of awe, this community of beings is let into ourselves. The regenerative universe free flowing within us—or we within it—is the full and easy breathing ensuing upon this. For Jews, the life-giving flow is sounded in vowels, particularly those of G-d's name that should never be written on pain of blasphemy—only cuts in the flow can be written, the consonants (YHWH). For Socrates the gasp of awe prompts aversion to writing: For it will implant forgetfulness in their souls. Buddhists discover the buoying and sustaining medium in the all-encompassing and pervasive, the all-enlivening presence, sounded in the breathing of OM. St. Paul writes of God as that in which we live and move and have our being. Black Elk speaks of Wakan Tanka, the pervading mysterious principle that animates all things.

In whatever form, this is the healing level, the shamanic level—wild beasts of the philosophic desert. This is where his academic colleagues would not or could not follow him. This is the challenge he leaves to us.

Notes

1. *The Principles of Psychology* (New York: Dover Books, 1950 [1890]), 1:184. William James, *The Principles of Psychology, The Works of William James* (Cambridge, Mass.: Harvard University Press, 1981) (hereafter cited as "critical edition"), 184.

2. *The Principles of Psychology*, 1:291 ff. Critical edition, 279–80. See also my *William James and Phenomenology: A Study of "The Principles of Psychology"'* (Bloomington: Indiana University Press, 1979 [1968]), 124 ff.

3. See Shaun Gallagher, "Mutual Enlightenment: Recent Phenomenology in Cognitive Science," *Journal of Consciousness Studies* 4, 3 (1997), especially 210.

4. "The Thing and Its Relations," in *Essays in Radical Empiricism* (New York: Longmans, Green and Co., 1958 [1912]), 93 ff. In my *The Essential Writings of William James* (Albany: State University of New York Press, 1984), 198. William James, *Essays in Radical Empiricism, The Works of William James* (Cambridge, Mass.: Harvard University Press, 1976) (hereafter cited as "critical edition"), 45–46.

5. "The Place of Affectional Facts in a World of Pure Experience," in *Essays in Radical Empiricism*, 144. Critical edition, 72. See also *The Essential Writings of William James*, 204 ff.

6. *A Pluralistic Universe* (New York: Longmans, Green and Co., 1958 [1909]), 266. William James, *A Pluralistic Universe, The Works of William James* (Cambridge, Mass.: Harvard University Press: 1977) (hereafter cited as "critical edition"), 118–19.

7. Page 305. Critical edition, 138.

8. "In Animals We Find Ourselves," *Orion: Nature Quarterly* (Summer 1990).

9. A neurobiologist I think of particularly is Antonio R. Damasio, M.D., Ph.D. (*Descartes' Error: Emotion, Reason, and the Human Brain* [New York: Putnam, 1994]). Notice also Bruce Mangan, "Taking Phenomenology Seriously," *Consciousness and Cognition* 2 (1993): 89–108. Refreshingly he sees the great relevance of James's idea of fringe to brain research. The focus of consciousness is very limited in what it can accommodate moment by moment. The fringe directs the movement of thinking and perceiving without having to be focal. For example, when unable to remember a name, this absence in consciousness is not an absence of consciousness. The fringe quivers expectantly, sometimes calling up the name, or at least able to recognize instantly when the right name is suggested. The fringe fades off into areas that are not conscious at all, but in which brain activity may be present. There is a conceptual tie binding thinking processes and brain, but the reverse of stifling empirical research, close phenomenological description of the fringe may point researchers in the right horizons to look for the whole ensemble of brain activity, some of it exceedingly subtle perhaps. Despite Mangan's contribution, however, he fails to make a clear distinction between thinking and thought-about, does not see the necessity of double-barreled mentalistic terms. Though he is right to relate James to certain "connectionist" theories in current brain science, and right to point out the distinction in these theories between serial and parallel brain processes, he does not see how the crucial thinking/thought-about distinction could relate to the crucial serial/parallel distinction. Prima facie, the thought-about experienced as remaining the same through time may best be conceived as running in parallel to various modes of thinking it, for instance, perceiving, remembering, anticipating,

hypothesizing. He is correct in thinking that connectionist theorists should come up with "rightness or goodness networks in the brain" (106)—networks that correlate with our felt sense that the right answer to our questioning or questing has been supplied. But he does not see the full phenomenological context required to help them to do this.

10. Quoted in Christiane Northrup, M.D., *Women's Bodies—Women's Wisdom* (New York: Bantam Books, 1994), 25.

11. *A Pluralistic Universe,* 133. Critical edition, 63.

12. "On a Certain Blindness in Human Beings," in *Talks to Teachers on Psychology and to Students on Some of Life's Ideals,* critical edition, 229 ff, and in my *The Essential Writings of William James,* 332. Critical edition, 132 ff.

13. *A Pluralistic Universe,* 152–53. Critical edition, 71–72.

14. Pages 158–59. Critical edition, 73–74.

15. *Seven Experiments That Could Change the World* (New York: Riverhead Books, 1995).

16. *A Pluralistic Universe,* 299. Critical edition, 135.

17. Pages 282 ff. Also in *The Essential Writings of William James,* 362–64. Critical edition, 127–28 ff.

James on Truth
The Preeminence of Body and World

James on truth may seem to be a worn-out topic. At least the epistemological aspect of James's thought has been thoroughly covered, has it not? Don't we know that James committed the howling error of confusing truth and confirmation of truth?

But I think this critical judgment on James has been passed within presuppositions foreign to James's own; his thought on truth has typically been misunderstood. We cannot look at James through the lenses of Descartes' dualism and mentalism and expect to see what's there. To get a clear view of what James believed, we cannot think there is a detachable epistemological aspect of his thinking, but must patiently reconstruct the evolving worldview that brought him inexorably to thoughts about truth.

The very idea of a worldview was not very congenial to him, given its suggestion of abstractness. Yet he developed one because through painful experience, both as scientist and thoughtful human being, he couldn't get minimal business done unless things wove themselves together and made sense in ways that were ultimate, irreducible. These weavings were useful at a rock-bottom level that most critics of his idea of truth as usefulness never imagined: a level without which all other ideas of usefulness make no sense, for without them there is no experience of world at all.

James believed that his critics missed the point: the absolute priority of the *meaning* of truth, and the urgent need to make this meaning *concrete*. Of course, what is needed is the truth about meaning! But ahead of Husserl, and critical of the absolute idealists' phenomenologies—and caught up in the toils and growing pains of his own clamoring thought—he couldn't spell out the phenomenological method of clarifying and establishing meanings that actually got him around in life and in thought. Nor was he consistently aware of primal or indigenous-like insights strained and funneled to him, particularly through Emerson.

As we have seen, the main focus of his professional life from 1878 to 1892 was the construction of a psychology that would avoid the metaphysical assumptions and presumptions of nearly all earlier psychologies. It would be natural-scientific and commonsensically dualistic: there are thoughts on the one hand and there are things on the other. We saw how his project failed. However, discarding what failed opened the way to creative achievement.

James discovers that thinker and thought are in a key way *identical* to the world of things thought about. He has landed himself squarely in metaphysics: a maverick version of Schelling and Hegel's identity-philosophy, a metaphysics he tried feverishly to complete before his death in 1910.[1]

He cannot accept the absolute idealists' belief in a through and through unity of the world formed in an Absolute Mind through its dialectical logic. He opts for a "pulverized identity philosophy": each bit of pure experience (anterior to and neutral between mental and physical, subject and object) is a "little absolute": it spreads into what intellectualistic logic says it is not, into its own others. To escape from the Absolute, James devises his own kind of phenomenology, one abetted by his never completely quiescent artistic abilities, and by his keen feeling of kinship with the natural world. I would call this feeling primal and pragmatic.

What do we actually have to think with? What are the resources of thought—not merely what we would like them to be if we were gods or goddesses. Assuredly it is not "sense data" supposed to be "in the mind"! Even in *The Principles* James had seen that such supposed mental particulars in the mind are derivative from particular interests and analyses (perhaps those of psychophysics). They are not building blocks of knowledge and reality. They are derivative, the fruit of abstraction from the immediacy of encounter with, and flow within, the world, abstraction that forgets itself. To think that philosophizing begins with sense data is to cheat at the start. It's to jump the gun and to deny with all apparent sincerity what one has done.

More and more he realizes the metaphysical implications of this idea. Before there can be any idea of mental particulars or sense data "in here," perhaps caused by something "out there," we must have an experience of simply being together with other things in the world. As we have seen, in immediate, moody involvement with things, it may not be clear that *I* regard *them.* We may feel as much regarded as regarding. "Objects" and "subjects" are abstractions that have forgotten what they are. (John Dewey elaborates, as we will see: sense data theories of knowledge are instances of *the* philosophical fallacy: mistaking what only emerges at a particular stage of inquiry for what antedates and provides the matrix for the inquiry.)

James struggles to describe our actual resources as thinkers: what is provided to be thought, given. It is assuredly not the sense data of British empiricism. We must penetrate the veil of supposedly private sensations, images, thoughts, and describe where we find ourselves anterior to any theorizing—that is, we are with things, co-participants!

James knows viscerally that he is caught up in the very substance of things, and that their identities—so neatly cut out and discriminated from one another by the logistic, verbalistic, and, too often, scientistic intellect—actually blur into one another. Talk of my personal and private experience presupposes a contrast with yours, presupposes that we both exist in the world. When we look in the sky and agree that it's blue, that is all the objectivity that we need for most of our purposes. "My mind" and "your mind" are reified bits of language, abstractions that forget the community of minding in the actual world that binds us together.

This is a community of minding bodies. In the radical empiricist essay "How Two Minds Can Know One Thing" he writes that knowing is a matter of being led in the world. When your minding or leading leads to the same place as mine, and this is the expected terminus for both of us, we simply know that we are knowing the same thing. He gives disarming examples. When you grasp me by my right wrist, I feel grasped at the same place you feel your grasping to be. To need more certainty than this for shared reference is to need the unneeded.

But of course, not all cases of actual or possible knowledge are so cut and dried. The last crucial phase of James's work includes his *Varieties of*

Religious Experience, a painstaking study of mystical experiences in which conversions occur because personal identities do alter and expand and merge. (Merge with what, ultimately? He doesn't exactly know.) Indeed, already in *The Principles* his sharp eye was laying the groundwork for his most direct of all direct realisms (the phrase is Hilary Putnam's[2]). When, for example, we are shamed by someone in authority, his or her total attitude, visage, or words work immediately on our inner organs, particularly the visceral—wrenching, turning, withering them: experienced, this just *is* shame.

James had a genius for sizing up and describing various situations in their wholeness, immediacy, passing and piercing actuality. Essential to his phenomenological abilities are his artistic. If asked whether things have determinate structures—molecular or atomic, say—we will reflect and affirm they do. But, as we have seen, what's actually experienced immediately may be no definite "what" but only a "that" *there* (though a "that" ready to become all kinds of "whats"). Our whole mental "machinery" may be momentarily disrupted as we are turned in a cusp toward the unknown. But we have a brute sense of the resistant world even though at times we may be mistaken about *what's* there.

Now no doubt the molecular structure of what disrupts us is just what it is. But if we think that such knowledge is more fundamental than that supplied in immediate sensuous experience, we risk misunderstanding ourselves, as well as the rest of reality—risk misunderstanding meaning and truth. We risk believing that real causation is something hidden in the cubic deeps, discoverable perhaps only by science, and that sensuous experience is a mere surface phenomenon to be explained by what is hidden. But James writes that water, say, just as really slakes thirst as it is really composed of H_2O, and that without causal relations on the "surface" level of human activity, experienced and known as such, we could not proceed to specify the particular sorts of causal activity that, say, chemical causes turn out to be.

> [A] philosophy of pure experience can consider the real causation as no other *nature* of thing than that which even in our most erroneous experiences appears to be at work. Exactly what appears there is what we *mean* by working, though we may later come to learn that working was not exactly *there*. Sustaining, persevering, striving, paying with effort as we go, hanging on, and finally achieving our intention— this *is* action, this *is* effectuation in the only shape in which, by a pure experience philosophy, the whereabouts of it anywhere can be discussed. Here is creation in its first intention, here is causality at

work. To treat this offhand as the bare illusory surface of a world whose real causality is an unimaginable ontological principle hidden in the cubic deeps, is . . . only animism in another shape. You explain your given fact by your "principle," but the principle itself, when you look clearly at it, turns out to be nothing but a previous little spiritual copy of the fact. Away from that one and only kind of fact, your mind, considering causality, can never get.[3]

Given the pervasive psycho/physical dualism of most modern philosophy, many philosophers today will dismiss this claim as of merely psychological—or merely epistemological—significance. But it is just the dualism inherent in these disciplines that James so fundamentally challenges. He is interested in recording primal, original, immediate *fact*—fact as the structure of appearance, or *meaning*. Descartes holds a coin before his eye, one that, small as it is, yet covers the apparent disk of the sun. Perhaps all our evidence for a world is merely like the apparent disk of the sun—sense data—that may mislead us about what's really out there?

But Descartes can begin to generate this doubt only by tacitly supposing that the sun really is—or very probably is—huge. His doubt is self-stultifying. Descartes smuggles in a view of the world he cannot declare. The concealment is not easily detected because of his pretension to doubt everything. But once Descartes "proves" that the Creator would not have created creatures who could not know His creation, he simply assumes that "the external world" must be as the Cartesian mechanistic physics describes it. But his physics is possible only on the basis of a pretheoretical sense of "world" that Descartes simply begs. James will not beg it.

Hegel aims to eliminate the cheating from the start that characterizes scientific-sounding psycho/physical dualisms: We cannot suppose that knowing and knowledge are like separate psychical processes—like a lens interposed between knower and known—that distort the reality out there—and all we have to do to get at the thing itself is to know the distortion caused by the lens and to correct for that in our account of the thing. All this begs the question of the nature of knowledge, truth, and world. For we must be tacitly supposing that we already *know* what lies *beyond* the distorting lens—the lens that we claim to be the knowing itself. We must be supposing some truth about the "external" world in our attempt to doubt its existence.

James falls within the Hegelian tradition, very broadly construed. Stung in *The Principles of Psychology*, he strives to avoid begging the most fundamental questions about knowledge and reality, cheating from the start. His focus is metaphysical or ontological (albeit in an unconventional garb); epistemology cannot be autonomous. The very nature of activity and causation must be known on the "surface" level of phenomena of human agency, however much we may then modify our account of this nature when we investigate activity and causation through the hard sciences, for example. Phenomenology may be insufficient for metaphysics, but it is absolutely necessary for it—necessary if science, also necessary, is not to pose as sufficient. That is, if we are to avoid the ideology of scientism.

This is the key idea in James's later approach to philosophy: He is basically concerned not just with the nature of activity, to be prized out phenomenologically, but with the nature of world in which any activity must occur—with what this tells us about this world and about truth in general. Falling into the psycho/physical and scientism trap, we believe that truth can reside only in mental (or linguistic) contents that somehow correspond to something really real out there in the deeps of the world. But this cannot be, writes James. Because the very meaning of "world" gets constituted in the meaning and truth that get made by us worldly sensuous beings interacting and interfusing with other things on the "surface" level.

It is all too easy to draw a picture on a blackboard in which ideas inside a head correspond to what they purport to be about in the "external" world, and hence are true. But the picture easily leads to skepticism: How can any of us get out of our heads without going out of our minds? James rejects the blackboard picture. We cannot be locked up in a private experience, because without things understood as experienceable by us interfusing, minding organisms we can form no meanings, not even "external" or "blackboard," or anything else. The blackboard picture tempts us to think of truth as an occult relation between two incommensurable domains. No, actual truth can occur only within the realm of the experienceable, the experienceable world. Truth must be a matter of coherence: the fruitful building out of one phase of experience into another. Truth is what guides us reliably in the world.

Meaning and truth get made, according to James. How? He acknowledges that concepts form a coordinate realm of reality, and that whenever a "what" appears at the intersection of personal and world histories, conceptualization is at work within perceptual experience.[4] But we must forever return to "the perceptual much at once" to replenish, modify, and augment our stores of meaning, which includes conceptualization itself. For concepts are ways of generating expectations and activities that sort out the experienceable world in the light of our evolving interests. Concepts are not visitations from an eternal realm of forms. They do not mark out changeless essences of things ("essence" is always put in scare quotes by James: in effect, the traits necessary to identify something within a historical period of inquiry and its particular needs and interests).[5] Moreover, early in *The Varieties*, James introduces a concept, that of religion, in terms of a wide "family resemblance" of traits (long before Wittgenstein), some of which are more important at one time, some at another. Needs of living organisms evolve within various whole situations in which we are caught up prereflectively, beyond our ability to reflectively grasp where exactly we are and what exactly moves us: Caught up in evolving expectations and leadings within a world experienceable in some ways to some extent—caught up in what James calls sciousness, not—again—consciousness with its gratuitous suggestion of awareness along with itself, or awareness reflecting itself.

Ponder the materials actually given to think with, according to James: Not only are there "thats" that are not yet "whats," though ready to become all sorts of whats—suggesting a radical creativity possible for us. Only by setting up tests, however rapidly, expectations that are either fulfilled or not, do we even know what we mean and where we are. (Some have said that the ultimate questions for human beings at all times and places are, Where are we? and What time is it?) The constitution of the meaning of the world is an evolving experimental activity, always open ended on some parameters, in which the meaning of things is established in terms of their experienceability. Without knowing what we mean by world, we cannot know about truth.

We are nearly ready to discuss what James means exactly by "truth." But there is one more point to be made first. An obvious and tempting way to think about truth must have seemed to James so obviously empty and misleading that he did not ever, I think, explicitly and carefully dismiss it. This is just to conflate the meaning of "truth" and "reality." If, naturally enough, we suppose that reality has determinate structure, this must be just *what* it is—right? If it is *what* it is, there must be this *truth* about it—yes? We may not know what it is, but that is irrelevant to what it actually is. The inference tempts and is nearly irresistible: If things are what they are, there must be the truth of this what, whether *we* know this truth or not. So truth must *be* regardless of what we know or do not know about it, for example, regardless of what we think makes it possible.

James resists this tempting inference with all his might. It mindlessly supposes that we do already know the ways the world might be determinate, and that these ways are accurately pictured in the propositions we might form. But what are the capacities and limits of our ability to determine what "determinate" might *mean*? Pretending to respect the majesty of truth by declaring it to be independent of our knowledge, it presumes that we already *know* what we should *mean* by "determinate." But we don't. There may be meanings of it crucial to grasping the world that we have yet to imagine. The natural tendency to equate in some general way "truth" and "reality" results in a gross tautology that is greatly misleading.

Now let us take up James's positive account of the meaning of meaning and of truth and how they get made. In the light of the labile and limited material of thought actually available to us, how is a meaningful, an experience-able, world formed? We are after an utterly primordial usefulness, without which no reliable awareness of a world would be possible, no survival, thriving, meaningful suffering, meaningful ecstasy, and none of that crass usefulness that most of James's critics *thought* he was talking about when he equated meaning and truth with usefulness.

What we expect to find, we do find. Within the *Essays in Radical Empiricism* themselves—not in a separate pragmatic theory of meaning and truth— James outlines what the conditions of meaning and truth must be.[6] In the second Essay, "A World of Pure Experience," with the subheading "The Cognitive Relation," he writes,

> Throughout the history of philosophy the subject and its object have been treated as absolutely discontinuous entities. . . . Representative theories put a mental "representation," "image," or "content" into the gap, as a sort of intermediary. . . . Transcendentalist theories left it impossible to traverse by finite knowers, and brought an Absolute to perform the saltatory act. All the while, in the very bosom of finite experience, every conjunction required to make the relation intelligible is given in full. Either the knower and the known are:
>
> (1) the self-same piece of experience taken twice over in different contexts; or they are
> (2) two pieces of *actual* experience belonging to the same subject, with definite tracts of conjunctive transitional experience between them; or
> (3) the known is a *possible* experience either of that subject or another, to which the said conjunctive transitions *would* lead, if sufficiently prolonged.

James is writing about knowing and knowledge, not explicitly at this point about meaning and truth. But as we shall see ever more clearly, for James there can be no meaningful talk about truth without assumptions about what we mean by truth, and no talk about meaning without assumptions about meaning-known, which is the point of his unnamed phenomenology to uncover: the "specific natures" of things (a chastened, family resemblance notion of "essence," if you will). There can be no truth floating in the blue: it must be rooted in a world constituted in its meaning through its experienceability by bodily experiencers. Truth can mean only reliable situational orientations, transitions, guidances, fulfillments—answers to meaningful questions, implicit or manifest. Truth considered to be merely a property of a statement or proposition is a vicious intellectualism that abstracts from the concrete reality of the situation and forgets it does so, substituting an occult relation, "truth," for concrete and concretely known and knowable relations, connections, processes. Since there is no gulf between "the mind" and "the world" to be jumped by "the mind" and its "mental representations"—such as propositions or statements—there can be no jumping of a gulf.

James's three levels of cognition must be taken in the strictest sense of logical and metaphysical priority: (2) presupposes (1), and (3) presupposes (1) and (2). (Or we could speak of constituting and constituted levels, as does Edmund Husserl.) That is, for (1) "the self-same piece of experience taken twice over in different contexts"—let us revert for the moment to his first example, the blue of the sky. It is primordial knowing of primordial sensuous meaning, simply truth as disclosure, whether articulated as such or not. Without this there could not be that orientation in situations that allows us to ask pointed questions, to expect something to be the case, and that leads us successfully to its fulfillment (when we have empirical truth)—the actual leading James speaks of as level (2). And without both these levels there could not be (3): the known is a *possible* experience either of that subject or another, to which the said conjunctive transitions *would* lead if sufficiently prolonged.

Now, establishing (3) gives James the greatest difficulty. For (1) and (2) are certainly necessary for it, but (3) has conditions of its own that must be met. It's a form of knowing a known in the wide world, but how could we ever know that the conjunctive relations or leadings in which we are caught up *would* lead to a *possible* experience of the thing to be known?

Clearly, multiple concepts are involved at this level, and James does not tell us enough about concepts as a coordinate realm of reality. Yes, they are teleological instruments that sort out the world pursuant to our needs and interests, but just how does this sorting take place so that what we're sorting is the real world, and—truly—not mere surface phenomena? How can they guide us reliably through the real world?

James is in a kind of bind here. He definitely does not want to fall under the spell of a kind of Platonism that supposes that "the mind's eye" has already seen the eternal Forms of all things and then projects them onto a physical world that must conform to them (more or less)—a sure leap across a chasm from the eternal into the temporal domain. He does not want to mindlessly suppose, for example, that the structure of our statements or propositions just does determine what reality must be. He wants to retain the concreteness and embeddedness in the thick, thick world characteristic of levels (1) and (2). He is afraid of anything that even slightly suggests a fantastic leap across a chasm or gulf. So afraid is he that he doesn't want to ascribe to thoughts, for instance, conceptions, any "self-transcendent" quality. They are "flat," they just lead us as they will within the thick, actual world.

But there are grave and fairly obvious difficulties with this approach. We *must* already know the sort of thing we *expect* to find in order to realize either that we have been led to it, or that we have been misled, that is, not led to it. Conceptions must be self-transcendent in this limited but funda-mental sense.[7] Moreover, there are situations to be known in which we seemingly could have no idea of the *possible* experience in which we *would* be led if we continued our inquiry. Take the belief, "There are no extrater-restrial forms of intelligent life." This is probably false, but just maybe it's true. We can't imagine experiencing all the angles on every point in the whole universe, or all the modes of interpreting "intelligence," that would be necessary to have the experience of no intelligent life being there. There are probably millions or billions of planets that might shelter intelligent life, and we can't hope to know them all.

Or take a case closer to hand. How can any belief about the past be true in James's view of truth? The past is past, is gone, how can we imagine being led up to it?

Since James's earliest days as a philosopher, he had described truth as "coerciveness over thought in the long run."[8] There is no single way that experience is true of the world by "agreeing" with it, because coerciveness over thought can take indefinitely many forms. But there seem to be sit-uations—as just above—in which we can't even imagine what form this coerciveness might take.

James was not altogether unaware of these difficulties. Let us patiently work our way through some of his texts and try to discern what he was trying to say. He acknowledged at the end that his philosophy was "too much like an arch built up on only one side," and we are right, I think, to believe that the main lack is insight into the workings of the coordinate realm of concepts.

I will be direct: Altogether, the three relations of cognition James sets forth in "A World of Pure Experience" are necessary to constitute the very meaning of the vast world. *They are necessary to hold the world together as experienceable—as what it means.* Nothing short of this. So truth cannot be some kind of occult relation between mind, or language, on the one hand, and world on the other. The different domains don't exist. To think they do is to be caught yet again in the snares of dualism.

But hasn't James confused confirmation of truth with truth? No. What we mean by truth is that it stands whether actually confirmed or not. Because what we mean by world is that it continues whether those members of it that are our knowing selves actually succeed or not in all our projects of knowing, all our searches for truth. (Without supposing that we are often right in the meaning and truth that get made, we can't suppose that we have a world at all in experience, and without that supposition, thought—whether true or false—is impossible.) We are not crazy enough to think that when we confirm that our dog, say, is in the garage, that this creates the dog! Or that if we confirm our belief that he is dead that this kills him!

James uses examples to illuminate the meaning of the vast world unfolding in time, its disclosure and experienceability a founding level of belief, the sense of the world's reality: "Though our discovery of any [thing] . . . may only date from now, we unhesitatingly say that it not only *is,* but *was* there, if, by so saying, the past appears connected more consistently with what we feel the present to be. . . . Julius Caesar was real, or we can never listen to history again. Trilobites were once alive, or all our thought about the strata is at sea."[9] But we cannot meaningfully believe that *all* our thought about the strata is at sea—taking "strata" as exemplifying a real world structured somehow. We must believe whatever is necessary to have a world, this generally reliable whole that has its own evolutionary process and structure, whatever our particular cognitive failures or successes might be. The very meaning of cognitive success or failure, and the very meaning of truth and error, depends upon it.

Still, so wedded to psycho/physical and subject/object dualism are most that the thought may persist that James does not adequately distinguish truth from its confirmation. Say I think now while in my study that there are no elephants in the kitchen. Surely if this is true, it is so now, before it is confirmed. James seems to be aware that his implicit use of founding and founded levels of meaning might not still such an objection. In the last sentence of what I think is his best work on truth as explicit topic, "Humanism and Truth" (first in *Mind*, 1904), he writes of this truth prior to confirmation as "virtual": "Pragmatically, virtual and actual truth mean the same thing: the possibility of only one answer, *when once the question is raised*" (the last sentence of the piece, the italics are his). And James, of course, is a pragmatist, and one who seems to know that we must make roughly the same commitments to the reality of the world—in terms of its experienceability—that our hunter-gatherer ancestors made.

This clause that he italicizes—"when once the question is asked"—rings down the curtain on the article, and sums up the pragmatism he actually uses in his own creative thought as a subset of his metaphysics of radical empiricism. There is truth, but its very meaning cannot stand independently of primally disclosive and orienting situations in which it comes as an answer to a meaningful question, explicit or tacit. If a question points to an answer that is the only one that does work out time after time—or could work out we believe, given some ideally prolonged inquiry and interaction we think at least we can imagine—then we must believe it is true *now*. It can be true now even if only later we confirm that it is. In the parlance of analytic philosophy, "truth" is a tenseless predicate, while "confirm" or "discover" is tensed.

James realizes his position appears to be paradoxical: we both make truth and find it. He resolves the apparent paradox with his stock-in-trade phenomenological skill: by describing actual situations of inquiry in their many-faceted wholeness. Truth is *found* when attention is placed on one facet of the situation, *made* when placed on another.

An example he uses is the second-magnitude stars so nearly equal in brightness that definitively make up the constellation "Big Dipper." One facet of the situation is the "stars themselves," another is the "counting and comparing mind." Notice the following (again in "Humanism and Truth"— at its close) where "fact" must mean "truth about the world": "A fact virtually pre-exists when every condition of its realization save one is already there. In this case the condition lacking is the act of the counting and comparing mind. But the stars (once the mind considers them) themselves dictate the result. The counting in no wise modifies their previous nature, and, they being what and where they are, the count cannot fall out differently. It could then *always* be made. *Never* could the number seven be questioned *if the question once were raised.*" We have here a quasi-paradox. Undeniably something comes by the counting that was not there before. And yet that something was *always true*. In one sense we create it, and in another we find it. We have to treat our account as being true beforehand the moment we come to treat the matter at all. We have to treat our account as true beforehand, because, again, we have to treat our account as *of* things in a *world:* an ongoing and fundamentally coherent whole that *must be thought to exist prior to all our projects and as situating them.*

He adds another paragraph to remind us of what he means by the counting and comparing mind, and how meaning actually gets made in this actual world. There is no mind in itself that might hold a copy of what pre-existed out there. Though the sheer *number* of stars doesn't change by being counted, nevertheless the very content of the world does get altered through the counting. That is, the stars themselves do get connected to a number tally, and to a dipper for our sight; they do get "built out" by it into a recognizable constellation. In other words, they are amplified in their sphere of influence—and reality is a matter of things' and events' radiating fields of consequences within the meaningful, the experienceable, world: "Our stellar attributes must always be called true, then, yet none the less are they genuine additions made by our intellect to the world of fact. Not additions of consciousness only, but additions of 'content.' They copy nothing that pre-existed, yet they agree with what pre-existed, fit it, amplify it, and build it out."[11]

Only because the world is really a somewhat more cohesive and vital place through being counted, for example, can it hang together in experience as a world. The truth about the stars means a peculiarly reliable hanging together in experience. Error must mean a leading to disconnection or disaster in the long run, whether we ever can confirm that it does or not.

Yet again (the crust of misunderstandings is so old and deep!): to say that a belief is true now, though not yet confirmed, is just to believe that experience would continue to hang together if inquiry were to be properly continued. If this looks circular—if "truth" is defined in terms of "properly" and "ideally long run," and these in terms of "truth"—then I think James would have to agree. But I think he would think it to be an unavoidable circle, so not vicious. If we won't simply reify an abstract word, "truth," and turn it into an occult relation across a fantastic chasm, we must bite the bullet and admit an element of ideality in the meaning of "truth" as used in the actual world.

But what of those difficulties for his view outlined above, situations in which we want to know about the past, or about possible extraterrestrial intelligent occupants of the cosmos? I think James's whole project suggests that he doesn't consistently think of concepts as "flat," and as just leading us one step at a time through very limited locales in almost total darkness, but that conceiving, like perceiving, is internally connected to, or essentially in, the world. That is, we cannot conceive a world at all, an experienceable one, unless we conceive that those concepts *must* apply that are necessary to form the meaning, "world."

James suggests at least that concepts of truth and reality are essentially or necessarily connected—though they are not isomorphic—and we cannot be sure if our language is sufficiently adequate even in its formal structure to grasp all the ways reality might be. Perhaps some realities elude the net of propositions as presently conceived and meant in their very form (and not forgetting the powers of mathematical logics)? Perhaps we have not yet imagined all the fertile questions that might be asked about the forms themselves!? Since the form of propositions is commonly taken to be the form *both* of statements equivalent in meaning *and* states of affairs in the world that the propositions are about, a deficiency in the notion of linguistic form must also be a deficiency in the notion of reality. But this would be concealed, and the concealing concealed, because the two senses of "proposition," the different "domains," cover for each other, bail each other out. What we cannot grasp or entertain with our propositions we will be unable even to imagine to be real.

There is reason for James to be suspicious of mere verbalism. "Proposition" as commonly used by philosophers does mean both the structure of thought or language and that of the world, of "what is the case." Floating and straddling as they do, propositions paper over the actual situations in which human organisms interact with the environment and sometimes eke out some truth. "True propositions" have some usefulness, of course, but the typical theorizings about them blur and fudge the relationship of organism and environment in which truth happens—and James is fed up with desiccation, a paper existence. (Recall Kant's insistence that the Idea of Pure Reason, which is that of the universe as the totality of determinate states of affairs, cannot be constitutive of this reality, but is only a heuristic device to spur us to ever more investigation on all fronts.)

But *are* there extraterrestrial forms of intelligent life?! Or, can we *know* the past?! Perhaps the greatest advantage of James's approach over others' is that his reveals just how limited and fallible our knowledge very often is. Whereas others who believe that our propositions either are or are not true, whether we know that they are or not—these others deceive themselves and us with a false sense of security. They simply assume that we already have an adequate idea of determinate reality, and probably also assume that science as we know it will ultimately apprise us of all that we want or need to know.

I think James would think this to be hubris, overweening pride, and I would agree. We do not float in the blue surveying the universe. We are humans sunk over our heads in the thingy and messy world.

James cuts through shiny verbal surfaces. For this reason, and others, he has greatly stimulated major thinkers of this century, Husserl—and through him Merleau-Ponty and Heidegger—and Whitehead, Dewey, Wittgenstein, and now Putnam.

Hilary Putnam is one of the very very few thinkers holding unimpeachable analytic credentials who also knows James quite well, acknowledges his greatness, and patiently works through the complexities and incompletenesses of his thought. I will close with a short review of Putnam's recent appreciation and critique of James.[12]

Putnam aptly terms James's view of perception to be direct realism. It cuts right through Cartesian psycho/physical dualism and representationalist ideas of knowing. This is an utterly fundamental point that, as any reader of this book must now know, I appropriate in my own way, in the most radical way I can imagine. I see it as a bridge that can finally connect European and indigenous thought. And by European I also include twentieth-century physics.

Black Elk explains how his cousin got his name, Crazy Horse. He was seeing his horse in a vision, in "a sacred manner." What does this mean pragmatically and concretely? As I've already suggested, if we go to twentieth-century field theories and quantum-field theories we get a big clue: the horse "itself" is not an isolated reality existing only within the envelope of its skin. But is rather a node-point in exfoliating shells of radiating energy that move through other nodes of fields of energy, and of course, through us. Perhaps "seeing in a sacred manner" includes experiencing these shells moving shimmeringly or "crazily" through us? If so, Crazy Horse was not perceiving crazily—nor was his horse loco or crazy—but he was perceiving more deeply and accurately than most of us usually do.

I'm probably extending direct realism farther than Putnam wants to take it. However, our points of agreement are fundamental. I agree with him about the basal level of perception. It must involve an "internal" connection to the world. That is, the very idea we form of reality is part and parcel of the idea we form of perception (when we are attuned to sciousness). Primal cognition is the very same pure experience that an instant later we can place in two different contexts or careers: my own history and that of the world at large. (Husserl speaks of perception as protodoxic, the most fundamental level of belief, as James had pointed out before him.)

I also agree with Putnam that James is not consistently a direct realist when it comes to conceptions. These form what James calls a coordinate realm of reality, but—and I agree again—he never really developed this realm, and that accounts pretty well for the incompleted or merely tacit parts of his philosophy. And I agree that this accounts for certain difficulties or uncertainties in his theory of truth.

Let's take something relatively easy to pin down in its meaning, something mundane—cut and dried, if you will. Putnam uses the example of the highly controversial Lizzie Borden ax-murder case. Did she do it back then? Putnam writes,

> If the immutability of the past means that it is a "reality" that Lizzie Borden committed the murders or a "reality" that she did not, *independently of whether one or the other of these judgments is ever confirmed*, then, if she committed the murders but the judgment that she did never becomes "coercive over thought," on James's theory of truth it will follow that
>
> > Lizzie Borden committed the murders, but the judgment that she did is not true—contradicting the principle that, for any judgment p, p is equivalent to the judgment that p is true.
> >
> > And similarly if she did *not* commit the murders, but the judgment that she did not never becomes "coercive over thought," we will have a violation of the same principle.[13]

I agree. If conception is not internally related to the world, if it is only a factual or happenstance leading, it cannot lead me to past things and events; they are gone. But if it is internally or necessarily connected, as is perception, then we can say that conceptions—as they figure in judgments about the past, say—can be true of the past. Just exactly which ones are, and which ones are not, we may never know.

Concepts, then, are minimally, but fundamentally, coercive over thought, because without supposing to be true some judgments about the past—replete with their concepts—we cannot have what we must have: an experienceable *world*, one in which the past is just what it was, regardless of what we happen to think, or not think, about it. Not all concepts need lead us anywhere, for some must apply immediately in our ongoing experience.

Perhaps James can be read as acknowledging this, though it's a stretch to read him this way. He writes, "Experience is only a collective name for all these sensible natures, and save for time and space (and, if you like, for 'being') there appears no universal element of which all are made."[14] And then again, "The great continua of time, space, and the self envelope everything, betwixt them, and flow together without interfering."[15]

It is not clear exactly what status James wants to give these terms. If we were to assume that he is talking about concepts, and if we assume that they always apply, then we might conclude that they must apply. But, again, the coordinate realm of reality, concepts, is not developed fully by James.

Putnam is completely right, at least as far as he goes. He may be more satisfied than I am that our judgments or asserted propositions, in their very structure, reveal all the reality that can be reliably revealed. His Lizzie Borden example is good, but we should not forget its limits. That case is fairly determinate in its meaning. The concepts needed—murderer, murdered, murdered by such and such means, and murdered at a time—are sufficiently clear to make the judgments we want to make about the case. So we must believe that one of the judgments—Lizzie did it, Lizzie did not do it—is true.

But what about extraterrestrial forms of intelligent life? The concept of intelligence, whether applied to terrestrials or extraterrestrials, is not nearly as clear as are the concepts in the Lizzie Borden case. What about forms of intelligent life or of action that may exceed our ability to imagine them and the many forms their interaction or interfusion with us might take?

What about a putative shamanic cure? On this level, the question, *Did it or did it not happen?* can be so uncertain in meaning that we cannot be sure whether the concept is putting us in touch with *it*. What *is* "it"? What is the cure? The scope of what is to count as a cure is not sharply etched in all the instances in which we wish to apply it. The sledgehammer question, Did it or did it not happen? may render us insensible to phenomena we should allow to burgeon and grow as they will, in their own time. As James would say, "Hands off! is the best advice in these cases."[16] Certain cures may come to fruition only when we do not ask the questions, "But has it really happened?" Or, "Is believing that it's happened true?"

Moreover, we mustn't forget that James distinguished knowledge by acquaintance from knowledge by description. He did not limit truth to the latter, to judgments or propositions that are true. Verbalizable or not, anything is true that "builds-out" in any way the past or present so as to develop, clarify, and better display it—moods, faces, silences, configurations in the forest.

(We must leave to another day the question of how concepts figure in knowledge by acquaintance.)

Moreover, *persons* (as well as other things) can be true if they habitually appear to be what they are, and if by developing themselves they develop their capacities, and enrich, draw out, and clarify what lies round about them as well (suggested, for example, by Aristotle in book delta of *Metaphysics*). James writes in *Varieties*, for instance, that he feels *truer to himself* if he respects his over-beliefs, his faith, if you will. I take this seriously. *Selves* can be true—or false. When indigenous Americans accused treaty-breaking Europeans of falseness, they did not refer only to their false judgments or statements. They meant that the Europeans were false in their *being*.

Finally, it is just because we must believe the world to be thick and obdurate and able to exist without us that we must believe that some of our concepts must apply to it, concepts like "she did it," or "she did not do it." But equally essential to our belief in the reality of the world is our conviction that concepts—teleological instruments—are limited in finding our way about within, and handling and sorting, the thick and often messy world. In immediate contact with the rest of the world, things are typically given as *thats* that may become indefinitely many kinds of *whats* (sorts or kinds specifiable by concepts). And there are kinds of experiences, notably religious experiences, in which the *thats* never become *whats*. We can only say, as James instructs us, that we contact "the more." That is, we contact "the more than can be conceptualized." This is absolutely essential to our visceral sense of the thickness and reality of the world, of our own bodies as organic members of the world, of our own actuality as finite beings.

We should not think that atavistic or archaic strands in James displayed in my account render him inhospitable to the needs and opportunities of science. There are reasons to trust in the long run and for the most part our gropings in this thick world. Our bodies have taken their structure from millions of years of prehuman and human adaptation within Nature. Good scientists grope, but not typically completely blindly. We know more than we know that we know, and it is reasonable to usually trust the body. James's friend Charles Peirce spoke at length about hypothesis formation. Ockham's Razor is typically taken to mean, Of two hypotheses equally plausible, take the simpler one. Peirce came to see "simpler" to mean "more natural." What is more natural for us bodily thinkers may be a clue to the truth of what we think. James helps us understand Peirce's insight.

William James allowed experience to speak in its richness and finitude, the strength of its finitude. He recalls ancient sage-philosophers who thought beyond facile sophistication into questions of personal and collective healing or salvation. He thought that the inability of many philosophers to understand his theory of meaning and truth was almost pathetic. And he closed his *The Pluralistic Universe* by noting that he didn't expect his academic colleagues to follow his pursuit of "wild beasts of the philosophic desert." His insight into pure or neutral experience has many more implications than classroom discussions of theories of meaning and truth tend to bring out. It is not merely the blueness of the sky that can possess us if we dilate to it. It is also animals and plants—those with great regenerative powers like snakes, or sage or red willow bark, or roots that regenerate themselves and grow in the dark.

At the turn of the century, James was embarking on a rational reconstruction of primal human involvements such as shamanism. Perhaps we can pardon him for not being perfectly clear about certain issues that preoccupy so many of us in this rootless age?

James begins and ends his intellectual life in wonder. Note chapter three of his last book, the unfinished *Some Problems of Philosophy: A Beginning of an Introduction to Philosophy*, "The Problem of Being":

> How comes the world to be here at all instead of the nonentity which might be imagined in its place? . . . One need only shut oneself in a closet and begin to think of the fact of one's being there, of one's queer bodily shape in the darkness (a thing to make children scream at, as Stephenson says), of one's fantastic character and all, to have the wonder steal over the detail as much as over the general fact of being, and to see that it is only familiarity that blunts it. Not only that *anything* should be, but that *this* very thing should be, is mysterious! Philosophy stares, but brings no reasoned solution, for from nothing to being there is no logical bridge. . . . The question of being is the darkest in all philosophy. All of us are beggars here. . . . Fact forms a datum, gift . . . which we cannot burrow under, explain, or get behind. It makes itself somehow and our business is far more with its What than with its Whence or Why.[17]

The world is just here, we find, we know not how or why. And so we *must* believe whatever is necessary to acknowledge this existence. The "must" has a "usefulness" more imperative and exalted than most of James's critics could ever imagine. Emerson declared that our identity is most deeply rooted in that which formed our bodies and nervous systems and to which we belong—Nature. Is it too much to say that Nature's ultimate gift is our ability to form the sense of *world* itself, and to be drawn out ecstatically into the horizon, *the everything else,* whatever it all might be?

We turn now to John Dewey, seventeen years James's junior, and of a temperament and style far more methodical than either James or Emerson. His most important work comes decades after James's death, and is imbued with a sense of science and technology. But as much as either thinker, he longs for a homecoming experience. He tries to integrate science, technology, urbanization, and our primal proclivities as organisms that must orient themselves in the whole somehow and feel that they belong. Visionary experiences of the sort we find in Black Elk—and even in Emerson, James, or Fechner—seem quite foreign to him, and yet he forms a vision inimitably his own in which "The unity of all the sciences is found in geography. The significance of geography is that it presents the earth as the enduring home of the occupations of man. The world without its relationship to human activity is less than a world. Human industry and achievement, apart from their roots in the earth, are not even a sentiment, hardly a name."[18] Dewey's homecoming is shorn of most of Emerson's and James's more obvious religious horizons. And its affinity to indigenous thought is almost completely concealed by its often dry, discursive mode of presentation. But it is infinitely more receptive to primal human experience than is the "analytic" quasi-scientific and narrowly focused philosophy that has taken over universities since Dewey's day. His work is a vast bridging operation, a great gift in its own right. It is just as much a gift as is Black Elk's vision and practice.

Notes

1. See my "The Breathtaking Intimacy of the Material World: William James's Last Thoughts," in R. A. Putnam, ed., *The Cambridge Companion to William James* (New York: Cambridge University Press, 1997).

2. "James's Theory of Truth," in R. A. Putnam, ed., *The Cambridge Companion to William James,* 175.

3. "The Experience of Activity," in *Essays in Radical Empiricism* (New York: Longmans, Green and Co., 1958 [1912]), 155 ff. Also in my *The Essential Writings of William James* (Albany: State University of New York Press, 1984), 216–17. *Essays in Radical Empiricism, the Works of William James* (Cambridge, Mass.: Harvard University Press, 1974) (hereafter cited as "critical edition"), 79 ff.

4. Though James never fully works out this idea of a coordinate realm of reality. See further in this essay.

5. *The Principles of Psychology* (New York: Dover Books, 1950 [1890]), 2:335, and fn. *The Principles of Psychology, the Works of William James* (Cambridge, Mass.: Harvard University Press, 1981) (hereafter cited as "critical edition"), 961–62.

6. It is lamentable that many professional philosophers limit their reading of James on truth to popular lectures that he published in 1907 as *Pragmatism: A New Name for Some Old Ways of Thinking* (Cambridge, Mass.: Harvard University Press, 1975). This tendency may have been strengthened by this being the inaugural work in the critical edition (!) of all James's work.

7. James seems to concede this in "Is Radical Empiricism Solipsistic?" in *Essays in Radical Empiricism,* his response to Boyd Bode's brilliant attack. Given some of James's statements— some of them careless—there is a danger of solipsism, of being cut off from the actual world. James comes up with a metaphor. An experience, for example, a conception, is like a compass needle: it "can point to the pole without moving from its box." This is a vivid metaphor, but it would be nice to have more description and explanation, more conceptual analysis.

8. See, for example, "Remarks on Spencer's Definition of Mind as Correspondence" (1878), in, for instance, my *The Essential Writings of William James.* Also of course in William James, *Essays in Philosophy, The Works of William James* (Cambridge, Mass.: Harvard University Press, 1978) (hereafter cited as "critical edition"), 7 ff.

9. "Humanism and Truth," in *The Meaning of Truth* (New York, 1909, and Ann Arbor: University of Michigan Press, 1970), 88, and in my anthology, 274. William James, *The Meaning of Truth, The Works of William James* (Cambridge, Mass.: Harvard University Press, 1975) (hereafter cited as "critical edition"), 54.

10. Page 94, and in my anthology, 277. Critical edition, 56–57.

11. Ibid.

12. I rely mainly on Putnam's "James's Theory of Truth," in *The Cambridge Companion to William James,* 166 ff.

13. Pages 182–83.

14. "Does 'Consciousness' Exist?" in *Essays in Radical Empiricism,* 27; my anthology, 173. Critical edition, 14–15.

15. "The Thing and its Relations," in *Essays in Radical Empiricism,* 94; in my anthology, 198. Critical edition, 46.

16. *Varieties of Religious Experience,* "Conversion," economically presented in my anthology, 239. Critical edition, 157.

17. William James, *Some Problems of Philosophy: A Beginning of an Introduction to Philosophy, The Works of William James* (Cambridge, Mass.: Harvard University Press, 1979), 26 ff. The critical edition is about four times the size of the original edition (New York, 1911). Since the book was left unfinished by James—and some of the "finished" portions in merely draft form—the critical edition performs an important function in this case. Let us hope it is widely read.

Echoing and amplifying James's assertion that our concern is more with the "what" of the universe than with its "whence" or "why," see Quentin Smith's very important, *The Felt Meanings of the World: A Metaphysics of Feeling* (La Fayette: Purdue University Press, 1986), 12 ff. The whole book should be read. It holds a fundamental phenomenological strand in need of being picked up by "Americanists" (how our great thinkers would have objected to such parochialism!).

18. *Essays on School and Society, John Dewey: The Middle Works, 1899–1924* (Carbondale: Southern Illinois University Press, 1976 [1899]), 1:13. Quoted more fully in the next essay.

PART TWO

Further Reclamations

rged into wild country, and the bright stars shown overhead in
 skies, unpolluted by staggering emissions of light from sprawl-
 during the night, and by continuous fossil fuel combustion. Oil
m vegetable contents of Earth that have been burned and the
own up into the sky. Now many millions have never seen Nature
 by human intervention—even the rain has been acidified, and
ave been so heavily veiled that these stupendous systems of energy,
e cosmic matrix, seem insignificant.

we find ourselves confined where wilderness is no longer directly
 the senses, some have said that we must find the wilderness in
They mean that through imagination we can resonate inwardly
ays lies somewhere beyond all sensory horizons, to *everything*
self-regenerating cosmos. There is something to be said for this
 are strange animals, not confined to what is immediately evident
s in the local environment. We stretch beyond all that is evident,
d imagine and dwell in possibilities, of whatever kind.

 beyonds—the beyond of the wilderness cosmos and the beyond
 body-selves—resonate with each other and intertwine so inti-
it is difficult or impossible to grasp the difference between them.
s adaptive resonance a remnant of the human species would not
d and we would not be here. The inner and the outer resonate
on to some extent even while we are lodged in cities. It may take
flight that disentrains our bodies' regenerative cycles, our "bio-
s," from the regenerative cycles of Earth to remind us of our
nt synchrony with Nature.

e level of primary experience, as Dewey puts it—or the primal,
dy as James does—a level of labile serpentine energies that blur
ding possibility from actuality, self from other, mind from body,
past, inner from outer, natural from supernatural, human from
is the fundamental level of interchange—call it the racial sub-
did Carl Jung—a level resembling deep ocean currents boiling
rwater caves and emerging on the other side of a boundary or

, the capacity "to find our wilderness within" is essential to
ut "within" suggests dualism and mentalism. It is easy to forget
ody-selves, habituated *body*-selves with essential perceptual
ough eons of adaptation we have been molded in and by the
/physical dualism is endlessly entrapping. Probably the loss
evident to the senses in the present and actual environment

John Dewey
Philosopher and Poet of Nature

The title of this volume, *Experience and Nature*. . . . To many the associating of the two words will seem like talking of a round square, so ingrained is the notion of the separation of man and experience from nature. . . . Experience reaches down into Nature; it has depth. It also has an indefinitely elastic extent. . . . That stretch constitutes inference. . . . "Experience". . . is "double-barrelled" in that it recognizes in its primary integrity no division between act and material, subject and object, but contains them both in an unanalyzed totality. "Thing" and "thought". . . are single-barrelled; they refer to products discriminated by reflection out of primary experience.
—John Dewey

But the glory of these forest meadows is a lily. . . . The tallest are from seven to eight feet high with magnificent racemes of ten or twenty or more small orange-colored flowers. . . . And to think that sheep should be allowed in these lily meadows! after how many centuries of Nature's care planting and watering them . . . yet, strange to say, allowing the trampling of devastating sheep. . . . And so the beauty of lilies falls on angels and men, bears and squirrels, wolves and sheep . . . but as far as I have seen, man alone, and the animals he tames, destroy these gardens.
—John Muir

Following Charles Darwin, and his own instincts and perceptions, John Dewey believes that experience can have integrity because it is integral with Nature. Yes, for better or worse, experience stretches beyond what Nature could provide without us, but its integrity requires recognition of its ineluctable rootedness in Nature. Fruitful experience digs back into its ground as it stretches toward its possibilities. It is primal and pragmatic.

Dewey died in 1952. Now we live at the cusp of millennia, and are vividly aware of the destruction of Nature. Many feel alone, bored, or disempowered, painfully aware of our loss of kindred in wild Nature, and dimly apprehensive that we will be left with only domesticated creatures, or worse, with Disney's humanoid ducks, rabbits, mice.

Some of us are more inclined now to think of animals as fellow subjects, not just entertaining objects, who experience the world in their own way. Shouldn't our experiencing of Nature, our meaning-making, include our experiencing of other creatures' experiencing of Nature, insofar as we can discern this? Though Dewey maintains we should emulate animal grace, he tells us something, but not very much, about animals' experiencing.

In any case, for him the concepts of human experience and Nature interpenetrate. At least a strong negative statement can be made about his thought. Human experiencing is not conceived along Cartesian lines, is not essentially self-reflexive and grandly isolated from the rest of creation. So the line drawn by some ecologists between "a human-oriented" approach to the world and "a thing-oriented" one is artificial and misleading. There is no Nature "in itself" or humanity "in itself"—whatever those phrases might mean.

John Muir in *My First Summer in the Sierra* points out how humans often behave as if they were out of place in Nature, wantonly disregarding her. This sets the problem for us: What is our place in Nature? Dewey gives us a tantalizing clue and a question: How can the stretching of experience, our powers of inference and imaginative symbolization, be wisely employed? So that we don't disrupt local environments that must always hold us, and without which we could not think, dream, plan, or do anything else?

Dewey's commentators have typically stressed our powers of logical inference, which includes science. But Dewey himself employed a vast battery of resources to try to reground us in Nature, to regain a sense of harmony and solidity. This includes his fugitive powers of metaphor and poetry—magical speech, if you will—aspects of Dewey's work that have been singularly ignored, and when not ignored, maligned. "Dewey a poet?! Ridiculous." Let us focus on salient points of his vast and somewhat problematical homecoming trajectory over the decades.

What is our place in Nature?—a formidable question, for we are ecstatic creatures who feel and imagine beyond horizons, and who construct and reconstruct ourselves and the world in the light of our feelings and imaginings. Our ecstatic transcendence into endless possibilities permeates our lives. Human verbal language, for example, is open ended: its creative powers cannot be precisely mapped. Plankton, other plants, animals, insects deeply affect the rest of Nature, but not, presumably, at the behest of imagination. The changes these other creatures make are profound but typically slow, giving Earth time in which to adjust itself and reach new equilibrium.

But humans, impelled by fear, imagination, greed, wild dreams, even some benevolent in intent, have set in motion abrupt changes that have destroyed vast areas of animal and vegetable forms evolved and regenerated through "how many centuries of Nature's care." We feel the dizziness of freedom

and an imminent fall. The rain forests cut dow[n]
porary grazing for beef cattle (a chunk larger [than]
every second). As people consume their fast-f[ood]
do not realize that they contribute to the d[estruction]
other species, of green growing things, of the[...]

So of course they do not realize how the[...]
depletion of our psychical resources: forests as[...]
brooding presences—waters refreshing and[...]
ecstasy—the materials of our dreams and[...]
modern technology and production too o[ften...]
our foundational dreaming and daydreami[ng...]

What is our place in Nature? The most p[...]
answer this ancient and now urgent questio[n...]
seventy years of publishing, teaching, and[...]
and academic-professional groups. He tho[ught...]
of cultural disintegration brought on by i[...]
and alienation from Nature.

Dewey knew that we are cultural being[s...]
of those who precede us, and evolving cul[ture...]
rate than biologically (although now, th[...]
beginning to dramatically alter our own[...]
tion we draw between culture and Natu[re...]
is not a product of a disembodied ima[gination...]
outer space, shouldering aside what's her[e...]
ported by Nature at every instant of ou[r...]
or not. Even a space capsule escapes Ear[th's...]
gravity of the solar system, unless it is g[...]
then it does not escape the gravity of th[e...]
the universe.

Dewey maintained that culture is[...]
replacement of it. With that insight, w[e...]
Nature as a transformation, and see[...]
remains of her resources. The question[...]
How do we alter Nature in ways that[...]
all involved?

There will always be some part of[...]
if, God forbid, it be only the stars.[...]
humankind's sojourn on Earth the wi[...]

6

John Dewey
Philosopher and Poet of Nature

The title of this volume, *Experience and Nature*. . . . To many the associating of the two words will seem like talking of a round square, so ingrained is the notion of the separation of man and experience from nature. . . . Experience reaches down into Nature; it has depth. It also has an indefinitely elastic extent. . . . That stretch constitutes inference. . . . "Experience". . . is "double-barrelled" in that it recognizes in its primary integrity no division between act and material, subject and object, but contains them both in an unanalyzed totality. "Thing" and "thought". . . are single-barrelled; they refer to products discriminated by reflection out of primary experience.
—John Dewey

But the glory of these forest meadows is a lily. . . . The tallest are from seven to eight feet high with magnificent racemes of ten or twenty or more small orange-colored flowers. . . . And to think that sheep should be allowed in these lily meadows! after how many centuries of Nature's care planting and watering them . . . yet, strange to say, allowing the trampling of devastating sheep. . . . And so the beauty of lilies falls on angels and men, bears and squirrels, wolves and sheep . . . but as far as I have seen, man alone, and the animals he tames, destroy these gardens.
—John Muir

Following Charles Darwin, and his own instincts and perceptions, John Dewey believes that experience can have integrity because it is integral with Nature. Yes, for better or worse, experience stretches beyond what Nature could provide without us, but its integrity requires recognition of its ineluctable rootedness in Nature. Fruitful experience digs back into its ground as it stretches toward its possibilities. It is primal and pragmatic.

Dewey died in 1952. Now we live at the cusp of millennia, and are vividly aware of the destruction of Nature. Many feel alone, bored, or disempowered, painfully aware of our loss of kindred in wild Nature, and dimly apprehensive that we will be left with only domesticated creatures, or worse, with Disney's humanoid ducks, rabbits, mice.

Some of us are more inclined now to think of animals as fellow subjects, not just entertaining objects, who experience the world in their own way. Shouldn't our experiencing of Nature, our meaning-making, include our experiencing of other creatures' experiencing of Nature, insofar as we can discern this? Though Dewey maintains we should emulate animal grace, he tells us something, but not very much, about animals' experiencing.

In any case, for him the concepts of human experience and Nature interpenetrate. At least a strong negative statement can be made about his thought. Human experiencing is not conceived along Cartesian lines, is not essentially self-reflexive and grandly isolated from the rest of creation. So the line drawn by some ecologists between "a human-oriented" approach to the world and "a thing-oriented" one is artificial and misleading. There is no Nature "in itself" or humanity "in itself"—whatever those phrases might mean.

John Muir in *My First Summer in the Sierra* points out how humans often behave as if they were out of place in Nature, wantonly disregarding her. This sets the problem for us: What is our place in Nature? Dewey gives us a tantalizing clue and a question: How can the stretching of experience, our powers of inference and imaginative symbolization, be wisely employed? So that we don't disrupt local environments that must always hold us, and without which we could not think, dream, plan, or do anything else?

Dewey's commentators have typically stressed our powers of logical inference, which includes science. But Dewey himself employed a vast battery of resources to try to reground us in Nature, to regain a sense of harmony and solidity. This includes his fugitive powers of metaphor and poetry—magical speech, if you will—aspects of Dewey's work that have been singularly ignored, and when not ignored, maligned. "Dewey a poet?! Ridiculous." Let us focus on salient points of his vast and somewhat problematical homecoming trajectory over the decades.

What is our place in Nature?—a formidable question, for we are ecstatic creatures who feel and imagine beyond horizons, and who construct and reconstruct ourselves and the world in the light of our feelings and imaginings. Our ecstatic transcendence into endless possibilities permeates our lives. Human verbal language, for example, is open ended: its creative powers cannot be precisely mapped. Plankton, other plants, animals, insects deeply affect the rest of Nature, but not, presumably, at the behest of imagination. The changes these other creatures make are profound but typically slow, giving Earth time in which to adjust itself and reach new equilibrium.

But humans, impelled by fear, imagination, greed, wild dreams, even some benevolent in intent, have set in motion abrupt changes that have destroyed vast areas of animal and vegetable forms evolved and regenerated through "how many centuries of Nature's care." We feel the dizziness of freedom and an imminent fall. The rain forests cut down for wood pulp and for temporary grazing for beef cattle (a chunk larger than a football field destroyed every second). As people consume their fast-food hamburgers, they usually do not realize that they contribute to the depletion of kindred beings of other species, of green growing things, of the very atmosphere we breathe.

So of course they do not realize how they are also contributing to the depletion of our psychical resources: forests as homes of archetypes—nymphs, brooding presences—waters refreshing and healing, birds companions in ecstasy—the materials of our dreams and imaginations. The ecstasies of modern technology and production too often undermine the ecstasies of our foundational dreaming and daydreaming life rooted in Nature.

What is our place in Nature? The most persistent effort in our century to answer this ancient and now urgent question has been by John Dewey during seventy years of publishing, teaching, and organizing political, educational, and academic-professional groups. He thought that we teetered on the verge of cultural disintegration brought on by irruptive technological innovation and alienation from Nature.

Dewey knew that we are cultural beings, building on the accomplishments of those who precede us, and evolving culturally at an immensely more rapid rate than biologically (although now, through genetic engineering, we are beginning to dramatically alter our own biology). But what of this distinction we draw between culture and Nature? Dewey reminds us that culture is not a product of a disembodied imagination that drops to Earth from outer space, shouldering aside what's here. Directly or indirectly we are supported by Nature at every instant of our lives, whether we are aware of this or not. Even a space capsule escapes Earth's gravity, for example, but not the gravity of the solar system, unless it is guided successfully to do so, and even then it does not escape the gravity of the galaxy or—try to imagine this—of the universe.

Dewey maintained that culture is a transformation of Nature, not a replacement of it. With that insight, we better understand the mutilation of Nature as a transformation, and see ourselves as dependent upon what remains of her resources. The question, What is our place in Nature? becomes How do we alter Nature in ways that are most beneficial in the long run to all involved?

There will always be some part of Nature that is unaltered by us—even if, God forbid, it be only the stars. This we call wilderness. For most of humankind's sojourn on Earth the wilderness was close at hand and obvious.

Farms merged into wild country, and the bright stars shown overhead in dark clear skies, unpolluted by staggering emissions of light from sprawling cities during the night, and by continuous fossil fuel combustion. Oil comes from vegetable contents of Earth that have been burned and the debris thrown up into the sky. Now many millions have never seen Nature untouched by human intervention—even the rain has been acidified, and the stars have been so heavily veiled that these stupendous systems of energy, nodes of the cosmic matrix, seem insignificant.

When we find ourselves confined where wilderness is no longer directly evident to the senses, some have said that we must find the wilderness in ourselves. They mean that through imagination we can resonate inwardly to what always lies somewhere beyond all sensory horizons, to *everything else*, to the self-regenerating cosmos. There is something to be said for this idea, for we are strange animals, not confined to what is immediately evident to the senses in the local environment. We stretch beyond all that is evident, and infer and imagine and dwell in possibilities, of whatever kind.

The two beyonds—the beyond of the wilderness cosmos and the beyond of our inner body-selves—resonate with each other and intertwine so intimately that it is difficult or impossible to grasp the difference between them. Without this adaptive resonance a remnant of the human species would not have survived and we would not be here. The inner and the outer resonate in imagination to some extent even while we are lodged in cities. It may take a long plane flight that disentrains our bodies' regenerative cycles, our "biological clocks," from the regenerative cycles of Earth to remind us of our bodies' ancient synchrony with Nature.

This is the level of primary experience, as Dewey puts it—or the primal, "neutral" body as James does—a level of labile serpentine energies that blur the lines dividing possibility from actuality, self from other, mind from body, present from past, inner from outer, natural from supernatural, human from animal.[1] This is the fundamental level of interchange—call it the racial subconscious, as did Carl Jung—a level resembling deep ocean currents boiling through underwater caves and emerging on the other side of a boundary or horizon.

No doubt, the capacity "to find our wilderness within" is essential to who we are. But "within" suggests dualism and mentalism. It is easy to forget that we are body-selves, habituated *body*-selves with essential perceptual capacities; through eons of adaptation we have been molded in and by the earth. Psycho/physical dualism is endlessly entrapping. Probably the loss of wilderness evident to the senses in the present and actual environment will finally induce habits of disengagement and inattention that will enfeeble most people's capacity to vitally resonate with wilderness and its mythic energies. It will leave them seriously divided, impoverished in their abilities to image and imagine, distracted, and addicted, at one level or other.[2]

Now, Dewey tries valiantly to integrate our lives, to integrate our powers of imagination and inference—embodied so often now in our technologies— with the fact that we are organisms that never escape the sensuously given local environment. He speaks of being "saturated" with things. The objects of technological consciousness may saturate and benumb us, often at the cost of breaking connections to the encompassing sensuous world and the whole gamut of our ecstatic capacities as thinking, dreaming, and moving animals.

In *Art as Experience*, Dewey writes of what we might call our **spiritual structure:[3] "In their physical occurrence, things and events experienced pass and are gone. But something of their meaning and value is retained as an integral part of the self. Through habits formed in intercourse with the world, we also inhabit the world. It becomes a home and the home is part of our every experience."[4] The meaning and value of events retained as an integral part of the self: we recall the meaning of the north wind retained integrally within the body-selves of Black Elk and the sick boy.

Through funded meaning we prefigure the spatiotemporal-cultural world at every moment, at every spot. It is a movable feast. The world is made our home through habits that are exhibited in an immense gamut of initiatives and reactions, from simple physiological responses such as the patellar reflex of the knee to the most complex working habits of a great artist. We take our habitual modes of generating space-time-culture with us from spot to spot. Ours is an ever-repeated but evolving pattern of inter-action. What we can expect from things, "The precantations of things," as Emerson put it, float in the air.

But we can entertain highly selected and isolated things in imagination, and embody them technologically so that our local environments are paved over and our habituated bodies disrupted—immune systems impaired, say, or torn up. How do we avoid turning our movable feast of meaning into a drunken whirl of destruction? Or how do we prevent loneliness or boredom from withering the feast?

Aware of the disruptive displacement of traditional orientations through the incursion of new ways of mediating the world technologically, Dewey devoted his life to restoring our feast's mobility and orienting and integrating our powers. Although his treatises take us far, only his fugitive poetry consistently and explicitly reveals the mythic or mythic-indigenous dimension of our lives. I will turn to these poems in due course.

The thrust of all of Dewey's work is toward continuity and integration. He writes in *Experience and Nature*, "The world seems to be mad in preoccupation with what is specific, particular, disconnected."[5] In the spirit of Greek ethics—and also, I think, of indigenous cultures—his master concept is *art;* by which he means the conscious employment of anything as a means to an end. It is impossible to tell at exactly what point culture begins within Nature, for Nature is transformed through our interactions with it before we know it. And Nature as it has been transformed is funded in our bodies as present habits of action and meaning-making resident in our nervous systems, most of which lie beyond the reach of direct consciousness (see the next essay). Dewey considers any habit to be natural (!) until it is employed consciously as a further means to an end and is caught up in art. Through the body's habitual as well as innovative commerce with the world, Nature is transformed into culture.[6]

By habits employed "consciously"—so that they become art—Dewey seems to mean voluntarily. Take our primal prefigurations of space and time ingrained habitually and coiled in our **spiritual body-selves: Dewey suggests at least that these habitual prefigurations are "natural," since their immediacy, spontaneity, and ubiquity make them practically automatic, or nonvoluntary. But the "natural" for Dewey blurs traditional distinctions and suggests James's notion of the primal and the "neutral." As no sharp cleavage divides the voluntary from the involuntary, so no such cleavage divides mind from body, consciousness from unconsciousness, subject from object, culture from Nature. Reality is continuous, is blurred in its momentous transitions.

Since Dewey is suggesting that our basal prefigurations of space, time, and residual culture are not voluntary, they fail to be art in the full sense of the word. Again, a primal, neutral zone is suggested in which the line dividing nonart (or pre-art) from art is blurred. The thrust of Dewey's great analysis of fine art is just to open up and illuminate this fundamental ecstatical area that functions as the fertile ground of all vital living and of all fine-art making. His reflection reveals just how fine art reveals the basal area, that is, the habitual prefiguration of space and time that we cultural and bodily beings both undergo and project.

This is the area in which fine art blurs into art of life, and into religion, broadly conceived. It is the ecstasy of being in Nature and enjoying it for its own sake. This area is what Edward Abbey means when he writes that there is something intimate though impossible to name in the remote.[7] In being ecstatically at home with Nature, we are at home with ourselves. As I develop in *Wild Hunger,* this ecstatic at-homeness is what narcotics addiction tries to simulate.

Plainly, Dewey is developing Kant's analysis of the a priori structures of experience, and implicitly criticizing Kant's mentalistic notions of "the mind" imposing its fixed forms on Nature. For Dewey, the bottom line can be neither the mind by itself nor the "external world" by itself. These dualizing abstractions are waived aside, and the philosopher tries to detect the moody quality that pervades and animates the evolving situation holding both organism and the rest of the world: the quality that conditions all activity and inquiry, the matrix within which our ecstasies, technological and otherwise, *might* approach harmonization. Congruently with all this, Dewey is developing the idea that all truth is co-created by the active organism and the ever active, abiding world. Even our prefigurations of space and time do themselves develop in time as we are led moodily and not fully predictably within evolving situations. And art's truth—*I* would certainly speak of truth—is essential to reveal all this.[8]

Now how are our various and sundry activities as imagining, symbolizing, and technologically outfitted body-selves to be integrated, so that the matrix of our lives in Nature is respected?

According to Dewey, habits may conflict with one another or be inadequately adaptive to the environment, but when they are employed consciously and voluntarily as means to ends, then art of some sort has *clearly* arisen and has a chance at least to harmonize behaviors. It has a chance if the arts are not divided hierarchically from one another. That a gulf is traditionally dug between the fine arts, on the one hand, and the "merely" useful, on the other; further, that the useful are divided into crafts, on one side, and social arts, on the other—all this is anathema to Dewey. For, as he puts it in *Art as Experience,* the hierarchies and divisions stem ultimately from contempt for the body [20]. Fine art is thought to be "higher" than any useful art, because the body's activities here are more refined and more closely associated with "mind." But even here some "low" bodily activity is involved in working up materials, so no art can be as high as pure thinking. And thinking today is usually considered to be pure calculation, often only scientific calculation, hence the dogmatism of scientism.

Dewey crusades to reinstate the body as body-self and to include as much of human life as he can under the domain of art. Ends in behavior, goals (whether easily articulable ends-in-view or not) pull on us, possess us to some extent, for we are ecstatic creatures. But given our complexity, ends often pull in opposite directions, or one pulls too strongly, the other too weakly.

Dewey writes in *Experience and Nature* that the subconscious of contemporary persons is "perverted, corrupted," mainly because meanings and expectations hatched by science are incorporated into body-self half-baked, indigestible, uncoordinated with primal, prescientific, or commonsensical meanings and expectations [298 ff]. Imagination is uncoordinated, ungrounded—to the point of narcissism, perhaps hysteria. Dewey focuses on the problem that is never adequately solved by Emerson: the body-self obstructs flowing participation in the Circular power returning into itself that Emerson revered, the cosmic flow of energy exchange and endless renewal, because the body-self is too often frightened, occluded, recalcitrant, perhaps split.

Science, Dewey believes, must be treated as one of the arts. Otherwise, it will lie upon us like an incubus, suffocating our dreams and aspirations [382]. It will jamb means, meanings, and behaviors into us that cannot be assimilated by the matrix, the anciently coordinated habits we bring with us to every situation. Claiming to liberate, science will finally oppress; our various means of control will go out of control, because they are undirected within a matrix of intrinsically and self-evidently valuable excitements, consummations of life. Again, science is just one of the arts—though a massively influential one: the art of using instruments to arrange Nature so that precise predictions about its behavior can be made and tested. But what we should make of all this as many-sided meaning-making creatures, science by itself cannot tell us.

Habits can be construed broadly as ingrained behavioral means that achieve ends. All means are meanings for Dewey, however far they may fall from voluntary and self-reflexive consciousness, and however primitive and repetitious the networks of meanings may be. Art emerges unmistakably with the conscious and voluntary employment of means as means to ends. Dewey tries to interweave sectors, levels, and moments—from the encounter with the automatic or spontaneous to the most explicitly artful and cultivated initiatives that seize possibilities; and from the most personal and private to the most public and corporate. Fine art blurs into an art of life in which the body achieves ever greater awareness and control of itself—insofar as control is needed. He tries to avoid those highly vulnerable stretches, gaping discontinuities, the black holes in time in which frightened addictions and compulsions develop.

For Dewey, the wisest ideal is "rectitude of organic action"—a formulation that deliberately connects the natural ("organic") and the cultural-moral ("rectitude") [301].[9] This formulation means the extension, development, and perhaps creation of arts. Since for Dewey arts are means that are no longer merely automatic but bridge involuntary and voluntary behavior, and unconscious and conscious minding, this extension of the arts marks an extension and development of human consciousness, and of our freedom, our being.

This extension is ambitious to be sure, but a necessary task, Dewey sees, if we are to fill the vacuum left by the decay of traditional patterns of coordinating life, the intricate networks of rite and ritual. Truth at its most basic—if least glamorous—is the lore by which we live, the names of things that guide us through the world day by day. Dewey remained intrigued by James's reports of religious experiences in which the individual self merges in a kind of chemical union with the world.[10] Dewey struggled to understand what this might mean for us today.

All art requires a medium, something that is used or worked up, however simply perhaps, by the art. Instinctive smiling, for example, is not an art because it does not work up a medium; it involves a channel of discharge, but the channel is not used as a means to an end. In contrast, the artful act of smiling that expresses welcome uses the smile, the lighting up of the face, as an organic means to communicate delight when meeting a valued friend.

Notice how subtly the natural, instinctive, and spontaneous shades into the artful, which is also spontaneous, but in its own way. There is some distinction to be drawn between the instinctive and the artful, but no gulf, and hence no supreme act of will required to leap such a gulf. Primal education is just what blends one into the other. "When the natural and the cultivated blend in one, acts of social intercourse are works of art," Dewey writes in *Art as Experience* [63]. This blending is essential to the art of life.

The task Dewey set himself is immense. It is not just instinctive smiles we must deal with, or artful but genuine smiles, but corrupted and perverted subconscious smiles. A body-self may have long ago been conditioned to smile because of others' self-serving expectations or demands insinuating themselves into us. But the smile is split off from the self's other needs and perceptions, and is unconscious and false. It resists perception and artful and fruitful control. For another example: faced with what is repugnant I hold my breath in a way that is not detected by me, for I have been conditioned not to name and identify what disgusts me. If the repugnant is something I myself am doing, I probably will not acknowledge this, but project it contemptuously, attributing it to others. How can art of any kind get a handle on all this?

Dewey writes in *Experience and Nature* of "immediate organic selections, rejections, welcomings, expulsions . . . of the most minute, vibratingly delicate nature" [299]. Although he does not spell it out, these responses surely include sickening recoilings at threatened pollution by alien things, or ecstatic welcomings of either expansion or purification by compatible things. He has exposed the domain of the archaic, the primal body with its labile and dangerous uncoilings of energy out of the viscera and burrowing through the world—or flying through it. How far the exposure goes we are trying to see. Already we sense the immense difficulties facing any art of life he tries to develop. How can destructive semiconscious or unconscious ecstatic responses, split off from the focus of voluntary attention, be detected? How can spontaneous aversive or panicked recoilings from the world—inverted and addictive ecstasies, as we might call them—be monitored, moderated, or eliminated?

If we happen to be happily conditioned and well educated early in life, no leap will be required to get from the natural as instinctively spontaneous to the cultural as cultivatedly spontaneous. But given abrupt cultural changes, and our vulnerability and our susceptibility to perverted and corrupted subconscious behaviors, the task of integrating and rectifying the gamut of human behavior, personal and corporate, is staggering. A minefield of chances opens for the artful to become mendacious or artificial, which is to say split off from deep intent or deep need—a debilitating addiction, say, or a mannerism cycling tediously in the void.

Only when we see how linear time is not the whole story of our cycling, recapitulating lives do we see how the past can be present. And present perhaps in fixated and perverted ways that keep us divided from ourselves, and divided as well from the present and actual environment. Dewey's insights help us grasp how meditational practices, developed at many places and times in human history, work to free us. To live in the present moment is to be alert to what is fresh and new within it, able to distinguish this from what is dead—deadly repetitious—in one's life. To live in the present moment is not to be cut off from the past—only obsessively linear thought would think so. But it is to be released from what the Buddha seems to have meant by attachment: the blind, and blindly repetitive, response to something in the past. Or it is to be redirected from the bad road of dependency, lethargy, and degeneration to the good road of connectivity, creativity, risk, and aliveness—as Black Elk limns the difference.

There is no way to simply sever ourselves from the archaic mythic level of experience. We are haunted by presences from the past, and our personal history blurs into the history of the race with its benign or malign archetypal presences. Either the sources are regenerative and freeing or they are not. After all, the voices of the authorities in our personal histories thunder out of the corporate body of the culture, as the voice of God is said to have thundered out of the burning bush at Moses. Only through assiduous practices can we build habits that counteract the bad habits of our lives. Fine art seems to have capacities to lead beyond itself into the art of life—if we are daring and diligent in extrapolating and applying its principles.

In *Art as Experience,* Dewey sees that the inspiration of fine art consists in the creative fusion of archaic subconscious materials from the past with current expressive actions, a fusion that "sets us on fire," as he says, and re-creates us [65]. Most significant this is. But it is not clear that Dewey in his published treatises ever squarely confronted the central challenge to an art of life: the mythic level funded in our adapted bodies since Paleolithic times, in which bodies' regenerative cycles are coordinated with regenerative cycles of Nature, daily, monthly, yearly, generationally. This level is disrupted today. Disoriented from a traditional corporate body that authorizes rites that conduct us through the stages of life, we are set adrift in vertiginous freedom. If oriented by a corporate body that is itself fragmented, fitfully changing, or merely obsessive, we will also be.

Dewey's view of fine art is such that he might have extrapolated it to an art of life that integrates all the arts pursuant to integrating ourselves. Fine art for him is not high, detached from everyday experience and the other arts; it develops and consummates the aesthetic quality of much of everyday experience itself. But without a thorough coordination of fine art and ancient regenerative rituals, I don't think fine art can bear the weight Dewey places on it.

In Black Elk, Thoreau, Emerson, and James, mystery is never far to seek. Mystery is there in Dewey, too, but often it lies some distance, and when we most need it, particularly when we must plumb our body-selves caught up in environments. Dewey introduces us to weird split-off states and subconscious impulses. How could we ever believe that such irrational things are going on in ourselves? If we can't believe they are possible, how could we ever know them? In fact we don't know them, but typically we have no idea of how to begin or where to look for them, or even whether to begin. These typically are not cases in which we know what we don't know (for example, I know I don't know Hebrew). The subconscious events and processes collapse within themselves in total darkness. This is mystery wretchedly close to home: we don't know we don't know them.

When some event somehow uncovers one of these gruesome blind spots, we experience a burst of liberation. From not knowing what *it* is, and so, of course, not able to imagine alternatives to it, we are explosively released into alternatives, into possibilities.

To be sure, Dewey experienced this liberation in his sessions with F. M. Alexander, which we are soon to relate. But I do not think the archetypal forms that structure the subconscious were ever woven by Dewey into his published treatises, which includes his treatise on art. (For example, I know a woman who was helped to discover that the more her mother did for her to express her love, the more the daughter despised her. Somehow the young woman had not been able to get from dependency upon mother to the mythic level of dependency upon Mother Nature. So she felt infantalized, trapped, by her mother's care. Once she discovered the absurdity of her response to her mother, she was freed into new possibilities of living.)

Dewey's treatise on art is important, but it cannot lead very effectively into an art of life because of inadequate treatment of archaic, archetypal material. His development of an art of life is interesting and important but limited. If this is correct, he could not succeed in his dearest project, the integration of that special art, science—and its twin, technology—into the whole body of the culture.

The media used by science are materials under tightly controlled instrumental manipulation. These materials either do or do not behave as precisely predicted. When they do, the basis for a technology for altering the earth can be set up. But without a life artfully integrated we will lack a network of intrinsically satisfying, releasing, consummatory experiences, and our scientific and technological means of control will have nothing to guide them and will go out of control. And how can we have reliable consummatory experiences if our chief sources of ancient mythic impulses and energies are gone? Technology cannot grasp its limitations, cannot assess the assumptions that drive it.

What *is* our place in Nature? What is place? Let us turn to Dewey's remarkable theories of education, for they are the heart of his overall project; if they fail, it fails. For all their greatness, they suffer, I believe, the weakness I am outlining.

He would educate us: *educe* from us our own deepest sense of what needs to be learned as we try to build vital and whole selves for ourselves in perpetual intercourse with the world during a fragmented time. Nature can be so transformed that we lose our sense of local environment, our sense of place. For Dewey, education should enable us to find our place, by integrating science, technology, fine arts, poetry, and perception of local environment. Education is the master art, another name for the art of life.

A vivid example of the cultural transformation of Nature is television. It is a triumph of science and technology that extends our knowledge in dramatic ways. But Dewey saw the untoward consequences of instant long-distance communication years before television itself was invented, and his theories of education, properly understood, are uncannily relevant to current debates concerning the educational significance of television.

Although we peek into remote corners of the world, one corner followed instantly by another, the corners rarely come together into anything like a structured whole. TV jumbles our experience into bright, disconnected bits. And it is not just the commercials that do this, jerking us about brutally and incessantly with their images.

How, then, can TV orient us within a world that extends continuously in every direction from our situated bodies? There are students in the university who do not know, for example, that Mexico—with its teeming masses of hungry and desperate people—borders on the United States. Sitting for hours in front of the set, we begin to lose our grip on the posture and location of our own bodies. Since at every instant we can only be this-body-within-this-total-environment, we lose touch to a great extent with both our bodies and the rest of the world. Inevitably, this must have a demonic dimension or coloration. As Norman Mailer once remarked, after a half-hour before the TV, something slips from the body, falls to the floor, and dies. It was once living skin, sheathing muscles and nerves, and coordinated with the world immediately around it, a world that should be exciting in its significance.

Dewey is suggesting, I think, that losing this basic orientation is like losing the primal person's sense of the magic number seven—a talisman that orients and locates us in the world around us. Why seven? Notice how the four cardinal directions establish the horizontal axis; then point down and then up to establish the vertical axis—that's six—then connect all the points at the center which is yourself, and you have the sacred number, seven. You have found yourself by finding your place in the world. Knowing, feeling, moving, and being are one. Black Elk, for example, finds himself and his people by locating them all relative to the Six Grandfathers and to the central Tree of the World that can bloom in our lives.

Dewey is practically obsessed not only by geographical but also by agricultural and animal metaphors for grasping our locatedness in actual environments and for guiding educational efforts. Goodness at a basic level is vitality, and vitality is unhampered growth—dynamic self-coordination and self-consolidation that prevent fixations, addictions, and various split-off states—a self dried out and disintegrating. Vitality is not just any growth— there are cancerous ones—it is oriented and integrated openness, growth forever more growth. It is not just getting what is desired, but getting what is desirable, that which is vital and which leads to more vitality over time. It is being fully alive and habitually coordinated, not self-defeating, paralyzed, seriously addicted, or spastic-of-self. Vitality requires the ecstatic, flexible, resonant body-self open to the circumambient world and to its ever-expanding horizons. So much of his work suggests at least an attempt to recoordinate us with our hunter-gatherer past and its funded proclivities.

This is why Dewey admonishes us in his book on art to emulate animal grace: The animal is "all there" in the immediate environment, existing in a continuous flow of sense into movement and movement back into sense, and so on [19, 25]. To move joyously and with abandon, but so that equi- librium is an ever-present probability for one's body-self, is to exist on an edge of dynamic balance in which many options for different activities remain open. It is to maximize spontaneity and freedom.

The crucial question for human education: Can we learn to emulate animal grace in our immediate environments—bonding dynamically with them? But also to coordinate this grace with the indefinitely broad range of our technologically outfitted imaginative lives—our technically assisted actions penetrating beyond horizons? Ironically, we penetrate electronically beyond horizons so quickly and easily that we are hardly aware of horizons as such. That is, we tend not to resonate to the *everything else* beyond the horizon, the unimaginable vastness of the World-whole. Hence the Internet, say, despite the fact that it expands and integrates on a certain immediate and obvious level, occludes the ever-remaining vastness of the World-whole that includes us and will, after all our clamor is done, fold us back into itself. On a funda- mental level, our awareness shrinks and loses weight. Our electronically mediated and manipulated symbol systems and abstractions are incarnated in social systems of myriad sorts springing up and evolving at incredible rates. Dewey faced a formidable task of integration! Insofar as he could sense it in the 1920s through the 1940s, and he struggled with it into his nineties.

How ironic when our vaunted scientific knowledge of Nature and our powers of communication fail to orient us within that very sector of Nature in which we live and breathe—the immediate local environment. Dewey writes, "While I was visiting . . . Moline a few years ago, the superintendent told me that they found many children every year who were surprised to learn that the Mississippi River in the textbook had anything to do with the stream of water flowing past their homes."[11] And we know that it is not only children who are comparably disoriented or lost. As if it were tomorrow, Dewey maintains that geography—presented in a particular way—is the unifying ground of all studies at every level of education. I quote this magnificent passage again, augmented:

> The unity of all the sciences is found in geography. The significance of geography is that it presents the earth as the enduring home of the occupations of man. The world without its relationship to human activity is less than a world. Human industry and achievement, apart from their roots in the earth, are not even a sentiment, hardly a name. The earth is the final source of all man's food. It is his continual shelter and protection, the raw material of all his activities, and the home to whose humanizing and idealizing all his achievement returns. [13]

Depicting Nature as protective, Dewey stands out starkly from technology mania and harks back implicitly to Emerson as well as to Black Elk. Geography surveys the land insofar as it is ownable (in some cultures), and insofar as it can't be owned—insofar as we belong to *it*, and it defines us on the deepest level of body-self. Nature is protective because it has formed our nervous systems and our primal needs and our means for satisfying them. He suggests that the habitually sedentary life leaves us like sitting ducks, and may be responsible for paranoic dissociations on the level of conscious or subconscious minding. The tragic possibilities of all this are typically muted in Dewey, but inferences can be easily drawn, and I discuss them in the next essay.

Dewey's vision in 1899 embraces work beginning with the one-year-old child through the graduate work of the university. So the invidious distinctions between the lower schools and the university, and between undergraduate and graduate work there, should be abandoned. Hard and fast distinctions between disciplines should be abolished as well, for Dewey envisions the unification of poetry, morality, and science, and "the necessary transition of science into philosophy; a passage that carries the verified and solid body of one into the large and free form of the other" [129].

If this seems like romantic nonsense to us, it is probably because we do not yet grasp our crisis and what must be undertaken to survive it. Particularly, many professional educators locked in various social sciences don't grasp the difficulty. Traditional rites of initiation, orientation, and purification that mediated between self and world and past and present are gone. Malcoordinations abound between our perceptual and our more obviously spiritual or mental capacities, between our behaviors in local environments and the vast reaches of distant environments brought near through scientific signs, symbols, technological appliances, electronically mediated global commerce. In general, the horizons beyond which an untouched and spontaneous wilderness excited resonances within us are no longer clearly and constructively available to us. Electronically mediated imagination in the form of TV and video is rootless and capricious. Even with the best intentions, we rattle around in nihilism.

World-girdling North Atlantic culture is off balance, and perpetually stretches and strains itself. Electronic technology, though great when measured by reach and speed, closes in upon itself and divides us from the local environments that always hold our bodies. The beyond of the inner body with its serpentine energies is not being taught to resonate dancingly with the wilderness beyond of the cosmos.[12] The need for ecstasy rooted in Nature is not being recognized, much less the wisest means of attaining it. We body-selves tend to be objectified and manipulated—indeed, treated as if we were objects. Or, we are treated as if we were isolated subjects, and this conduces to a kind of barely repressed panic or hysteria. The basic problem is not recognized. How are the deeply rooted energies of our wilderness and mythic past—funded in our bodies and subconscious minding and meaning-making—to be coordinated with our local present reality, on the one hand, and our explosive technological projects, our production and commerce, on the other? How are civilization and wilderness to be mediated?

Dewey demands the reconstruction of intelligence, what I like to call the regeneration of intelligence. But the coordination of mythic wilderness energies and contemporary body-self is demanded for that. Otherwise we get addictive and degenerative ecstasies. To reiterate: "Human industry and achievement, apart from their roots in the earth, are not even a sentiment, hardly a name." Fecund names are needed to root and empower us. And especially it is what names the *mythos*—names for mythic beings and presences that coordinate our experience of the whole—that must be included in our repertory. Take, for example, Mother Earth. What if this were given new life? If mythic energies are not acknowledged and included, erratic pulses of them move abortively.

Dewey is betting that we do have a chance of regaining our coordination in the archaic background of sensuous experience in which we feel at home—

a background that should be complemented by our scientific concerns, not drowned out by them. When Dewey regards Earth as our home, to whose humanizing and idealizing all our achievements should contribute, he is trying to entice us off the linear track of the detached intellect and into a cyclical participation in our sources. He is trying to revive natural piety and reverence, but he is reluctant to use such terms. He also wants to be "progressive" and "relevant"!

Dewey presents diagrams of the ideal school in his seminal work of 1899, *School and Society*. They are spatiospiritual. The school is adjacent to a garden, and avenues into the community are plainly marked—to business, to universities, to civic and government institutions, to homes. On the four corners of the first floor are placed industrial shop, textile plant, dining room, kitchen. In the center is the library. Dewey engages in a kind of spiritual geography: "The centre represents the manner in which all come together in the library, that is to say, in a collection of the intellectual resources of all kinds that throw light upon the practical work, that gives it meaning and liberal value. If the four corners represent practice, the interior represents the theory of the practical activities" [48]. Dewey is refurbishing and maintaining our "home" that "is part of our every experience," our prefigurations of space-time-and-culture coiled in the body, which guide our intercourse in every situation, our deepest habits that should be fostered, not paved over or managed in a ham-handed way. Through the meanings, skills, and values retained from the past and integral to the self "we inhabit the world."

According to Dewey, the upper story of the ideal school extends the work of integration. In two adjacent corners are laboratories, physical-chemical and biological, and in the remaining two corners, studios for art and music. In the center is the museum. "The questions, the chemical and physical problems arising in the kitchen and shop, are taken to the laboratories to be worked out. For instance, this past week one of the older groups of children doing practical work in weaving which involved the use of the spinning wheel, worked out the diagrams of the direction of forces concerned in treadle and wheel, and the ratio of velocities between wheel and spindle." And "The drawing and music, or the graphic and auditory arts, represent the culmination, the idealization, the highest point of refinement of all the work carried on (and the fruits of past creative effort are placed within the central room, the museum)" [52–53]. Dewey's labors of integration in 1899 are astonishing—self and body, self and others, self and world, self-of-the-past and self-of-the-present-and-future. Sensuous metaphors rooted in an archaic past need not merely illustrate what is already known, but can open new areas and create understanding. Dewey gives examples of students' language that is both poetic and scientific, because they have "a clear image and personal feeling" for the way in which a scientific theory is formed. Niels Bohr will later assert that science at the all-important level of hypothesis formation progresses by image, parable, and metaphor.

But are even Dewey's achievements in integration as deep and comprehensive as we need? Is the central room, the museum, active and powerful enough? Can it restore us to an intelligent involvement in mythic resources and ritual? Or will they erupt randomly and demonically? Is Dewey adequately attuned to the archaic-ecstatic? Is performance allowed sometimes in the library? Is ritual? I think of the need for ritual in particular. Most significant it is that though he pictures the school adjacent to a garden, there is no suggestion of wilderness anywhere within his diagram![13] This absence means occlusion of ancient forebears' ritualized acknowledgments of the gifts of Nature.

Nearly every utterance from Thoreau, Emerson, Black Elk, and the later James is bathed in a halo or fringe of tendrils or tendencies reaching into "the more," as James put it in *The Varieties of Religious Experience.* This far and yet so near domain holds possibilities of renewal. Similar to the Hoop of the World for Black Elk, the horizon for Emerson points beyond itself to the fertile and mysterious fastnesses of Nature, a horizon as beautiful as our own nature. Without openness to Oversoul—in Emerson's language— we shrivel up, we lack helpers, auxiliaries.

Only occasionally are Dewey's utterances bathed in this halo. Moreover, he sometimes reads "the more" as the "unconquered domain," suggesting that it would be better if it were conquered by science and technology. The possibility that grace might issue from it is not emphasized.

Dewey, of course, is complex. He does write in *Art as Experience,* "Through the phases of perturbation and conflict, there abides the deep-seated memory of an underlying harmony, the sense of which haunts life like . . . being founded on a rock."[14] Moreover, in a vivid passage he speaks of a kind of cosmic comfort: "These encompassing continuities with their infinite reach. . . . Religion as a sense of the whole is the most individualized of all things, the most spontaneous, undefinable, and varied. For individuality signifies unique connections in the whole. . . . Yet every act may carry within itself a consoling and supporting consciousness of the whole to which it belongs and in some sense belongs to it."[15]

Nevertheless, Dewey exhibits a distinct shift in attitude from the earlier thinkers, a shift toward the secular and away from the mythic and the religious.

Some might construe this as a difference in emphasis merely, but I regard the shift as very significant, and will continue to develop the point in this essay.

On the "neutral" or primal level, the body generates ineffable impulses and cravings (nameless at least for the scientific secular mind); it is taboo. Only the language of archaic myth and rituals grasps what is going on, and here Dewey the great philosopher does not give us the consistent support that we need. Without this there can be no ritualistic-habitual way of being, no way of bringing the vast, unmappable unknown into a primal or mythic mode of awareness that energizes, opens, and orients us.[16]

On the mythic level, the body is not just another object to be managed and manipulated. Nor is it a subject that can inventory and manipulate itself. When manipulated, the self either withers in repression and addiction or explodes in random rebellion. The self can delude itself that it is a disembodied spirit that maps and objectifies the world, while containing and directing itself as it wills, but the price for this delusion will be paid at some time, some way.

The immediately lived body-self, which is more fundamental and polyvalent than our common distinctions and dualisms imagine, is powerful, labile, knife-edge, dangerous. It will resonate with wilderness—the will of the place—one way or another.[17] "Hands off!"—it seems to say—"unless you're prepared to come to grips with something powerful and dangerous" (greatly ecstatic sexual experience taps into this power).

All we can do is locate ourselves practice-wise and ritualistically in the world that is experienced as whole, and trust that our anchorings and resonatings in proven namings will evoke responses from the "neutral" body, responses that contribute to our integration and integrity and are beneficial to all over the long run. As Freud and Dewey and others know, the body cannot be repressed without danger and loss. It must first be listened to, and then guided in response.

I do not think Dewey listens adequately to ancient voices. Nor does he touch and feel archaic patterns, the ancient mythic matrix of the human body-self directly, immediately, intimately engaged in the world. Although he often refers to the "uncannily precarious" aspect of Nature-experienced and experienceable, he does not really link this to the mythic proclivities of our lives. Whether we are thematically aware of it or not, the body-self moves snakelike with wilderness energies, and can make connections archetypally and mythically, if it is allowed.

Dewey is in a bind. On the one hand, he will not, for example, dismiss James's observations that in religious experience we melt in a kind of chemical union with the world at a fundamental level, and that this enlivens and supports us, if it is not merely sporadic. And as seen above, he realizes that religious experience touches "encompassing continuities with their infinite reach," and that religion as "a sense of the whole" is the most individualized of all things, the most spontaneous, undefinable, and varied. Religion need not be escapist or sentimentalist. It works in an area in which intellection does in fact break down—the domain of unique connections in the whole and of spontaneity. All of this is indefinable, the events unpredictable.

On the other hand, however, there were forces at work in his life that countered these inclinations. First, his commitment to democracy, which entailed a commitment to public education. Given the constitutional separation of church and state in the United States, how could he provide for anything remotely resembling religious ritual in the schools? Including ancient Nature observances, which despite claims to their universality would be regarded in a traditionally Christian country as pagan? Second, he was committed to science. True, science construed in the broadest and most flexible way as an art, but it did carry the idea of progress. How reconcile scientific progress and archaic modes of mythic-religious thought and practice? Third, to be mentioned at least, Dewey reacted strongly against his mother's early attempts to force upon him evangelical Christianity.

His way out of this bind was inventive and resourceful, even if not in the end completely satisfactory. We will see how, in a period of crisis, he betook himself to the body-worker, the psycho-bio-therapist, F. M. Alexander. This man's mode of therapy roots in ancient practices of healing, ones that derive from times in which our kinship with all living things was ingrained in us ritualistically. Developing this lead, we add more substance to his recommendation in *Art as Experience* that we emulate animal grace.

Dewey's hesitations and limitations are due to no lack of courage on his part. His personal problems, which he faced, converged on the theoretical problem that yanked and tugged on his writing and demanded the attention it never triumphantly received: How are we to grasp the primal body-self and its labile, ecstatic involvement in the world? At the age of fifty-seven, already famous, Dewey entered a period of personal as well as intellectual-professional crisis. Like Dante's lament in *The Divine Comedy,* "Mid-way upon the journey of our life I found myself in a dark wood, where the right way was lost," life for Dewey was stale, flat, pointless, somewhat frantic—something was missing. All his efforts to achieve a theory that integrated body, self, and experience were blocked by the experience of his own life.

Dewey detected a rude discontinuity between his powers of inquiry and perception, and the very conditions of these powers in his functioning organism. Although he had brilliantly criticized psycho/physical dualism, his own consciousness seemed to split off from its conditions in his organism. This imperiled his vision of goodness as vitality, as integrated, dynamically interactive living. Since he was a person of vision, his life was imperiled.

Dewey began to suppose that there are factors at work in our bodily selves that condition and limit consciousness to such an extent that it cannot grasp these factors. He suspected that consciousness is a closet lined with mirrors. As had James before him, he became suspicious of the pretensions of our "voluntary careers." In 1916, in a kind of desperation personal and professional, Dewey consulted the pioneering psycho-bio-therapist, F. M. Alexander.[18]

Alexander had discovered means for altering minding by altering bodily movements and postures. He had made advances in the art of life, the conscious use by the body-self of its own organism to achieve ends of fuller vitality, integration, orientation, consciousness. He was a great educator. Judging from the way Dewey talked and held his head and neck, Alexander said Dewey "was drugged with thought"—as if his mind were dissociated from his body.

Does seventeenth-century psycho/physical dualism return? No, Dewey thought, but he knew he faced immense personal and theoretical difficulties. It was here that he discovered something fundamental about the limits and conditions of his own consciousness and his free will: It was only *after* Alexander manipulated Dewey's body into unaccustomed positions and postures that Dewey could imagine the possibility of them!

As in fine art, so in the art of life, *the body must take the lead* if consciousness is to become aware of its closet; it must be jolted and prompted by the body. But how can the body do this without being conscious, and how can it imagine new ways of living if it must do so with the old consciousness? A new consciousness requires a new body, if you will, and it cannot be the body merely thought-of. It must be body freshly thin*king* and act*ing*, freshly springing out of the earth that formed and is forming us, the creative body.

In fact, a leap of faith seems to be required. And it may also require intervention from another conscious body-self. Only then, perhaps, can sensations be generated that both form revealing hypotheses about one's body-self and test these. Dewey pushes out the envelope of what can count as science.

Fine art is a way the body-self reveals itself and its world. But more than fine art may be needed. Emerson: "Fate then is a name for facts not yet passed under the fire of thought: for causes which are unpenetrated."[19] However, Dewey discovers that the most brilliant and penetrating thought cannot penetrate directly into the bodily matrix in which one's thought occurs, and which, if undetected, is as much fate as Fate itself.

It is self-deceivingly abstract to limit truth either to the mind inventorying itself, or to statements writable on a blackboard. Nor can self-knowledge be limited to a set of facts that a consciousness spies in the outer world, facts that imply something about the self. The truth of self-knowledge demands that body-self intimately and courageously interact with itself-in-environments to lead to consummations revealing of itself. Fine art supplies at least a clue for the art of life. As artists working up materials, we live in a feedback loop that progressively echo-locates ourselves in the world—echo-location, a capacity we share with our distant cousins, dolphins and bats.

Alexander concentrated on altering the way in which Dewey's head rested on his neck. His habitual positioning was so integral to his self's identity that—as I've said—Dewey could not imagine the new positionings until Alexander effected them manually. Caught up by the tacit belief that consciousness floats free from the body, the body-self is not open to its own impulses to integrate itself—either with its own past or with the surrounding environment. It is not open to its own residual impulses to free and heal itself.

When the head—the heavy head—is not balanced atop the backbone as a dynamically integral part of the body, the most intimate continuity of self—experiential time—is knotted and disrupted. One's senses are constrained and warped by fixed ideas, unable to grasp new possibilities of growth. Instead of acknowledging one's origins, and building on them, one is captured by some of them. Head tilted up perhaps, cramped, gritting teeth, holding back breath, holding back tears, the little child's tensions and fears still held in the muscles and joints of the middle-aged man's jaw. Lacking a strong body and a secure position in the world, the child as head has tried to go it alone.

To reconnect and readjust the head and neck properly may be sufficient to release this archaic fixation and to free the self for mature behavior. To straighten out the body is to begin to straighten out lived time, to undo fixations and addictions. The past is not always present beneficially. Such therapy may be sufficient to liberate consciousness by opening it to some of its own conditions here and now in the body. Once aware of them through feedback dynamics, we can begin to curb impairing and deadening behaviors and to strengthen others. Persons must grope and intuit trustingly if they are to open their consciousness, allow their body to move as it will, to *be* with their body, and begin to behave intelligently.

To balance the head atop the backbone, and to move flowingly thus! This principle is found in healing traditions in immensely diverse times and places. Why is it so fundamentally healing? From ancient Nature religion in China, Taoism, and the Tai Chi meditation in movement that arose from it, through yoga practice in India, and now in many places, to the cyclic drawing in of the six directions in the Lakota's, Black Elk's, healing ceremony, and to many other healing traditions.

Why its healing power? Because it ritualistically relocates us in our Source, in the six-directional world cycling regeneratively to which we and our pre-human ancestors adapted over millions of years and which formed us.

Head balanced, we can move spontaneously in any of the directions as appropriate and pulsing with possibility. Head balanced—in some moving and secure abode—we turn up into the sky, sky-i-fied—when there's no need to scan the horizons for predators. Head balanced, not thrust forward in some rapacious, rampaging project that defies the natural cycles of stress and restoration built into our bodies by the ever-cycling earth: what consigns us to unremitting stress and burnout and addiction. With head balanced and body flowing, we emulate in each stage of movement the Tree of the World that connects lower, middle, and upper worlds—the circulating sap of things. Head balanced, we emulate the cobra rising erect from its coils, vibrant with potentiality. Tai Chi exhibits and exercises the wilderness body, but now caught up in the disciplines of later civilization, become civilization's intimate other.

Now, all this lies at the roots, I believe, of Alexander's body-work, accounts for its effectiveness, and helps account for Dewey's attraction to it. Dewey had fairly regular sessions with Alexander for decades after his initial encounter in 1916. His most important philosophical work followed this encounter, and a detailed study of this would show, I am certain, Alexander's greatly beneficial influence.

But no place in these major works does the truly archaic background of Alexander's work show itself. Dewey's way out of his bind was to integrate in his person Alexander's methods, and to allow this work to fuel his decidedly modern, secular, discursive prose in his later works, without the mythic or archetypal elements showing themselves nakedly.

We can infer along biographical lines to the prehistoric origins. Soon after Dewey's first meeting with Alexander, he sailed to the Orient and spent two and a half years there. He saw first hand the Zen Buddhist background still alive in martial arts training. At a women's school in Tokyo he observed, "We went to the gymnasium and saw the old Samurai women's sword and spear exercises, etc. The teacher was an old woman of seventy-five and as lithe and nimble as a cat—more graceful than any of the girls. . . . The modernized gym exercises by the children were simply pitiful compared with these ceremonies."[20]

Dewey was aware of the very ancient Taoist tradition, and thought it had some important lessons in natural piety to teach the West. He briefly summarizes his understanding of the insights of Lao-tzu, thought to be the founder of Taoism:

> The important thing is the doctrine of the superiority of nature to man, and the conclusion drawn, namely, the doctrine of non-doing. For active doing and striving are likely to be only an interference with nature. The idea of non-doing can hardly be stated and explained; it is a kind of rule or moral doing, a doctrine of active patience, endurance, persistence while nature has time to do her work. Conquering by yielding is its motto. The workings of nature will in time bring to naught the artificial fussings and fumings of man. Give enough rope to the haughty and ambitious, and in the end they will surely be hung in the artificial entanglements they have themselves evolved. [500]

This feeds directly into his insights concerning later civilizations' jamming of meanings half-baked into consciousness and subconsciousness and these being corrupted thereby. And, as noted, it emerges directly from his discovering in his sessions with Alexander that liberating movements cannot even be imagined before his body is placed in certain positions and incited to move in certain ways.

Moreover, as the individual body-self cannot imagine this beforehand, we see it follows that the corporate body of the culture, the society as a whole, cannot see in its unliberated state the value of techniques like Alexander's. Ironically and perversely, they are thought of as "occultist" or "mystical," in the worst sense. The society, sensing that something is missing, and wedded to the conviction that something we want we will get, pursues the occluded goal with addictive frenzy.

I should mention an experience of Dewey's, which I would call religious in the profoundest sense. As a young man in Oil City, Pennsylvania, on his first teaching assignment, he experienced one evening a tremendous lifting of a burden previously unperceived as that. He suddenly realized, There's nothing to worry about! He was released into an immense domain he couldn't describe. I take this to be a version of nonattachment, found in all religious traditions at their best: that is, it is one thing to be engulfed in upsets and troubles as we usually are. It is something else—poles apart—to just let them be, to *be with them,* to pump free air around them, as James had it. We discover that we survive! This is a transcendence so primal or primary, so elementary, that most of the time the culture, caught up in some glorious Transcendence, completely overlooks its possibility. As Jesus put it, "Let not your hearts be troubled" or "You must become as little children." Nothing is more difficult to reach, nothing more a matter of grace—of being open to receive the gift!

Nevertheless, Dewey never really explores in his great published works the prehistoric and archetypal background of all this.

Only in Dewey's fugitive, discarded poems do we directly perceive the mythic horizon that pulled at him so profoundly if sporadically and unclearly. These were written at the height of his maturity. They have been tracked down and published by Jo Ann Boydston. She writes of how M. Halsey Thomas found them: "From 1926 to 1928, Thomas was librarian of the Butler Library of Philosophy [at Columbia University]; access to Dewey's office was through the Library. Thomas wrote me that he was 'addicted to Boswellizing,' and 'usually looked in Dewey's wastebasket at the end of the day, particularly when it was full.' He was 'rewarded at one time by finding a sheaf of poetry which he [Dewey] had written.'"[21] The sheaf contained treasures, the mythic sources nakedly revealed, the hidden fuel that had powered Dewey's published treatises. Among the poems we find new—and very old—paradigms of connections between Earth and us earthlings. Gone from the poems is the dominating Transcendent deity of patriarchy, Jehovah or Zeus, archetypes of thought and feeling that have dominated most of our technological civilization's thinking of what is right and proper for us: little creators modeled on the greatest Creator. Instead, we find new ways of weaving into the Earth: a female archetype of Earth, the ever-regenerating goddess who is decentralized and noncontrolling, the ultimate matrix. In "Two Births" we read:

> Or ere I sought the golden fleece
> Seized in the fever'd clutch

Of youth, that screened caprice,
Nine months I dwelt in a dark hutch
Of warm and precious solitude.
Sweetly bedded in that soft haven
I fed on wonder food
Miraculous more than that the raven
Brought Elijah, God's nested brood. . . .

No thief is nature but mother
Whose power shall not lack
to turn me in time to clean brother
Worm and sister flower and laden air
To feed the tender sprouting plants
Till in their mingled life I share
And in new measures tread creation's dance

Tho unshelter'd is the tomb
Of the rude and thoughtless clods of earth
That make my second secret womb
Yet e'en there is miracle of birth
And wondrous food for the mysterious life
With which the world, our God, is rife.

                                             [46]

As did Emerson—and James at certain moments—Dewey in his discarded poems equates the world with a kind of pantheistic divinity—"my second secret womb." Unlike the patriarchal tradition, this divinity is protecting (if we are properly receptive and careful and fortunate) but nondirecting, enwombing, nurturing, dark, ever-regenerative, female. In this earthy world he finally mingles his life with nonhuman forms—"in new measures tread creation's dance." As poet, he touches the ultimate horizon through which wilderness sounds. Circular power returning into itself, death and rebirth. It is just the poet, Emerson declared, who can integrate all the parts entailed by the horizon. And, as we saw in the second essay, the horizon for both Emerson and James is very close to the hoop of the cosmos for Black Elk.

Dewey seeks deliverance from the customary divisions of the intellect, the divisions encased in our institutions and in constricting habits of the thinking, squinting body—"the fierce divisive sun"—and gravitates toward an "all embracing night, Mystic mother." An untitled poem:

Now night, mother soul, broods the weary hours,
Flutt'ring fugitives from the tasks of day,
Worn and wan creeping to her waiting wings . . .

And groping were clasped together within
The capacious stillness of her bosom.
Merged in oneness of the first creation
They gather strength against the shock and strain
Of day's wedge-like doom of separation
Ever new enforced. All embracing night,
Mystic mother, in her patience endless
And unconquerable, makes them her own,
As within death's majestic solitude
Blend the struggling spirits of severed men,
While fretful time, subdued, waits in worship
Wond'ring at the enduring womb of God.

[60]

People are severed (amputated from the trunk, Emerson put it), and can only be reintegrated on the primal level of Mother. How is this to be accomplished? Dewey never maintained that calculating and managing one's life would be sufficient—through some behavior modification program, say. All doing emerges from prior undergoing that we can never completely comprehend and that sometimes disposes of our best-laid plans in ways we cannot imagine. To be caught up in short-term goals and calculations and to forget the environing and enduring matrix is foolish. Always in Dewey there is the moment of piety, of acceptance of the mysterious and incalculable whole, of allowing what *will* happen *to* happen.[22] But in his published writings this strand is certainly not fully developed.

The moment of piety occurs within his critique of Pavlov's program of animal conditioning. In the introduction to Alexander's *The Use of the Self*, Dewey writes that since there are central organic habits that condition every act we perform, we can hope to locate these, bring them under conscious direction, and convert "the fact of conditioned reflexes from a principle of external enslavement into a means of vital freedom." He means auto-conditioning—procedures such as Alexander's, and more recently those developed by Moishe Feldenkrais and Joseph Heller—in which our behavior is reflected and fed back into us in various ways, making its alteration possible. With this idea of freely reconditioned reflexes, Dewey connects scientific thought to the ultimate goals of all education—freedom, informed choice, ethical responsibility, even religious sensibility of indigenous sorts, to some extent. Opened is the door to the ultimate art, the art of life.

In Dewey's fugitive and discarded poetry, we see the female archetype of a decentralized, pluralistic, and noncontrolling ground of being. It is reminiscent of Mother Earth in Black Elk's thought and practice—the ultimate support system and source of nourishment, energy, endurance. What is seen is immensely important. Furthermore, it illuminates everything in Dewey's writings, latent and manifest, undeveloped and developed. Why the abiding emphasis placed by him on democracy unless it is, at bottom, a religious emphasis—and a very archaic one at that? It is no great stretch to be again reminded of Black Elk: "And I saw that the sacred hoop of my people was one of many hoops that made one circle, wide as daylight and as starlight, and in the center grew one mighty flowering tree to shelter all the children of one mother and one father."[23]

But, of course, Dewey's vision of an interdependent whole in which responsible individuals emerge is not visionary. That is to say, it lacks the mythic punch of the "one mother and one father" delivered repeatedly on the trancelike, prereflective level of immediate experience, the level at which we gasp, our breath is taken away for an instant, and we inhale, inspire: we are restored to the universe that formed us, and to which we belong. Dewey's vision cannot be as behaviorally compelling, and this is a resounding limitation of his published writings.

Only in the philosopher's poetry is this mythic power boldly revealed, and the poetry is discarded.

Notes

1. Exploration of this "neutral" zone has barely begun, but it did not stop with James and Dewey. For example, Bernie S. Siegel, M.D., writes of the power of visualization to impede or stop certain diseases, "Visualization takes advantage of what might almost be called a 'weakness' of the body: it cannot distinguish between a vivid mental experience and an actual physical experience." (By the latter he must mean "an experience of the physical"; experience is just experience—always in itself actual.) See his *Love, Medicine, and Miracles* (New York: HarperCollins, 1986).

2. Silas Goldeon writes in "The Principle of Extended Identity," "[Some] think it would be the 'natural' extension of the 'human adventure' to create space colonies where people could live in controlled, self-sustaining environments. . . . [But] the planet—and more specifically, the place we live on it—is our main source of spiritual and biological information, and to do without it for ANY AMOUNT OF TIME WOULD affect us in much the same way that starvation

influences morality." References to Goldean, particularly to his *Pantheist Practice,* can be found in Dolores LaChapelle, *Sacred Land, Sacred Sex, Rapture of the Deep* (Silverton, Colo.: Finn Hill Arts, 1988), and extracts from his work can be obtained from Way of the Mountain Learning Center, Box 542, Silverton, CO, 81433.

3. I use two asterisks before "spiritual" in the attempt to dislodge the ingrained assumption that only the nonbodily can be spiritual.

4. *Art as Experience* (New York: G. P. Putnam's Sons, 1980 [1934]), 104 (*page references to future citations from this book will be found in brackets in the body of the text*). John Dewey, *Art as Experience, John Dewey: The Late Works, 1925–1953* (Carbondale: Southern Illinois University Press, 1987) (hereafter cited as "critical edition"), 10:109. Note how this relates to the north wind that Black Elk sucks through the sick boy's body (see Chapter 3). A residuum of the north wind experienced frequently or habitually remains in the boy's nervous system as the visceral meaning of north wind. This is activated in the healing ceremony. A more contemporary example: A president is shot in Dallas. The rifle's reports send the birds on nearby telephone wires flying. They soon return. But the meaning of this event stays within the body of the corporate organism of the nation.

5. I use the version used, I believe, by most people: (New York: Dover Books, 1958), 295. This is the second edition. *Henceforth page citations from this volume will be found in brackets in the body of my text. Experience and Nature, John Dewey: The Late Works, 1925–1953* (Carbondale: Southern Illinois University Press, 1981) (hereafter cited as "critical edition"), 1:224.

6. All cultures seem to contrast and to mediate Nature and culture. And all seem to entrust the mediation to the body's deepest practices and rituals. This emerges starkly with the Yanomami of what Europeans call Venezuela: "The Indians do not eat the animals they raise, and when this possibility is suggested to them, they declare that only true cannibals are capable of such an action. . . . The Yanomami . . . have tame animals. But they have no domestic animals, and it is probably for the following reason: What good is it to assemble a herd or raise a flock if it is impossible to eat the animals produced? Food received from a human hand is the agent that makes possible the transition from the state of nature to the state of culture; it transcends the original reality. A newborn that has not yet nursed is still of neutral status, a thing in transition; it is not altogether a being, and it is possible to kill it if it displays a patent congenital malformation or if it is not wanted by its parents. Infanticide becomes impossible as soon as the child has sucked the mother's milk even once" (Jacques Lizot, *Tales of the Yanomami* [Cambridge and New York: Cambridge University Press, 1985 (1976)], 15).

7. *Desert Solitaire* (New York: Random House-Ballantine, 1971 [1968]), 45.

8. In *Art as Experience,* Dewey writes that successful art intensifies and clarifies experience. But he is reluctant to call this the truth of, or about, experience. This may indicate an undue influence of science in his work. The same breadth of vision linked nevertheless to a restricted use of "truth" can be found in a younger American philosopher, Justus Buchler. See his important *Toward a General Theory of Human Judgment* (New York: Columbia University Press, 1951).

9. As Samuel Todes puts it in his remarkable *The Human Body as the Material Subject of the World* (New York: Garland Publishing, 1989), xiii: "As our erect stance gave us our original sense of actually being in the natural world, our *possibility* of upright principled conduct comes to give us our sense of being in a moral social world." We can go on to develop this (as Sam did not have the chance): What's right is what's upright, what connects the dark earth through the middle zone we mainly inhabit and thence into the heavens. Namely, the mythic World Tree with which our rituals can identify us, for it brings everything into connection with our hearts, our understanding, and our empathy. That is, the World Tree is the magical seventh direction, wisdom. The World Tree conducts mana power throughout the whole experienced and experienceable world—as if it were an organic dynamo. Walt Whitman: "I sing the body electric."

10. "The Philosophy of William James," in *Problems of Men* (New York: Philosophical Library, 1946), 391. The date of this essay is given as 1942.

11. *Essays on School and Society* (Carbondale: Southern Illinois University Press, 1976 [1899]) (hereafter cited as "critical edition"), 46. *Page references will subsequently be placed in brackets in the body of the text.*

12. See my *Wild Hunger: The Primal Roots of Modern Addiction* (Lanham, Md., and New York: Rowman & Littlefield, 1998).

13. Of course, *School and Society* is a fairly early text. Particularly in Dewey's later work, wilderness is not named, but it is meant, for example: "Our liberal and rich ideas, our adequate appreciations, due to productive art, are hemmed in by an unconquered domain in which we are everywhere exposed to the incidence of unknown forces and hurried fatally to unforeseen consequences." (Note, however, that he speaks of this domain as mainly something to be conquered—indigenous people would demur.) *Experience and Nature* (1958 [1929]), 372.

14. *Art as Experience,* 17; critical edition, p. 23.

15. *Human Nature and Conduct* (New York: Modern Library, 1930 [1922]), 331. John Dewey, *Human Nature and Conduct, John Dewey, the Middle Works, 1899–1924* (Carbondale: Southern Illinois University Press, 1983) (hereafter cited as "critical edition"), 14:226–27.

16. See Jack Turner's marvelous *The Abstract Wild* (Tucson: University of Arizona Press, 1997), 49.

17. See my *Wild Hunger* 8–9, for the etymology of "wilderness."

18. See Frank P. Jones, *The Alexander Technique: Body Awareness in Action* (New York: Schocken Books, 1976), particularly the chapter on Dewey and Alexander.

19. "Fate," in *Ralph Waldo Emerson: Selected Essays,* ed. Larzar Ziff (New York: Penguin Books, 1982), 379.

20. Quoted in Stephen C. Rockefeller, *John Dewey: Religious Faith and Democratic Humanism* (New York: Columbia University Press, 1991), 342. *The next page reference is to this book and will be inserted in brackets in the body of my text.*

21. *The Poems of John Dewey* (Carbondale: University of Southern Illinois Press, 1977), xi. There is a grave ethical issue here. Dewey's privacy was not respected by Thomas. Indeed, should *I* use this material? I decided to do so for two reasons: (1) the material has been published, and (2) it is exceedingly important, I believe, for better understanding both Dewey and the world in which we live. *Subsequent page references for the poems will be inserted in brackets in the body of the text.*

22. So complex, rich, varied, and prolonged is Dewey's thought! We have to be exceedingly careful with him. For example, in *Art as Experience,* he beautifully describes the moment of piety as "being lured on by an aura" [73; critical edition, 80]. And later in the book, "Art is a mode of prediction not found in charts and statistics" [349; critical edition, 352].

23. *Black Elk Speaks* (Lincoln: University of Nebraska Press, 1979), 43.

Body-Mind and Subconsciousness
Dewey and Tragedy

It is not easy to think of John Dewey as a tragic figure. There are too many photos of his kind grandfatherly face, of his dandling schoolchildren on his knee, or of his meeting notables. He achieved influence fairly early, and ultimately fame comparable to that of Emerson or James. He lived to a very old age, active and honored practically to the end.

But there is another side to the picture. Before World War I, two of his children died quite young, and the advent of the war itself was profoundly shocking. Its gruesome absurdities shook Dewey's optimism, and its occurrence coincided precisely with his midlife crisis. At fifty-seven he had pretty well summed up his views in the magisterial, tightly organized *Democracy and Education* (1916). He had no way of knowing he would live for thirty-five more years, and he entered a period of depression (his views on the war prompted harsh criticism, which did not help). He became romantically involved with a woman not his wife (although the relationship was probably

not consummated), and, as we will now see at greater length, he hied himself
to the psycho-bio-therapist, F. M. Alexander.

Dewey had been criticizing Cartesian psycho/physical dualism for decades.
But when his personal problems were confronted in the startling light that
Alexander's body work threw upon the limitations of consciousness, Dewey
produced a much deeper critique. In 1918 he accepted an offer from Stanford
University to give a series of lectures on morals (published in expanded form
in 1922 as *Human Nature and Conduct*). Dewey acknowledged Alexander's
influence, but it would be clear to the attentive reader even if he had not.
Also, vivid allusions occur both to psychoanalysis and the war. What could
drive supposedly reasonable people to such insane carnage? Dewey notes
James's seminal "The Moral Equivalent of War," and observes that the traditional motives—glory, heroism, fame, booty—have been complicated and
attenuated by the nation-state organized technologically. Anticipating to
some extent Hannah Arendt's idea of the banality of evil, Dewey writes,

> The activities that evoke . . . a war are of . . . a collective, prosaic polit-
> ical and economic nature. . . . Universal conscription, the general
> mobilization of all agricultural and industrial forces of folk not
> engaged in the trenches, the application of every conceivable scientific
> and mechanical device, the mass movements of soldiery regulated
> from a common center by a depersonalized general staff: these factors
> relegate the traditional psychological apparatus of war to a now remote
> antiquity. . . . [T]he more horrible a depersonalized scientific mass
> war becomes, the more necessary it is to find universal ideal motives
> to justify it. . . . The more prosaic the actual causes, the more neces-
> sary is it to find glowingly sublime motives.[1]

On the eve of his sixtieth year, Dewey reconsidered the very meaning of
individual identity and behavior—essentially socialized group members that
we are. And he wonders what we are to make of groups when they are
organized according to scientific and technological principles. Moreover, he
reconsiders the meaning of science itself. And it is no surprise that he examined the ability of psychoanalysis to peer behind our cheap talk about motives
and to disclose what really makes us tick. But he can give psychoanalysis
only a mixed review:

> It exhibits a sense for reality in its insistence upon the profound impor-
> tance of unconscious forces. . . . Every movement of reaction and

protest, however, usually accepts some of the basic ideas of the position against which it rebels. So . . . psychoanalysis . . . retain[s] the notion of a separate psychic realm or force. They add a . . . statement of the existence and operation of the "unconscious," of complexes due to contacts and conflicts with others, of the social censor. But they still cling to the idea of a separate psychic realm and so in effect talk about unconscious consciousness. They get their truths mixed up in theory with the false psychology of original individual consciousness. [86–87]

Despite Jung's and Freud's creative work, they are stuck, Dewey believes, in unsuspected Cartesian assumptions. In effect, Dewey launches himself on a new career that will see him expose "the false psychology of original individual consciousness" with a severity and thoroughness never before seen in his work, or perhaps in anyone's. But if the conception of the unconscious or subconscious that he puts in its place is right, any in-depth knowledge of it will be terribly difficult to achieve, as will be any effective educational program, any sane reconstruction of persons and culture. At seventy, long a famous and influential educator, Dewey writes of consciousness, and by implication, subconsciousness:

We have at present little or next to no controlled art of securing that redirection of behavior which constitutes adequate perception or consciousness. That is, we have little or no art of education in the fundamentals, namely in the management of the organic attitudes which color the qualities of our conscious objects and acts. As long as our chief psycho-physical coordinations are formed blindly and in the dark during infancy and early childhood, they are accidental adjustments to the pressure of other persons and circumstances which act upon us. They do not then take into account the consequences of these activities upon formation of habits. . . . Hence the connection between consciousness and action is precarious, and its possession a doubtful boon as compared with the efficacy of instinct—or structure—in lower animals.[2]

In 1938, nearly eighty, Dewey published *Experience and Education,* an attempt to explain to his many followers in "progressive education" what he was up to. But most of them, despite their good intentions and hard work, had not a clue to what this very difficult philosopher was doing. Nor did most professional philosophers, for they, too, despite their apparent intelligence and logical rigor, had left Cartesian psycho/physical assumptions in place, and had succumbed to simplistic ideas of human identity, science, learning, and knowledge. They could not grasp body-mind. Exhibiting a kind of professional deformation, they equated mind with consciousness, and consciousness with what's essentially reflectable by it! They could not grasp the foggy area in which mind is not accessible to consciousness—in which organic adjustments move toward ends that are not monitorable by consciousness. Moreover, these means may clash with other means, with consciousness unable to adjudicate the conflict. We develop a dirempted and perverted subconsciousness, as Dewey puts it, and we go out of touch with the involuntary bases of our ancient being in Nature.

There is something tragic about Dewey's career, and it centers on his penetrating, but never rounded out, views on subconscious mind. It is not just that his views were not widely understood for lack of definitive clarity, or for lack of sympathetic and truly intelligent readers, but also that he exposed mountainous difficulties for gaining self-knowledge, difficulties that stagger au courant "with it" educators or statesmen today. And, most important, Dewey himself, I believe, has a limited grasp of the archetypal and mythic means and meanings at work in us body-minds.

This essay on Dewey builds on the previous one. We saw how he equates human civilization with the rise of manifold arts. These use organic processes and adjustments—inherited from millions of years of prehuman and human evolution in Nature—as means to achieve ends-in-view. The arts mark the rise of voluntary behavior.

But the concept of the voluntary is exceedingly broad and foggy on its edges. Exactly when and where does it begin to apply? This indeterminacy connects essentially to indeterminacy in the concept of ends-in-view. Dewey says that instinctive smiling (over agreeable sensations in one's stomach, say) becomes voluntary and an art when used as a means for welcoming a friend, for example. But there are undecidable cases. What if one has some doubts whether this visitor is a friend? This is neither a case in which one is convinced that the visitor is a friend, nor convinced that the visitor is not (when one may put on a false face and know perfectly well what one is doing). But one may smile anyway, perhaps because one must show some reaction, and one fears instinctively any delay. Is one's behavior voluntary in the sense that one knows what one is doing, knows what one is aiming at, trying to achieve? The situation is in fact exceedingly murky, and anxiety producing

because of that. There very well may be what Dewey calls perversion of consciousness—or more likely subconsciousness—that goes much deeper, and
is much more disintegrative and troubling in the long run, than is conscious,
fully voluntary dissembling and deceit.

Thus appears the absolute necessity for humans to become habituated
in group ways through rites and rituals and manifold habits. These autho-
rize and inculcate definite modes of response, which are adequate for most
situations and which allay much anxiety. Particularly important are the group's
rites and rituals at those cusps of development when the person's status is
itself problematical, from infancy to childhood, from adolescence to young
adulthood, from that to parenthood, and so on. The group lays down patterns
of behavior in the bodies of its members so that they can count on their ability
to act and react in most problematical situations.

Now Dewey knows that science and technology develop so rapidly that
cultural habits laid down deeply for untold centuries are breaking to bits.
Habits of face-to-face interactions of various sorts to, for example, deper-
sonalized scientific mass war. Or habits of face-to-face interactions between
elders and initiates during rites of passage, say, to adolescents today communicating with other adolescents in "chat rooms" on the Internet—to
bring things up to date nearly fifty years after Dewey's death.

Dewey in the 1920s is prophetically aware of what is plain for us to see at
2000: "As long as our chief psycho/physical coordinations are formed blindly
and in the dark during infancy and early childhood, they are accidental
adjustments to the pressure of other persons and of circumstances which act
upon us." Perversions of subconsciousness and our deepest psycho/physical
habits mean disintegration and degeneration of persons. Moreover, it's not
just a matter of trouble for individuals, but for the whole society—and now,
because of marvels of communication, transportation, and trading, societies
interlocked globally.

Let us follow Dewey's development of the concepts of habit and the subconscious, so that we see how, as he says, habits are what we *are*. And then
we will be positioned to see how profoundly bad, bad habits are. Given our
loss of archetypal myth and ritual practice, they may be intractably bad—
that is the tragic dimension of the great philosopher's work.

"Know thyself!"—words inscribed on the temple of Apollo at Delphi.
These words that haunted Socrates haunted Dewey and, along with many
lessons from Alexander, enabled him to deepen his thought during the next
three decades of his life. Science that does not lie upon us oppressively stifling

our freedom and dreams, science that becomes intelligence and an art, cannot be divorced from patience and courage, or from that aesthetical-ethical satisfaction that is rectitude of organic action. These virtues are not merely "values" inside some subjective consciousness, but structures of the body-in-the-world, and they must emerge if we are to live sanely and vitally. To achieve this rectitude, Dewey writes in *Experience and Nature*—a key passage that we quote again—we must get in touch with "our immediate organic selections, rejections, welcomings, expulsions . . . of the most minute, vibratingly delicate nature. We are not aware of the qualities of these acts. . . . Yet they exist as feeling qualities and have an enormous directive effect on our behavior" [299]. Dewey puts his finger on the nub of subconscious mind, that point at which we begin to understand people's irrational exclusions and aggressions, their ecstatic engulfments in groups, and even the ways they can be numbed or hypnotized, inured in routines, dulled into mindlessly obeying orders, and cast into the banality of evil. We can begin to understand all this without reifying "consciousness" as some strange entity or nonphysical substance, and then imagine that there is an even stranger incarnation of it that is somehow not conscious, "unconscious consciousness," as Dewey derisively calls it (thereby anticipating Jean-Paul Sartre's critique).

Now let us follow the main contours of Dewey's inquiry into mind—or rather, body-mind—and those of its workings that do not involve consciousness. He completely reverses Descartes' procedure. Instead of beginning with consciousness as the most certain reality and somehow tying knowledge of everything else to it, Dewey articulates a view of the world in which consciousness is understood as momentary and highly derivative. His is a developmental view in which consciousness emerges from mind—most of which is not conscious. And mind emerges from the psychophysical, and the psychophysical emerges from the physical. The question is reversed: Instead of, How is anything but consciousness possible? the question becomes, How is consciousness possible?

Dewey describes *the* philosophical fallacy as the tendency to think that something achieved eventually through a process existed prior to the process and caused it. It is true that at some stage, under certain circumstances, there can be some consciousness of consciousness. But it does not follow that an essentially self-reflexive consciousness exists on its own prior to what is achieved under certain circumstances, and that it lies behind this process, simply unveiling itself through it. Believing that consciousness is a self-sealing, self-illuminating "substance" of some kind is a remnant of substantialist metaphysics and its tendency to reify the reference of nouns. Since we can quantify and speak of "one consciousness," we tend to infer mistakenly that consciousness is some kind of individual thing referred to.

There is an echo of Aristotelianism in Dewey's view. *What* something is (its "form") is best understood as a realization of some of the potentialities of the organism. But for Dewey mind itself comes into being, is formed, and "can be understood in the concrete only as a system of [habitual] beliefs, desires, and purposes which are formed in interaction of biological aptitudes with a social environment."[3] Dewey's idea of what something is differs radically from Aristotle's. For Dewey, "form" evolves, *gets formed,* through habits of interaction building up between organism and a total environment. There is no showcase of finished, eternal forms. Mind itself is an evolving pattern of habits of interaction. It is a realization of the potentialities of stages of habits prior to mind-habit, and it itself may or may not become "material" for realization as consciousness. Characteristically Dewey writes, in *Human Nature and Conduct,*

> Habits may be profitably compared to physiological functions, like breathing, digesting. The latter are, to be sure, involuntary, while habits are acquired. . . . Walking implicates the ground as well as the legs; speech demands physical air and human companionship . . . natural operations . . . and acquired ones like speech and honesty, are functions of the surroundings as truly as of a person. They are things done by the environment by means of organic structures or acquired dispositions. . . . They involve skill of sensory and motor organs, cunning or craft, and objective materials. They assimilate objective energies, and eventuate in command of environment. . . . They have a beginning, middle, and end. [14–15]

Mind is not a substance, it is minding: the habitual ways an organism and environment assimilate, interact, and coordinate so that needs of the organism (and typically also the environment) have been satisfied over the millennia. At what point in complexity of interaction does minding emerge? Is an earthworm adjusting to its environment minding it? It is essential to Dewey's approach—and no mere defect of learning on his part—that he cannot tell precisely what this point of emergence is. There are untold numbers of borderline cases. Continuity or continuum is the key concept in Dewey's worldview—as it was for Charles Peirce—and a continuum is defined as that which is not constructible out of discrete units or stages. Dewey's practice is to take leaps along the continuum until he locates positions that clearly exhibit different properties. Not that this consistently dissolves difficulties. For example, he says that minding emerges when an organism interacts and becomes habituated in a social environment, or when it engages in a language. But don't chimps, for instance, have their own society and their own language? "Language" remains vague in Dewey's writings, at least as far as I can see.

But he is telling us something very important about human beings. Even if we say somewhat arbitrarily that minding in the full sense emerges with humans engaged in human language, we must also say that minding emerges within a background of human and prehuman organic habits that is never simply discarded and left behind. Minding, he says, involves *meanings,* and meanings are always tied up in some way with *means*—the means whereby an organism interacts in some way with the environment. Dewey profoundly undercuts psycho/physical dualism. Minding is the activity of body-mind organizing itself and the world around and within it so that dominant needs are satisfied (when things are going right). The *means whereby* this is accomplished include the responses of others—present and actual, or remembered or anticipated—which the organism incorporates within itself to deal with the world and to make sense of it. "Objects" are events with meaning; that is, individuations or "cutouts" emerge within the processing, interfusing world as the co-creation of organism and environment. The means whereby adjustment is achieved show up on "the other side" as the meanings of *things.* As he writes in *Human Nature and Conduct,* "Objects are habits turned inside out" [182]. But a habit of adaptation may cease to be fruitful, and may be superseded, in whole or part, by another habit pattern, and so a new inventory of the items of the world must be toted up, an inventory that can never be final.

Dewey writes in *Experience and Nature,* "'This,' whatever *this* may be, always implies a system of meanings focused at a point of stress, uncertainty, and need of regulation" [352]. There must always be an element of uncertainty because there is no assurance that ongoing, habituated means and meanings will achieve accustomed satisfactions. Due to changes in organism or environment, old habits may be disrupted. If so, consciousness may arise, says Dewey, for consciousness emerges only when there is some hesitation or some failure in habitual adjustments.

The limitations of consciousness are immense. It's no good to say that consciousness can run ahead in imagination and anticipate certain of its probable failures or hesitations. For its ability to imagine is limited by adjustments already achieved. Its ability to imagine is limited by bodily and other material conditions that typically lie beyond the scope of any present consciousness. There is no reason to think that consciousness can predict which meanings will arise, so of course no reason to think that consciousness can predict which meanings will become conscious.

Dewey is indebted to his experience with Alexander: he could not imagine certain bodily movements or postures until Alexander moved his body for him. As Dewey stretches science to include self-knowledge, he draws the stunning conclusion that in the psycho/physical complex that is body-self, body must take the lead in both forming and testing hypotheses about self. We must somehow relax and let things happen. What William James emphasized as a condition for religious experience, Dewey discovers to be a condition for any reliable self-knowledge.

This is what Dewey learned so surprisingly and sometimes so painfully from Alexander, and what he is trying to theoretically reconstruct in his treatises. "Immediate givens of consciousness," "sense data," enjoy no primacy—for if these figure in consciousness it is because they are factored out of the processing continuum and come to be as "individuals" only when the occasion for a certain kind of focusing analysis arises. But if that occasion arises, it is the result of circumambient stimuli and organic adjustments that cannot at that moment be precisely or exhaustively known by anyone. Consciousness cannot reliably predict its own course. There must always be some not yet adjusted to stimuli as well as some organic adjustments, means, and meanings that are not conscious. As James put it famously in *The Principles of Psychology,* "The present moment is the darkest in the whole series." Consciousness is conditioned within a matrix that is not itself conscious, nor is it immediately accessible to consciousness.

Again, Dewey recalls Emerson: We belong to Nature before anything can belong to us, and recalls also Black Elk's discovery of the mystery of growth. But Dewey's density of empirical detail and his close association with science also distinguish him from them.

We begin to see what Dewey means by subconscious mind, and it's an enormity. He cannot describe it as some backwater or far corner of consciousness that a sedulous reflexive or introspective consciousness could detect just by "looking." Most of body-mind—or body-minding—never becomes conscious. To miss being consciousness, all that need happen is that organic adjustments or means "work" in some minimal or short-range sense. They may permanently stifle growth of self; they may cause vague suffering or boredom or elusive malaise. No matter, the trouble does not focus itself enough, is not sharp enough, to call for consciousness. The best consciousness may be able to do is to stand open to the possibility that body-mind will reveal something surprising if allowed to spontaneously display itself.

To be sure, consciousness may help prepare the ground for discovery by dilating and relaxing, by allowing, say, the body to be manipulated by another body-mind who knows the sorts of things to look for—another body-mind in the unusual language community of therapist and patient. Consciousness can perhaps prepare itself to be startled. By incorporating the other's attitudes and manipulations, the other's means-by-which, one's own behaviors may be given conscious meaning, stand out, finally be noticed.

But one's consciousness "by itself" cannot change one's person at will. I put "by itself" in scare quotes, because there is *no such thing* as *a* consciousness. Such a meaning is a trick of language, not a precipitate of an effective means of adaptive behavior that leaves an effective meaning, an actual individual, cut out, individuated, in the world. *A* consciousness is not a bona fide individual. Organisms caught up in some way with other things are the actual individuals.

Dewey grapples with the concept of subconscious mind in two key chapters of *Experience and Nature,* "Nature, Life, and Body-Mind," and "Existence, Ideas, and Consciousness." Note well these trenchant words from the opening pages of the latter chapter: "There is thus an obvious difference between mind and consciousness; meaning and an idea. Mind denotes the whole system of meanings as they are embodied in the workings of organic life; consciousness in a being with language denotes awareness or perception of meaning. . . . The greater part of mind is only implicit in any conscious act or state; the field of mind—of operative meanings—is enormously wider than that of consciousness. Mind is contextual and persistent; consciousness is focal and transitive" [303]. Several points must be emphasized. Although Dewey writes of "a system of meanings," this misleads if it suggests a coherent system. It's not necessarily that at all! Notice next the vague locution, "consciousness . . . denotes awareness or perception of meanings." He does not tell us if he means awareness of meanings *as* meanings—reflexive, semi-reflexive, or, to various degrees, thematic awareness—or, on the other hand, whether it is awareness merely in the sense that means are bringing about ends, but it does not follow that the person need be able to be aware of the means and ends *as such*. He seems to allow for the latter when he writes of "sense:" "Sense is . . . different from signification. The latter involves the use of a quality as a sign or index of something else, as when the red of a light signifies danger, and the need of bringing a moving locomotive to a stop. The sense of a thing, on the other hand, is an immediate and immanent meaning; it is meaning which is itself felt or directly had" [260–61]. The distinction is important, but in terms of Dewey's own emphasis on continuity, it can be made overly sharp. It is not clear where sense ends and signification begins, or the reverse. The lived reality is itself vague. Immediately felt senses involved in being one's bodily self can lead us in directions and toward ends that we cannot consciously reflect and acknowledge. Insofarforth, they are significatory. To sense—usually on the margins of consciousness—the muscles clenching, as if on the verge of attack, say, is to sense them as the means to attack, that is, as meaning, as signifying, attack. (Never to attack, even when one believes one should, is to be conflicted—which may manifest in psycho-somatic symptoms.)

Without trying to make these difficult points, we can never understand how subconsciousness can become as conflicted and maladaptive—as perverted—as Dewey observes it to be. I have tried to bring greater clarity to the matter by employing the phenomenological distinction between thematic and non-thematic meanings. With the former we are aware of meanings and means *as* what they are; with the latter we are not. Alexander can be construed as aiming to make thematic *the means by which* certain effects are generated. Only then can ill effects and bad habits be detected and perhaps superseded by better, more fruitful and harmonious behaviors. Without this transfor-mation into thematization, bad habits seem normal, for no alternative is imaginable.

Subconscious means and meanings easily become incoherent. He thinks the "soul of modern man" is a hellish mess. I will quote at some length from pages in *Experience and Nature* that should forever dispel the illusion of the kindly, grandfatherly, benign, and optimistic Dewey. That these pages are seldom quoted by commentators reveals the typical squeamishness of intel-lectuals brought face to face with messy and disturbing facts of body-mind and subconsciousness. In this material are some key lines already quoted:

> Apart from language, from imputed and inferred meaning, we continu-ally engage in an immense multitude of immediate organic selections, rejections, welcomings, expulsions, appropriations, withdrawals, shrinkings, expansions, elations and dejections, attacks, wardings off, of the most minute, vibratingly delicate nature. We are not aware of the qualities of many or most of these acts; we do not objectively distinguish and identify them. Yet they exist as feeling qualities, and

have an enormous directive effect on our behavior. If for example, certain sensory qualities of which we are not cognitively aware cease to exist, we cannot stand or control our posture and movements. . . . Meanings acquired in connection with the use of tools and of language exercise a profound influence upon organic feelings. In the reckoning of this account are included the changes effected by all the consequences of attitude and habit due to *all* the consequences of tools and language—in short, civilization. Evil communications corrupt (native) good manners of action, and hence pervert feeling and subconsciousness. The deification of the subconscious is legitimate only for those who never indulge in it—animals and thoroughly healthy naive children—if there be any such. The subconscious of a civilized adult reflects all the habits he has acquired . . . all the organic modifications he has undergone. And in so far as these involve malcoordinations, fixations, and segregations (as they assuredly come to do in a very short time for those living in complex "artificial" conditions), sensory appreciation is confused, perverted, and falsified. . . . Activities which develop, appropriate, and enjoy meanings bear the same actualizing relation to psycho-physical affairs that the latter bear to physical character. . . . The actualization of meanings furnishes psycho-physical qualities with their ulterior significance and worth. But it also confuses and perverts them. . . . the casual growth and incorporation of meanings cause native need, adjustment, and satisfaction to lose their immediate certainty and efficiency, and become subject to all kinds of aberrations. There then occur systematized withdrawals from intercourse and interaction . . . : carefully cultivated and artificially protected fantasies of consolation and compensation; rigidly stereotyped beliefs not submitted to objective tests; habits of learned ignorance or systematized ignorings of concrete relationships; organized fanaticisms; dogmatic traditions which socially are harshly intolerant and which intellectually are institutionalized paranoic systems; idealizations which instead of being immediate enjoyments of meanings, cut man off from nature and his fellows. [299–302]

All of Dewey's herculean efforts in education are aimed at avoiding this mess. More and more, meanings are incorporated casually, without regulation. He realized that well-founded educational projects, effective cultivation of persons, must grow out of the genetic legacy. If civilization is not to jam means and meanings half-baked into a precariously balanced, fearful, conflicted body-self, it must develop the tendencies built into us over millions of years of adaptation in Nature: our natural curiosity and exploratory urges, our joy in making connections, and in feeling sound, whole, competent. The first job of the teacher is to discover where the child is at that place and time of his or her life. What interests and concerns the child? The world as experienced grows, and it grows in connections that ramify from the particular things that sting our interest here and now. We need not know why these sting our interest. They do. Out of them springs the mystery of growth.

If growth is to be sound and vibrant, it must be organic, coherent. There are cancerous growths. Organic growth vitally interconnects the world as experienced and one's growing capacities as an organism to accommodate and enjoy an expanding, ever-complexifying world. Too much ingestion of subject matter too soon produces disintegration—split-off states, or total numbing, or premature crystallization: the child learns something, but the very accomplishment blocks further learning. The ideal is growth forever more growth. Fixation can be produced by "too much too soon," by too much unearned gratification. Or by too little gratification: the child is balked and stymied in hopeless boredom, knowing *something* is not forthcoming, budding, but not knowing what.

Again, the growth of the individual is the growth of that person's experienced world. It tends to grow all through itself and on its edges. Dewey's ingenious siting and design of the ideal school—noted in the last essay—fosters this beautifully. The rooms are arranged to facilitate the transmission to the laboratory of actual questions and problems arising in work in kitchen and shop; they are worked out there. The so-called fine arts are just the ultimate refinements of the other arts, including science of course, and the fruits of past creative efforts are placed within the central room, the museum. The building as a whole is sited to look out in various salient directions at the encompassing world—to businesses, to universities, to civic and government institutions, to gardens, to homes.

But as I noted in the preceding essay, Dewey does not site the school to look out on wilderness. And I mean this in its etymological sense: will-of-the-place—the Nature to which we have belonged, and will belong, before anything can belong to us. The wilderness that formed us. I don't mean wilderness as just something to be conquered (of which Dewey sometimes speaks). It is wilderness generating its own piety from its own members, a piety he honors, but, I think, inadequately develops.

Thoreau wrote that in wildness is the preservation of the world. Paul Shepard in our day continues this probe. He also was acutely aware of the

dangers of rampaging technological civilization jamming means and meanings half-baked into our body-selves, disrupting and perverting deep organic
adjustments dearly obtained over the millennia. Shepard: "Learning means
a highly timed openness in which the attention of the child is pre-directed by
an intrinsic schedule, a hunger to fill archetypal forms with specific meaning.
Neotony is the biological commitment to that learning program, building
identity and meaning in the oscillation between autonomy and unity, sep-
arateness and relatedness. . . . [Learning] is a pulse, presenting the mind
with wider wholes, from womb to mother and body, to earth, to cosmos."[4]
Archetypal forms interlaced with the genetic legacy: Dewey does not say
enough about this. Archetypes interdigitate and move with our ancient lives
formed in wilderness and funded in our bodies still: Artemis, hunter and
protector of animals; waters bathing and healing us; trees regenerating—and
stories of people turning into trees; goddess figures with pendulous breasts
and heavy thighs, that mean succor, protection, and fresh life; the moon
emptying and filling, emptying and filling; and countless mandala inscrip-
tions generating the sensing and sense of the interdependence of things; and
on and on, without apparent limit.

It is particularly the loss of wild animals that Shepard laments: "The
growth of self-identity requires coming to terms with the wild and uncon-
trollable within. Normally the child identifies frightening feelings and ideas
with specific external objects. The sensed limitations of such objects aid his
attempts to control his fears. As the natural containers of these projected
feeling receded with the wilderness, a lack of substitutes may have left the
child less able to cope and thus more dependent, his development impaired"
[33]. And:

> All children experience the world as a training ground for the encounter
> with otherness. That ground is not the arena of human faces but
> whole animals. Nonhuman life is the real system that the child spon-
> taneously seeks and internalizes, matching its salient features with his
> own inner diversity. . . . The city contains a minimal nonhuman fauna.
> Adequate otherness is seldom encountered. A self does not come
> together that can deal with its own strangeness, much less the aberrant
> fauna and its stone habitat. . . . The world to the child—and adult—
> is grotesquely, not familiarly Other. [98]

Let us close this allusion to Shepard with his terrifying image of institutionalized deracination and immaturity:

Like land birds instinctively setting out on transoceanic migration, given assurance . . . from the experience of the species that there is land on the other side, the human adolescent organism reenters the dangerous ground of immature perception on the premise that society is prepared to meet his psychic demands for a new landing—that is, that society is organized to take these refractory youths through a powerful, tightly structured gestation; to test, teach, reveal; to offer . . . things worthy of their skill; to tutor their suffering and dreaming; and to guide their feelings of fidelity. If . . . the adult group is not prepared to administer the new and final birth, then the youths create autistic solutions to their own needs and . . . sink finally, cynically, back into their own incompetent immaturity, like exhausted birds going down at sea. [65–66]

To subsume both the fine arts and science under the rubric of art, to assign such a fundamental role to art in our being in the world, and to integrate this in a system of educational theory—all this is Dewey's great achievement. But without a major role for archetypal myth and ritual, his work will not be sufficient, I believe, to reintegrate and reconsolidate us. The near absence of the archetypal in Dewey is the tragic dimension of his work. That with all my and others' efforts to re-myth and reground our lives in the primal . . . that this may not be achievable—that is the tragic dimension of our work.

Notes

1. *Human Nature and Conduct* (New York: Modern Library, 1930 [1922]), 113 ff. *Page numbers for subsequent references will be in brackets in the body of our text. Human Nature and Conduct, John Dewey, the Middle Works, 1899–1924* (Carbondale: Southern Illinois University Press, 1983) (hereafter cited as "critical edition"), 14:81.

2. *Experience and Nature* (New York: Dover Books, 1958 [1929]), 316–17. *Subsequent page references will be placed in brackets in the body of our text. Experience and Nature, John Dewey, the Late Works, 1925–1953* (Carbondale: Southern Illinois University Press, 1981), 1:239.

3. *Human Nature and Conduct*, preface. Critical edition, 228 ff.

4. *Nature and Madness* (San Francisco: Sierra Club Books, 1982), 110. *Subsequent page references will be placed in brackets in the body of our text.*

Passion for Meaning
William Ernest Hocking's
Religious-Philosophical Views

William Ernest Hocking is a major thinker unjustly forgotten. The reasons for this neglect are several, and throw light on our current situation: His addresses and publications, spanning the first years of this century to the 1960s, are of great subtlety, complexity, and variety; we live in the age of the fast read. We are as much driven as our European ancestors who colonized this continent and who—compulsive, acquisitive—disgusted and terrified indigenous people.

If one were forced to play the labels game, one might call Hocking a rationalist and a mystic and a genuine public servant. With the neglect of all these roles in our secular, hyperspecialized, often cynical age, it is not surprising that a thinker who somehow combines them should be dismissed as eclectic and consigned to the dustbin of history. Hocking seems to be one of those old-fashioned thinkers who had the temerity to feel responsible for assessing and maintaining the fabric of civilization. But what knowledgeable person in the fast lane of today's multi-laned relativistic world would

even use the singular, "civilization" (but probably without much understanding of other civilizations)?

Finally there is his great hospitality to the world, the many powerful
philosophers East and West whom he received gratefully, and whose influence is clearly evident (his ego is not fragile): For example, both William
James and Josiah Royce (!), and in about equal degree, and Edmund Husserl
and Gabriel Marcel. All these get woven into a tapestry that is huge, original, distinctly American, and hard to take in at even several glances.

Trying to get an initial fix on the whole pattern, I will employ at crucial junctures a phenomenological lens. Even without knowing that Hocking spent
three months of his formative years studying with Edmund Husserl, we
could see a version of phenomenology in his works themselves.[1]

But Husserl is a German philosopher, and the word "phenomenology"
has a distinctly continental flavor (though Charles Peirce used it or a cognate
term). What does this have to do with this book, which is entitled *The Primal
Roots of American Philosophy*? A lot. First, the classic American philosophers
with whom we deal are greatly influenced by continental thinkers of the
nineteenth century, particularly the identity-philosophies already mentioned.
This is true even though they interweave these influences with distinctly
American concerns and enthusiasms. Second, and even more important,
phenomenology responds to a crisis of meaning and living felt throughout
"advanced" North Atlantic culture. The crisis arises over the very successes
of science and technology. So totally do they take over our lives that the vast
prescientific matrix without which life cannot be meaningful and vital is
eclipsed and begins to crumble. Indeed, without prescientific meanings and
practices to supply a matrix for living, science and modern technology
would themselves be impossible.

Very simply, phenomenology is the attempt to see clearly what we typically
take completely for granted, what we feel we can ignore. In other words, it is
the attempt to see the primal and pragmatic: the meaning of being selves that are
bodies, selves ineluctably in situations or circumstances, selves ecstatic or
depressed, gripped by responsibilities and enlivened thereby or wayward and
listless; selves often very different from moment to moment, yet ones who
remember what they've been through, and what they've promised, and know
they will die. It is completely understandable that indigenous peoples, torn from
their land and their lives, send up a lament that mingles achingly and strangely
with the lament of thoughtful Europeans or Euro-Americans who, caught in
vast tides of history, also feel dispossessed, alienated, uprooted, desiccated.

The connection between phenomenology and existentialism, on the one hand, and primal or indigenous life, on the other, is deep and direct. These ways of thinking aim to see deeper into the life we actually lead, to unmask what seems to be obvious and evident. Particularly clear in the later work of the existential phenomenologist, Martin Heidegger, is the connection to indigenous lifeways. Heidegger writes of "the play of the fourfold," of thinking as thanking, of dwelling as being open to the sky; of the pouring out from the jug of wine as a giving that echoes the giving which is Being itself; of the spring from which the water is drawn for the wine, which reflects the sky; of the earth into which the wine grapes root.[2] Earlier than Heidegger—or Marcel—Hocking's unique phenomenology opens the way for recovery of primal values: of ecstatic expansiveness, holism, kinship, reverence, basal gratitude, ultimate responsiveness, and responsibility.

As an advanced graduate student at Harvard, Hocking was the beneficiary of a traveling fellowship to Germany. Once there, Paul Natorp suggested he study with the barely known Edmund Husserl in Göttingen. None of Hocking's advisers had suggested this, but Natorp's sketch of Husserl's attack on psychologism—his critique of the assumption that an empirical science of psychology can speak definitively on meaning and truth—resonated strongly with Hocking's "gropings," and with trepidation he went to Göttingen and was warmly received into Husserl's sparsely attended course on logical investigations. When he sent to his superiors at Harvard the mandatory report on his activities, he was told in effect not to waste the university's money on this "unknown" phenomenologist, and sadly he moved on after three months. But in this time Husserl made a profound impression, and my entry into Hocking's work will be by way of it.

How do we begin philosophizing without cheating? How do we avoid being sucked into the magnetizing and dazzling funnel of natural-scientific explanation that must reduce or ignore our sensuous, immediate situations in which primal meaning gets made? This meaning-making contributes massively to our very being. Just because it is presupposed so unquestioningly and completely, seems so obvious and banal, we tend to think that we don't need to think about it, protect it, discover its ways of working.

Husserl was developing a way of unfolding and protecting it. He amended Hegel at a fundamental level, an amendment much appreciated by Hocking. How does the world "give itself out" primordially, how does it appear initially as phenomena and phenomenon? Hegel replies that it is the poorest content or *what;* it is merely the phenomenal certainty of the *that,* sheer existence, "something there."

With daring genius, Husserl makes a distinction that allows him both to appreciate Hegel's point and to supersede it: Yes, it's a *that,* but it's not completely empty of content, and, moreover, this content is not given isolated and alone, but rather in a fundamental network of meaning, ultimately the primordially given world itself—difficult to describe just as it appears. To expose this content, to avoid burying it under the epithets "obvious and taken for granted," we no longer *simply* assert or assume its existence in the everyday tunneling and practical way, but we just entertain this world-assumption as what it gives itself out to be—as phenomenon—namely, "unquestioned assumption." In Husserl's technical language, we suspend (without eliminating) the assertive or *positing* aspect of minding in order to allow the *constituting* aspect (constitutive of meaning) to freely unfold itself.

Paradoxically, perhaps, but really, release from everyday tunneling behavior that benumbedly asserts existence allows the meaning of existence to billow out. This disclosure is augmented by what Husserl calls free variations: we freely vary in imagination how any phenomenon presents itself, and when we encounter the limits of variation along its various parameters, these points mark out its essential structure, its scope, meaning, or essence. In other words, when a phenomenon presents itself as one of a certain sort, its essential features (essence) are those that can't be varied beyond certain points without destroying the identity of the phenomenon presented. For example, we cannot vary anything presenting itself as *actual thing* beyond "presents itself incompletely to any glance or series of glances," hence that pertains to the meaning or essence of "actual thing."

Hocking's most famous book is *The Meaning of God in Human Experience,* 1912.[3] Nearly six hundred pages, it is an epochal, multifaceted achievement: in intellectual sophistication, breadth, and sensuous depth without parallel in this century. I will treat it as a de facto phenomenological study. He gives a clear clue in the heading of Part III: "The Need of God: A Series of Free Meditations." Free meditations for Hocking do much the same work as free variations do for Husserl: they allow primal meaning to exfoliate and exhibit itself.

Hocking does not try to assert and to establish the existence of God until page 301 and the chapter following. Clearly, it's as if he had first suspended the positing or asserting of God's existence in order to display how the phenomenon of Deity is constituted, what it means. When he finally offers a "proof" of God's existence ("proof" always in quotes), it is a rich, highly motivated version of the so-called ontological argument, not the threadbare, glaringly abstract schema of argument that most philosophers from Thomas Aquinas to Kant to those of our day love to explode.

If one comes to Hocking's book of 1912 after having been steeped in mainstream analytic philosophy in this century, it is like being let out of a barrel into the open air. Even the less rigid forms of analytic thought seem pinched, pale, and reductivist. Not only do we find in Hocking a kind of Husserlian billowing out of meaning, but, unfettered by that philosopher's mathematicism (if I can call it that), Hocking anticipates in certain ways the existential phenomenologists Marcel and Heidegger, besides developing key points in Royce and James. Heidegger, for instance, reminds us that humankind has grown up and taken shape in the presence of the gods, in the richest panoply of presences that draw us into themselves and constitute us ecstatically. Do they *exist*? But why raise the question until we know how our existence and experience feels and what its intended subject matter means?

The primal given is not some circular coin-size visual sense datum, say—such data are not building blocks of knowledge and being, but are derivative from analyses and assumptions furtive and unacknowledged. The primal given is the primal gift. Given before all reflection and analysis, is that we are environed, environed moodily and totally, before any analysis can begin to pick our environedness apart. For Royce we begin as world creatures and end that way, hoping only to have thematized some of the embeddedness before we die. For James we are engulfed in the world of practical realities, which is the baseline against which all other worlds—mathematical, fictional, insane—are to be judged: an engulfedness or circumpressure that he calls belief, the feeling of reality. This he develops later as pure experience, primally given "thats" and "whats" that antecede the very distinction between self and other. For Husserl perception is the protodoxic basis, the foundation upon which all other belief, no matter how sophisticated and complex, must find its place or be wayward and nihilistic. For Heidegger, again, we cannot be understood apart from how we find ourselves having already been found by the world, given back to ourselves moodily by the world that has already held us and assessed us in some way—*Befindlichkeit*. This includes, of course, our having already been-engulfedly-with-others—*Mitsein*. For Marcel recuperative reflection can only try to comprehend where we already are caught up in and by the world. It requires the most personal digging and rumination, work that we try to make understandable to ourselves and others. Rumination for Marcel is like tilling soil, as we will see in the next essay. No simplistic division should be made between appearance and reality. Likewise, no simplistic line should be drawn dividing the personal and the universal.[4]

Hocking knows that every mood has its idea, its notion of where we are and how we stand in the whole, and that every feeling moves to consummate itself in some ideation-realization of this place. Profound pleasure is finding ourselves confirmed as whole beings in the whole place, in the world-idea, as he calls it. He writes with amazing perception: try as we might to find ourselves isolated, "the undertone of Nature's presence never leaves us, even in deep sleep" (*The Meaning of God* . . . [269], which book I will quote extensively). This Harvard professor speaks in a way an indigenous person would immediately appreciate.

Again, Hocking writes of that "one background field" that is "beyond all use" [119]. Here he criticizes James's pragmatism, and would outdo his mentor's notion of environedness and circumpressure. Yes, things must work and work out: that is necessary for meaning and truth; Hocking holds to a "negative pragmatism." But pragmatism itself cannot be sufficient, for the very reason that the one background field within which all uses and triumphs and failures must occur is itself beyond all use, beyond all manipulation and comprehension (though he will speak of world-idea). Differently put, it is presupposed by all that we typically mean by "use," so cannot itself be just another use. James is not blind to this point about *world,* but does not make enough of it.

Hocking's phenomenology of where we find ourselves in primal experience is patient, penetrating, and relentless. Our original sin, he writes, is failure to be engaged and aware: "We still live in semi-savage dreaminess, incredulous of the distant contingency, incredulous therefore of the present moment, veiled from the actual conditions of action, circling at planetary distances about our own practical center. . . . The evil that is in this world, and especially in this spirit of meaningless accident—the luck that we hope will be *for us* good luck—this evil does not rouse us: it benumbs us, rather, and confirms our somnambulism" [515].

Awake, Hocking unpacks everyday phenomena (but I'm not sure what he means by "semi-savage dreaminess"—"savages" have to be intensely alert most of the time if they would survive). But to his unpacking: for example, "Every [generalized] optimism implies a judgment about a reality which has a character and is therefore One" [168]. Or again, every generalized resentment implies—though we may be shocked to realize it—a personal character for the world as a whole [145–47]. For we can feel resentment only toward persons.

Hocking penetrates to the uncanny level of immediate involvement, and banalities and stereotypes lose their grip. He develops (without naming it, I think) William James's phenomenology of pure experience, of experience so fresh and perhaps so shocking that it is only a "that" though ready to become all kinds of "whats."[5] Probably influenced by James, Hocking gives an example of being dazed [66]. Husserl, probably likewise influenced, gives perhaps the best example—consider it again: Absentmindedly reading at table, I reach for what I think is a glass of water. It is really fruit juice, say. At the moment the liquid touches my tongue, it is neither water nor juice; it is a mere "that," mere "sensuous matter." So alien to us creatures who must identify and form ideas of *what* things are, no wonder we may spit it out!

Or, again, James gives examples of *thats* that are simultaneously floating *whats:* Watching the moon through the clouds I may not in the instant know whether it is the moon, the clouds, or I that moves.[6] But if in that instant I do not make the primal distinction between self and other, my own self loses its everyday identity. It is uncanny. Or take the pure experience of regard. It is not yet clear that *I* regard the *other,* or that the *other* regards *me.* Regard floats in the situation. At the primal, immediate, or primitive level of experience, I attend to the world and, strangely, it attends to me. Though things may appear to everyday practical awareness to exist independent of one another, they do not. Everything draws out everything else. Everything is a means for the fulfillment of everything else. To sense that is to sense what is of final importance.

Hocking takes this idea and develops it far beyond James (and way beyond Husserl's monadism). His first vantage point is on interpersonal phenomena of the human sort. I think we can call it the first free variation on the nature or meaning of God, the-person-but-more-than-person. For this idea must be built up on a founding level of human persons being-together. As the human phenomenon immediately gives itself out, it is a necessary condition for understanding the divine. And on the human level, no isolated I-self presents itself to fresh perception, no Cartesian egocentric predicament presents itself. Hocking writes,

> How would it seem if my mind could but once be *within* thine; and we could meet and without barrier be with each other? And then it has fallen upon me like a shock—as when one thinking himself alone has felt a presence—But I *am* in thy soul. These things around me are in thy experience. They are thy own; when I touch them and move them I change *thee.* When I look on them I see what thou seest; when I listen,

I hear what thou hearest. I am in the great Room of thy soul; and I experience thy very experience. . . . This world in which I live, is the world of thy soul: and being within that, I am within thee. I can imagine no contact more real and thrilling than this; that we should meet and share identity, not through ineffable inner depths (alone), but here through the foregrounds of common experience; and that thou shouldst be— not behind that mask—but *here,* pressing with all thy consciousness upon me, *containing* me, and these things of mine. [265–66]

Directly evident to sharpened perception, we contain others' objects of experience, and can modify these and others' experience of them. We participate in each other's lives. Insofarforth, we contain each other.

We may think ourselves alone, but suddenly with a shock, the presence of the other is with us. In certain circumstances, we may be unable to identify just who the other is. Hocking builds on the example given by Emerson: riding horseback into the woods, we feel we have interrupted something, and are now being observed. By whom exactly? We may have no idea. We feel contained in the largest Room, the Whole. The phenomenon to be seized and described is this: we may feel ourselves regarded by the Supreme Reality, the Ground of all that is.[7]

Here the meaning of God in human experience obtrudes itself, a fascinating, fearsome, perhaps protective all-surrounding presence and power, which can melt down, recast, and unify the self. Though not necessarily a focalizable object, nothing could be more objective in its sheer presence and meaning. Dewey maintained that every "this" is a system of meanings focused at a point of stress. Perhaps he would disallow the encompassing presence in question the status of a "this," on the grounds that it is not focused at a point of stress. Hocking would not be thus deterred, I think. In any case, Hocking believes that the worship or reverence induced by this overwhelming presence is the primitive propulsive source of all distinctly human accomplishments in art, religion, science, and philosophy. But regard on this all-engulfing immediate level floats dangerously. It can also result in the most destructive fanaticisms in corporate and personal bodies. One feels regarded by Divinity, but the regard is attributed to groups or corporate individuals less than the Whole that pretend to be the Whole. Groups can be caught up in genocidal madness.

He uses what he calls a "rapid survey of . . . historic phenomena" as a de facto free variation on the experience of this stunning, all-pervasive regard and mana power.

If man's religion is first embodied in his exclamations, these . . . were at once cognitions and prayers, incipient transactions . . . but behind all these pictures [of rewards and punishments] there is, even from the beginning, a residual importance in being right with deity which we might call an ontological importance, i.e., affecting somehow the substance of one's self, the soul and its destiny, opening up some bottomless depths of being such as the eye is hardly fitted to gaze into. The amount of power that can be released when the religious nerve is pressed is quite out of proportion to the belief in the more definable pleasures and pains. . . . To keep God friendly there are few efforts that men will not make. . . . But these necessary moments of approach have their own terrors, when some one must take it upon himself to break through the habitual taboo of Holiness; a cloud of oppressive gravity deepens over the event, supportable only by fierce resolution, wrapped probably in mutilation and blood. And when the act is accomplished in safety, an exultancy equally fierce floods the brain; exhibitions of savage gaiety, the license of supermen, can alone satisfy the spirit. We are stranger now to this vehemence, whether for better or for worse; but we can still catch from afar the pulse of this ancient ocean, its terrors and its glorious liberations. We can understand how this strange sense of ontological importance must condense in any phase of human experience in which the actual remoteness of deity seemed overcome. We shall expect to set excessive value upon those states of enthusiasm, ecstasy, intoxication, in which heaven and earth were felt to flow together. [346–47][8]

At this primal level we can expect Hocking to have little respect for arguments for God's existence that assume a contingent Nature in itself and argue to a necessary Being, a Creator, as its source. For there can be no Nature in itself. Nature as it is actually given as phenomenon in experience is Nature-regarded. It is Nature interpreted by and within itself, Nature pictured, storied, sung.

So arguments that go from contingency or design, "Because Nature is, God is," are out. Hocking writes piquantly, "Because Nature is not, God is" [312]. That is, tuning in reverently on Nature regarding itself through its members sets us beyond the mere abstraction, "Nature," and the participatory naming of this all-pervasive regard—God—*must be* one with the immanent being that is named: so it must be true. Hence Hocking's "broader empiricism": his phenomenological insertion in world-process-as-meaning-returning-into-itself delivers its own version of the ontological argument. But, as always, the "argument" is not so much that as it is insight: the universe celebrates itself through us as God—comes home to itself—and shows itself perfectly adequate and self-sufficient in doing so. How could this feeling-awareness of conjunction possibly be false? So it must be true. Hocking makes that point clearer than ever before in history.

If one must play the traditional labels game, Hocking is first a rationalist. His idea of ideas grows up within the tradition of Hegel, Schelling, and Royce broadly conceived: Ideas as concrete universals. Concrete, as they take shape within individuals residing in definite cultural situations and institutions of the period. Yet also universal as that life of consciousness that sorts the world into kinds, symbols, archetypes that determine not only the expectations of the period in which they arise, but have a life of their own and cumulate through history as a kind of destiny.

Yet Hocking is also a mystic: one who doesn't believe that the logistic intellect in any form can build up an Absolute system of necessarily connected ideas that subtends—or *is*—the Whole. He doesn't believe we can think God's thoughts after Him, in the manner of Hegel. Also he is a mystic who attends keenly to the sensuousness and moody kinship of daily life, which leads him into a kind of existential phenomenology, or what he calls his broader empiricism.

This mix holds in solution metaphysical elements that are more traditional. He designates these the Self, the Other, and the Thou.[9] Let us hazard a sketch of how he tries to put all this together.

The scientistic strand of analytic philosophy in this century constricts meaning-making and hence our lives. Hocking opens us up—throws the windows wide onto a broad sky and singing air. The extent of a person is the extent of his or her ability to grasp the world. Or, much better, the extent of his or her ability to be grasped by the World-idea. The value of any particular thing in the world—a hat, say—is the extent to which we can find our self's nature, our "idea-stuff," instantiated, confirmed, extended in the hat [131].[10] We grasp the hat zestfully if it simultaneously grasps us and draws us out. A recent ad for a car touches the nerve of this point: "What am I looking for in a car? Myself." If only our advertisers could put things together and help us be wise!

The life of our ideas is voluminous, enwrapping, and propelling. He gives the concept of idea an exceedingly broad range: from sensuous images to the vastest universals or mathematical systems, each section of the range needing to be balanced and supplemented organismically by all the others if a human life is to be cohesive and effective. What is most distinctive about us, he thinks, is that we make pictures (and not merely "in our minds" as sense-data). Imagine on a wall a picture of a tree. How far up from the floor is the top of the tree (and he doesn't mean the bit of pigment that iconically signifies the top)? The question is absurd. But we have no trouble keeping the world of the tree and the world of the room in which we stand distinguished, and they nicely complement each other. We are creatures of interlacing systems or worlds of meaning.

The expansive life of new ideas has the power to break through closed systems of them, and through ossified behaviors [472–73, 482, 489]. We can't help but think today of addictive systems, short-circuitings of what Emerson called "Circular power returning into itself," "the inexplicable continuity of this web of God" (and which Hocking echoes in his own way). The bodily self fails to trust the regenerative powers of the world; it generates sure but short-term pleasures and satisfactions—by addictively ingesting drugs, say; but this impairs the regenerative powers of that part of Nature that is our own bodies and brains. One is dependent. One's freedom to choose—or, better, freedom to be grasped by alternative possibilities or ideas—one's very self is impaired.

Addiction is a tough test for Hocking's view of Self and the life of ideas. Can he show us how to break through the body's self-closing addictive circuits: an emptiness in the stomach and a falling away that demand instant support by any means *now;* an urging in the groin that might find satisfaction in an appropriate situation, but the self lacks the momentum and assurance to wait; a waning of energies that might signal an upcoming period of dormancy within the regenerative cycles of Nature, but one cannot trust these cycles and becomes a workaholic, say.[11]

Or, related in the most intimate ways to individuals' addictions are the society's, the corporate body's: groups caught up and intoxicated in their false Whole-idea, their insecure and counterfeit totality, ethnically cleanse any other groups who threaten to pollute their purity and hegemony. The experience of Divinity easily short-circuits into terror and aggression.

The sixteen years that elapse between *The Meaning of God in Human Experience* and *The Self: Its Body and Freedom* include the agony of World War I and Hocking's pursuit of the question, Can persons be basically modified?[12] His interest in instinct, in the primal and atavistic, always deep, is deepened, and he confronts the human body in a way he had not done before. I will give only the sketchiest account of the horizons he points to.

Very significantly, Hocking writes, "Whatever my [whole] body does, I do" (*The Self* . . . [ix ff]). But he does not affirm the converse: Whatever I do, the whole body does. He does not assert a simple equivalence between self and body. Perhaps his reasons are these: For him, again, "Nature itself" and "bodies themselves" are abstractions. The reality is Nature-and-bodies-regarded-or-regardable. So when that part of Nature that is my bodily self regards itself, it transcends itself as a mere physical thing presented at any moment. I—my self—am the whole body regarded through the whole-Idea, so we cannot affirm a simple equivalence between what I do and what the body does, though there is profound overlap.

In other words, the functioning of mind cannot be reduced to the functioning of the body, no matter how essential the body's functioning is. To take perhaps an overly simple example, if I perceive the twelfth stroke of a clock, it is not just that stroke that occupies my mind and myself at that instant, but also, at the very least, the eleven that preceded it. The twelfth stroke perceived as such is not just one sound in my ears or one demarcatable electrical event in my brain.

He extrapolates: I cannot be merely a causal mechanism, because any cause perceived as such is not merely a cause. Reflected upon, it must receive my consent, tacit or explicit, in order to work. He anticipates the field of psychosomatic medicine: As certain advanced physicians have suggested, the body is the "outside of the mind" [80].[13]

But Hocking goes on, "Now there is nothing in the field of natural causation entering into me upon which I may not thus reflect" [151]. That claim seems to me to be an inflation of the powers of mind that is metaphysical in the objectionable sense. He himself pointed out that a feeling may consummate itself in a false idea. And as John Dewey, for example, found through decades of sessions with the psycho-bio-therapist F. M. Alexander, it is maddeningly difficult to even begin to enlarge the veridical awareness of one's own bodily reality. Before another person manipulates one's body so that certain new sensations are generated, one could not even have imagined them. Recall the crucial passage in Dewey where he says we engage in an immense multitude of immediate organic adjustments of which we are not aware.[14]

We need a phenomenology of the body—a highly applied phenomenology, if you will—which might reveal the actual scope of our abilities to disclose its workings. Interestingly enough, Hocking himself initiates at least such an approach to body as we actually live it and regard it in the first person, before it is objectified by the sciences. It is not "the biologist's body": not

Körper, as the Germans put it, but *Leib*, the body lived, its capacities my self's. He writes in *The Self: Its Body and Freedom*, the chapter "Why the Mind Needs a Body": "I open the gate with so much exertion: I walk with ease at such a rate, and not much faster. These are my coefficients. And . . . it is only by some afterthought that they are referred specifically to my body: the power of my limbs is my power—and in fact I never learn the physiology of my muscles: as I use it, I seem to live in it" [79–80]. Marvelous, but notice he does not say I "live in" the body that I *am*.

Now just how—according to Hocking—does thought penetrate and grasp with its ideas this pre-objectified and prereflective body? (I assume here that *Leib* is the sense of body most germane to his observations just above.) Perhaps he confronts the question, but I do not find it yet. His view of mind and body seems to me to remain parallelist, for the most part, with mind over matter, and matter conceived at times in a somewhat mechanical way as a reliable appliance for the use of mind (body conceived as *Körper*).

I do not find a univocal sense of "body" in Hocking, or a clearly multiple sense. And I confess I keep wanting him to affirm a double aspect rather than a parallelist-with-mind-dominant view, keep wanting him to say that what we call thought and what we call body are but two aspects of one energy. One of the advantages for him if he would say this, I think, is that he would connect what he says about body as *Leib* with his powerful thought about God. If he emphasized more body as lived, as what *I*-my*self* do (*Leib*), he could more easily connect with potent divine regard. What if my regard for myself melds in experience with the personified Whole's or God's potent regard for myself? Swelled and buoyed by this grace, what might be the disclosure of body-self's workings then? Expanded and deepened?

A religiously informed phenomenology of body-self suggests itself, a far horizon pointed to by Hocking but not much explored. Indeed, I don't think it has been really explored yet by anybody (though Marcel must not be ignored): a phenomenology, a rational reconstruction if you will, of yogin and shamanic experience of the body as phenomenon, just as it is experienced. Such a phenomenology might, for example, flesh out, refine, reform Alcoholics Anonymous's dictum that belief in "a higher power" is necessary for recovery from addiction. For "higher than the body" might itself be addictive, may leave the person free of drink, but still burdened with addictive traits and personality.

Hocking's Gifford Lectures of 1938 have never been published as they were delivered. A piece in *Review of Metaphysics,* "Fact, Field, and Destiny" (vol.

9, 4 [1958]) develops points in the second series. It's a powerful expression of what might be called religious existentialism, with even a qualified nod to Nietzsche's will to power. Most significantly, taken together with his lectures published as *The Meaning of Immortality in Human Experience,* it might be read as presenting a third view of body, neither *Leib* nor *Körper,* neither body-subject nor body-object, as inchoate (so it seems to me) as it is fascinating.

What if—I may be pressing too hard here—body-subject and body-object are but two aspects of a single energy, a more basic free energy that, gropingly, we might call body-mind? This may be what he is suggesting. Recall the epigraph I have used for this volume, which comes from *The Self* . . . . Hocking writes: "If the impulse which is I is a 'racial impulse,' there is no reason to ascribe age to it: it is presumably, like energy, always new as on the first day" [120–21]. Body-self or body-mind as energy always regenerative, always new!? I believe Black Elk would understand instantly and completely.

Hocking offers a fascinating piece of speculative metaphysics coupled with some volatile pieces from twentieth-century physics. The world of art-inspired energy and imagination may open onto *another system of space-time.* How about the tree's world in our picture on the wall! Yes, the possibility boggles the mind, but why not unboggle the mind, try out at least that seemingly impossible possibility? Might absolutely strange transformations occur in a universe that passes through "black holes," say, and through the unmappable domain generally of what we don't know we don't know? Perhaps, as Hocking says, the body is a hinge, a vinculum, that—as body-mind—might take another form in another space-time when its death in the space-time system of this room occurs. There might be a form of immortality.[15]

Couple all this with his general phenomenological, existential, and pragmatic approach to philosophy: what we must posit if life is to be meaningful. He writes in *The Meaning of Immortality* . . . , "To be able to give oneself whole-heartedly to the present one must be persistently aware that it is *not all.* One must rather be able to treat the present moment as if it were engaged in the business allotted to it by that total life which stretches indefinitely beyond."[16] Might systems of space-time and energy, which most of us today cannot even imagine, have already opened themselves to such passion and commitment? Yes—but of course I don't know.

Hocking is an inspiring explorer, a marvelous antidote to the straitened and desiccated world of most professional philosophy today. Perhaps nothing better sums up the flames and generosities of his heart and mind than his remarks celebrating John Dewey's eightieth birthday:

Ten years ago, when Mr. Dewey was only seventy years old, a session of the Association meeting in this place was devoted to a phase of his philosophy. I seem to remember reading a paper at that session in which I recounted the tragedy of thirty-two years occupied in refuting Dewey while Dewey remained unconscious of what had happened!

I have now a different and happier report to make. Not, I hasten to say, that Dewey has changed, but that I have largely ceased to read him with polemical intent: I read him to enjoy him. In this I succeed far better, in fact I am almost completely successful! Only, the question continues to trouble me whether Dewey, if he knew about this, would regard it as an improvement on my part or as a retrogression.[17]

This passage exhibits the faith that both philosophers showed in unfettered dialectical exchange no matter where it might lead, the faith in each other, the faith in the world and the beckoning horizons it displays to us, the faith that might yet save humanity from its fear of awareness—its original sin, as Hocking put it—a faith lacking which the prospects are bleak.

Notes

1. See Hocking's "From the Early Days of the 'Logische Untersuchungen,'" in *Edmund Husserl: 1859–1959* (The Hague: Nijhoff, 1959).

2. *Poetry, Language, Thought*, trans. A. Hofstadter (New York: Harper & Row, 1971), throughout.

3. (New Haven: Yale University Press). It is no longer in print! *All page references are to the original edition, and are given in brackets in my text.*

4. For Marcel's indebtedness to Hocking, see *The Philosophy of Gabriel Marcel* (LaSalle, Ill.: Library of Living Philosophers, 1984), "Autobiographical Essay," 54–55. Marcel's image for rumination as tilling soil is found in his introduction to Henry Bugbee's *The Inward Morning*, which we consider in the next essay.

5. *Essays in Radical Empiricism* (New York: Longmans, Green and Co., 1958), "The Thing and its Relations," the first two pages. *Essays in Radical Empiricism, the Works of William James* (Cambridge, Mass.: Harvard University Press, 1974) (hereafter cited as "critical edition"), 46.

6. See *Essays in Radical Empiricism*, "The Place of Affectional Facts in a World of Pure Experience," 72. Critical edition, 35–36.

7. Trying to express the numinous, mythic, or archetypal meaning of key terms, I capitalize them. For Peirce's version of Husserl's free variations that encounter a residual background phenomenon of world that cannot be eliminated, see Chapter 13.

8. Compare Jonathan Edwards: "I often used to sit and view all nature, to behold the sweet glory of God in these things; in the mean time, *singing* forth, with a low voice my contemplations of the Creator and Redeemer. . . . [I]t was always in my manner . . . to sing forth. . . . I was almost constantly in ejaculatory prayer." *Devotions of Jonathan Edwards* (Grand Rapids: Baker Book House, 1959).

9. *Edmund Husserl*, 7. See note 1.

10. The taproot of value seems to be delight in unfolding our being. Compare Dante: "In every action . . . the main intention of the agent is to express his own image; thus it is that every agent, whenever he acts, enjoys the action. Because everything that exists desires to be, and by acting the agent unfolds his being, action is naturally enjoyable" (quoted in M. Csikszent-mihalyi, *The Evolving Self* [New York: HarperCollins, 1993], 191).

11. Hocking retrieves regenerative cycles in his "principle of alternation," *The Self: Its Body and Freedom* (New Haven: Yale University Press, 1928), 404 ff.

12. *The Self: Its Body and Freedom*, 120–21. *Subsequent page references will be placed in brackets in the body of our text.* In the 1920s, Hocking recommended to Marvin Farber, a graduate student of his at Harvard, that he study with Husserl and write his dissertation on Husserl's philosophy. Farber subsequently founded the journal *Philosophy and Phenomenological Research* and became known as the foremost Husserl scholar in the United States. See Peter H. Hare, "Marvin Farber," in *Dictionary of American Biography* (New York: Oxford University Press, forthcoming).

13. Candace Pert, former chief brain biochemist, National Institutes of Health, writes, "Consciousness isn't just in the head. Nor is it a question of mind over body. If one takes into account the DNA directing the dance of the peptides, [the] body is the outward manifestation of the mind." Quoted in Christiane Northrup, M.D., *Women's Bodies—Women's Wisdom* (New York: Bantam Books, 1994), 25.

14. *Experience and Nature* (New York, 1958 [1929]), 299. *John Dewey, the Late Works, 1925–1953* (Carbondale: Southern Illinois University Press, 1983) (hereafter cited as "critical edition"), 1:227.

15. Notice below in Chapter 14, "Shamanism, Love, Regeneration," how I discuss non-locality phenomena as they figure in quantum physics. I am not sure that this matches exactly what Hocking means.

16. (New York: Harper & Row, 1957), 155.

17. "Dewey's Concepts of Experience and Nature," *The Philosophical Review* 49, 2 (1940): 228.

Henry Bugbee
The Inward Morning

As true stillness comes upon us, we hear, we hear, and we learn that
our whole lives may have the character of finding that anthem which
would be native to our own tongue, and which alone can be the true
answer for each of us to the questioning, the calling, the demand for
ultimate reckoning which devolves upon us.

—Henry Bugbee

Of all the ringing, luminous, consummatory expressions Henry Bugbee
delivers in *The Inward Morning,* the above is the one I have settled on for
epigraph. It summons each of us to discover what is most fulfilling—to discover what would explain each of us to our own selves, whether the explanation would impress the scientific researcher or not.

I was tempted, however, to use another bright patch of his words:

There is this bathing in fluent reality which resolves mental fixations
and suggests that our manner of taking things has been staggeringly a
matter of habituation. Metaphysical thinking must arise with the earliest dawn, the very dawn of things themselves. And this is the dawn
in which basic action, too, comes into being. It is earlier than the day
of morality and immorality. . . . No reason for acting can supplant the
depth of true affirmation. This is not to disqualify the giving of reasons, or the having of reasons for acting; it is only to suggest the comparative lateness, and so the relative force of reasons had or given.[1]

I decided against using this as epigraph because without proper context crucial terms are off-putting. Particularly "metaphysics" stymies or misleads. For it suggests what is beyond the physical, whereas Bugbee is thoroughly immersed in the eventful physical world within and around us, immersed in its presence. The whole point of metaphysical thinking for him is to alert us to this worldly presence that circulates around and through us enlivening us, and that makes possible the small focus of what we directly attend to. He desires energy, new as on the first day. Recalling Hocking's elaboration that Nature is an abiding background presence—even in our sleep!—Bugbee recounts fishing for steelhead trout in a river in the redwoods of northern California. The vast whole gives birth to the dazzling focal moment:

> It is a glorious thing to know the pool is alive with these glancing, diving, finning fish. But at such moments it is well to make an offering in one's heart to the still hour in the redwoods ascending into the sky. . . . Now the river is the unborn, and the sudden fish is just the newborn—whole, entire, complete, individual and universal. . . . To respect things *qua* existing, may indeed be *vision*, but it is vision *enacted*, a "seeing with the eye of faith." At its heart existence and decision interlock. One is himself the leaping trout. [86, 130]

With this we get the meaning of "Metaphysical thinking must rise with the earliest dawn, the very dawn of things themselves," and the meaning of "faith." Without a primal affirmation, anterior to all reasons, in which we open ourselves and allow things to disclose themselves in the fullness and freshness of their reality, without this leap of faith, the world goes dead for us, and we grow dead within it. Bugbee is operating on the level of Black Elk's seeing in a sacred manner, Thoreau's and Emerson's wakefulness, James's pure experience, Dewey's basic qualia of situations, and Hocking's ever-present background Nature brought to thematic awareness. He is profoundly phenomenological and existential, and thereby opens the door for us of European lineage to touch indigenous peoples. Thoreau: Only that day dawns to which we are awake. Hocking: We wake to energy new as on the first day. All primal peoples welcome, celebrate, and thank the dawn.

Henry Bugbee, still alive as I write, but ailing, keeps an ancient and ever new flame burning—though it is extinguished now in most academic philosophy in the United States. It is what *he* means by metaphysics. Since many academics take metaphysics in the old sense of beyond the physical, and since they style themselves scientific and do not believe science can refer to such a domain, they drop metaphysics in any sense of the word.

But in doing so, they drop what Gabriel Marcel, stimulated initially by Hocking and later by Bugbee, called a new and fresh style of realism (see his introduction to the original edition of *The Inward Morning*). It is a realism that keeps us in touch with our hunter-gatherer ancestors, and with our actual lives as we are actually living them each moment.

Taking its lead from Descartes, much academic or analytic philosophy is profoundly alienating, so profoundly so that it cannot imagine it is alienating. We are supposed to be subjects over against a world of objects. But we would be unable even to imagine this if we weren't profoundly involved in, and stabilized and grounded by, the reality of the world around us and through us.

The world appears primordially in the vibrating margins of consciousness. In the alienated view, things that nourish our being become merely objects to be surmounted or manipulated. Ironically, this attitude is harmful to science itself. To ask too soon, But are there testable predictions derivable from your thought? is to pinch off the budding and flowering of fresh hypotheses in science itself. As Bugbee says, the heart goes out of ideas, and they lose their actual exploratory cast [9].

Emerson saw a core truth: each person is a stream whose source is hidden. And Black Elk discerned that persons' true growth is mysterious. To think of oneself as a subject over against a world of objects is to be fixated, obsessed with the problem of reference. At its baldest we ask, Is there a world at all out there? It is not merely to be careful but to be obsessed with gaining a reliable method of inquiry and a reliable focus for consciousness. The obsession runs: Can we in principle get everything at last in front of us, fixed, objectified, skewered, catalogued, at least as to its type?

But all the while our busyness and wondering occur within an enwombing surround that is and must remain largely unknown. Philosophy in the tradition I am tracing delves into what is behind, beneath, through, and around us and all that we do, the implicit, the encompassing fringe and suffusing nimbus that is the world's presence to us and within us. With deep and true affirmation we can sense it, darkly numinous and strangely attractive and reassuring. There is the domain of what we know, and the domain of what we know we don't know. But then also an unmappable domain of what we don't know we don't know. It is Bugbee's hope to find himself at home in the unknown [155]. Only then could we know what it means to be responsible, that is, to be responsive to what moves in its vastness around, within, and behind us—and all other things. Which means that then we could grasp what it means to stand behind what we say and do.

But he is anything but obscurantist. Like Marcel and Hocking, he is pursuing an arresting realism. Reminiscent of indigenous thinkers as well, he finds too much of the Western tradition to be highly abstract, to lead us away from the actuality of our immediate involvement in the world and, of course, ourselves. When he writes of the inward morning, he is not—emphatically not—speaking of some subjective experience that only he can know and can never really communicate. Not a small image or sense datum of the sun arising inside his mind! But an awakening of the whole person when, in primal affirmation, we allow the sun, the sun itself, in its arising to awaken us in our entirety. We must take the initiative in this allowing, yet it is the rising sun itself that lifts us and our fellows. This is the energy, new as on the first day—the ancient truth that our hunter-gatherer ancestors knew— and that we are smugly forgetting.

Only when firm in what we feel and know can we acknowledge the unmappable numinous domain of what we don't know we don't know. Acknowledged, it sustains, grounds, illuminates, and refreshes us. We are placed, defined in a unique and consummate way, authorized as tiny but vital members of the mysterious Whole.

In a recently published collection of articles on Bugbee (*Wilderness and the Heart: Henry Bugbee's Philosophy of Place, Presence, and Memory*), the editor, Edward F. Mooney, publishes a tribute to him by Willard Quine, perhaps the most famous academic and "scientific" philosopher today. The tribute opens the book. Quine describes Bugbee as having a "mystical sense of the pure poetry of being." He goes on, "Henry is the ultimate exemplar of the examined life. He walks and talks slowly and thoughtfully, for he is immersed—a Bugbee word—in the wonders of the specious present."

Now, I have no idea what *Quine* means by "the pure poetry of being." And I find his phrase "the specious present" troubling. Actually it is James's phrase from his earlier period. James wanted to mean that all experiencing is drawn out, elongated, by the "specious" presence of the immediately past and the immediately futural or expected. When as natural scientist he clocks it, he finds we hold at most about twelve seconds in this "specious" togetherness.

But what is specious about it? It is the actual tissue and muscle of our immediately evident living, our experiencing, our stretching in time. It is the Newtonian or Cartesian "point instant" that is the abstraction and that is specious (though useful for the purposes of mechanistic physics). We witness here the inversion of ontological values so typical of "scientific" philosophy:

abstractions are made from a basis in experiential reality, and then the act of abstracting is forgotten. Kierkegaard called it the lunatic postulate, and the existential-phenomenological tradition follows his lead. This is the line of work sorely imperiled today in academic or analytic philosophy.

When Bugbee ruminates on his experiencing—so like tilling the soil [33]—he is not immersed in something specious, but in the very reality of things insofar as this reality is evident, and can only be evident, in our immediate experiencing when that is opened to us. (Even an analytic reductionist will have to admit that any scientific explanation—in terms not immediately experienceable—of immediate experiencing will, at the very least, have to describe just what is to be explained.)

Consider this account from Bugbee of a near-calamity on a beautiful day on the North Fork of the Trinity River in California. Bright sun streams down from the tops of the pines, people bask by a marvelous pool, and the roar of the rapids below "might have been but a ground-bass of contentment filling us all" [172].

There came a cry for help, seconded with a cry of fright. A young man flails at the tail of the pool, then is sucked under a huge log, and is carried down into the rapids. He bobs up for a moment, but there seemed no avoiding "an impending execution on the rocks below." Desperately he grabs at a willow branch, holds, and is carried in a wide arc toward shore.

> He had barely the strength and the breath to claw himself up on the muddy slope onto firmament. . . . I had run across the log and arrived on the opposite side below the willow, where he now paused, panting and on all fours, unable to rise. Slowly he raised his head and we looked into each other's eyes. . . . Not a word passed between us. As nearly as I can relive the matter, the compassion I felt with this man gave way into awe and respect for what I witnessed in him. He seemed absolutely clean. In that steady gaze of his I met reality point blank, filtered and distilled as the purity of a man. [172]

The reality, needless to say, is the unspeakable preciousness of life evident in the young man's eyes, the cleanness is the absence of any pretense or distraction.

Awe and respect can turn into reverence: the experience of being embraced by a fathomless significance. For we find ourselves as co-participants in a universe the existence, extent, and source of which we cannot explain. But it and we are here, inexpressibly preciously here—here and alive rather than not here and not alive. Ultimately for Bugbee, reverence is for reality, and reality is what sustains responsibility, which is our ability to respond truly, in a way that is not arbitrary [215]. These are primal affirmations and disclosures, and not to be derived from reasonings about isolable characteristics of things "objectively" determined. "There could be no appeal to what we might conceive as demonstrable characteristics of things as warrant for construing love and respect as their due. Neither reality manifest as things, nor its ultimate mode of intelligibility, can be pocketed by the mind. Only as we may be ripe for it in our entirety does it seem that reality may dawn on us concretely and anew" [129].[2]

And are we to conclude that reverence, responsibility, and awe are not fully real, but are merely epiphenomena cast up like fizz water from the stream of the specious present? It is hard to imagine words more grossly and baldly question begging and fallacious.

Henry Bugbee clings to life as I write, and so does the tradition of thought and being that holds some possibility of maintaining contact with primal experience, that which formed our species and various protospecies over millions of years. American thought has interwoven itself with European existential-phenomenological thought for 150 years, and the pattern is evident, if one cares to look. Emerson's work fed into the young Nietzsche's, Kierkegaard's into the later James's, James and his work into the just emerging Husserl's, Husserl's into Hocking's, Hocking's into Marcel's, and Marcel's into Bugbee's and reciprocally. And we should mention the Americans John Wild, William Earle, William Barrett, James Edie, and the Europeans with whom they interwove, Martin Heidegger, Maurice Merleau-Ponty, Aron Gurwitsch, Jean-Paul Sartre, Michel Foucault, Luce Irigaray.

This lengthy tradition is almost totally unknown to the dominant analytic-academic philosophers today, for they cling to ossified polarities of thought: mind/matter, appearance/reality, historical/current. The fluency and fluidity of experiencing are used by them, of course, but repressed in their professional thinking. It is above all the dogma of scientism that detaches them from lived reality. As we have seen, this is the unscientific view that only science can know. But science, in any of its current states, cannot even know all the fruitful questions to ask.

So, it is thought, since science progresses, and philosophy is parasitic upon science, philosophy must progress. Nothing could be more unprovable, metaphysical in the worst sense. But it's a powerfully real belief that blocks the continued cultivation of the tradition traced in this book that I write. For any attempt to reclaim primal experience and, moreover, to establish linkages with indigenous thought and behavior is construed as reactionary, primitive, superstitious.

Now, any historical awareness would reveal that the thinkers we study are deeply rooted in venerable traditions of thought and exhibit a rigor appropriate to their concerns. But, in effect, philosophy is bifurcated by analysts into real or current philosophy, on the one hand, and mere historical scholarship on the other.

Ignorance of crucial features of phenomenological thought is usually cloaked as contempt for it. But the underlying cause, I think, is fear. Fear lest we come too close to primal experiences, feelings, moods, and intimations with which we cannot deal in the accepted modes of inquiry and analysis in which the world is automatically objectified and kept at a safe distance.

After the defense of my dissertation at New York University in 1966, I was walking with William Barrett in Washington Square. His voice shifted to another level, and I sensed that something that had been left unsaid for years was about to be said. Within this aura, it surfaced—as if out of a rising globular skin of smooth and shining ocean water a great back would appear. "You know, Bruce, one can lose one's job for being a phenomenologist." Phenomenology, of course, I knew. At that time, for me, indigenous thought was beyond the pale of possibility.

Henry Bugbee was denied tenure at Harvard in 1952. Edward Mooney informs me that one of the tenured professors said goodbye with tears in his eyes. He recognized the man's quality, but is reported to have said, "Henry, you haven't published enough."

The assumption is unquestioned: only written and published work can be evaluated by peers nation- and worldwide. Basically, only the written word matters. The loss of the immediately human is palpable. As if philosophy were science, and every theory and its predictions must be testable by all qualified inquirers. Bugbee belongs in a different world. One that includes Socrates, who never published anything. Indeed, Socrates expressed apprehension about the growing power of the written word. In *Phaedrus* Plato reports him saying, and let us quote it again, "If men learn this, it will implant forgetfulness in their souls; they will cease to exercise memory because they can rely on that which is written, calling things to remembrance no longer within themselves."

This is a remainder and a reminder from primal times, and the thought is echoed by many indigenous peoples even in this century: what is written cannot have the force of memory and the vow. Despite his great knowledge of the history of western philosophy that *The Inward Morning* evidences on nearly every page, Bugbee derives also from an ancient preliterate tradition of rumination, counseling of elders, story telling. Or as if a Paleolithic hunter were about to die, and is making a final reckoning of his life.

Bugbee's critique of academic-analytic philosophy flows seamlessly from his ruminating, his turning things over in his mind to find what deeply moves him, renders him whole, grounded, his thought like a prayer and a vow, momentous. Abstraction and argument too easily become abstractedness, detachment from the de jure, the valuable, and the moving, a mere collecting of reasons, theories, and facts—as if one were a spiritual ragpicker.

> [T]here must be a background, necessarily implicit, from which whatever becomes explicit for us can derive intelligibility and *de jure* force. . . . We cannot rub each other's noses in immanent reality by argument. Adversarial attitudes entail argument which can be resolved only by conversion of attitude. An argumentative attitude, as we know, is as inflexible and unrealistic as can be. . . . The kind of "objectivity" of mind which distresses me philosophically is that kind of abstractedness of mind from immanent reality which entails the reduction of what is explicitly attended to, to an exclusively *de facto* status. [99]

The *elan* of one's most personal life—recollecting, ruminating, stretching—fusing ecstatically past, present, future . . . a mere "specious" present? Never has one of James's words been more ill chosen and ill repeated. Time really lived is more than duration, for it is also the enduring and the durable. It partakes of the heart of our reality, *durée*—Henri Bergson's word. Bergson, whose metaphysics dictates we install ourselves empathically in moving things. Bergson, to whom Gabriel Marcel dedicated his *Metaphysical Journal*—with Hocking as co-dedicatee. Marcel, whose example later encouraged Bugbee's journal, *The Inward Morning*. Bugbee, who flashes before us like a shooting star that leaves its trace on the patinate air. We do not forget you.

Notes

1. *The Inward Morning: A Philosophical Exploration in Journal Form* (Athens: University of Georgia Press, 1999 [1958]), 52. In this essay, only this one of Bugbee's publications is used, and *page references are given in brackets in the body of my text.*

2. As Hilary Putnam once remarked, if we look for demonstrable characteristics of things as warrant for construing respect as their due, we can argue that since these characteristics aren't present, we may therefore exterminate what fails to possess them. Is a root of genocide the desperate, fearful inability to respect the sheer existence of things? And does this inability derive from a failure of deep affirmation, as Bugbee would put it?

PART THREE

Taking Stock

Ways of Knowing

Western people are children of inner poverty, though outwardly we have everything. Probably no other people in history have been so lonely, so alienated, so confused over values, so neurotic. We have dominated our environment with sledge-hammer force and electronic precision. We amass riches on an unprecedented scale. But few of us, very few indeed, are at peace with ourselves, secure in our relationships, content in our loves, or at home in the world.

—Robert A. Johnson

To think of knowledge today is to think mainly of scientific knowledge, and of this as distinctly Western or European science. Many centuries ago, the Chinese made important scientific discoveries: chemical, to produce gunpowder; astronomical and technical, to produce navigational instruments, and the like. Around 3000 B.C., astronomer-priests or priestesses in what is now called England and Ireland set up vast mounds and temple-observatories to precisely determine the turning points of the yearly cycle, winter solstice, spring equinox, and so on. In a great feat of observation and calculation, the irregular cycles of sun and moon were discovered to conform to a master cycle of fifty-nine solar years, when again the two would be in a particular relationship. Centuries before European incursions into Africa, indigenous peoples on the eastern shore of what Europeans call Lake Victoria had discovered methods of smelting iron out of rocky ore, and using it to produce tools and artworks.

But these non-European scientific-technological accomplishments were not directly tributary to the ever-welling mainstream of Western science as it brims to the top today and spreads over the world (though Babylonian and Egyptian astronomy did influence the Greeks). There is something peculiar about Western science and its ability to penetrate to certain underlying features of Nature. This is evident in some sixth century B.C. Milesian Greek thinkers, those who reduced all natural phenomena to the action of a single natural substance, air or water, for example. Though perhaps not apparent to sight, *all* things, they said, are composed of water, say, in its various states, solid, liquid, gas. And water will operate in its predetermined way regardless of any of our attitudes toward it, whether of entreaty or appreciation, or awe or ignorance. Universal laws are to be discovered by the highly focused observer who grasps water "in itself," particularly in terms of stable, quantifiable units of it.

It is sometimes thought that emotional detachment is a further salient characteristic of Western science. This is understandable but greatly misleading. For the scientist is typically intensely involved, but very narrowly so, and the narrower the involvement the greater the intensity. That is, this person is involved emotionally with the world, *but only insofar as the world reveals itself in its quantifiable aspects.*

Equally important, as William James observed, the effective scientist's intense desire to verify a hypothesis is counterbalanced by an intense desire not to be duped. This dynamic intercourse of desires bores into the world in an immensely intense way, and so brilliant and absorbing is its focus that aspects of the world that lie outside the quantifiable are eclipsed, and the eclipsing is eclipsed. Concealed is that aspects of the world are being concealed. The shadow cast by the dazzling light is typically deeper than can be imagined.

The Chinese pursued their science, but within a whole metaphysical system that was never totally absent from their consciousness. Taoists postulated the complementary actions of cosmical principles, Yin and Yang, which were never fully quantifiable, and only partially understandable within a universe that eluded precise formulation, and for the very existence of which no reason could be given. We are in over our heads in this awesome whole, Taoists believed, and to pretend to be otherwise is to be disoriented at an ultimate level, is to lose one's placement in the whole, lose touch with what is valuable for life in the interdepending universe.

As for ancient priests or priestesses in the temple-observatories of what is now England and Ireland, they were never only scientists, presumably, but simultaneously religious and civil officials. As for Africans rhythmically working their bellows for many hours into the furnace buried in the Earth, heating it to the point of liquefying iron and separating it from stone, they were never only scientists or technicians, but were also engaging in a religious rite in which the symbolism of sexual intercourse with Earth was appropriate, explicit, and treasured.

The staggering, world-girdling success of Western science is predicated on scientists qua scientists no longer feeling themselves participants in a vast ensemble of fellow beings of mysterious origin. They set upon Nature-as-quantifiable-and-calculable and challenge her. Francis Bacon epitomized the attitude: we are to put Nature on the rack and force her to answer precisely our questions and to respond exactly to our probes. Kant, scientist and philosopher, in his most influential work sees Nature as subjugatable by calculative, technologically enhanced human mind. Indeed, science is just the theory of technology: what we must suppose about Nature's objects if we would grasp how our techniques for enumerating and calculating them— inquiring into and manipulating them—are able to expose them. The world is no longer a community of fellow participants or subjects, but a collection of objects to be penetrated, exposed, *perhaps* marveled at.

Marveling, feeling awe and wonder, reverencing, are optional—mere subjective reactions and preferences. Scientific and technological power is bought at the expense of denying full reality and importance to our "inner states." As Robert Johnson puts it, we have inner poverty and outward riches. If Black Elk and his young patient had been party to this, the cure would not have happened; they would not have believed that the north wind that teaches endurance could be drawn through the boy's body.

Again, Western science exhibits intense emotional involvement in the world, but only insofar as the world is revealed in its precisely quantifiable and manipulable aspect. The dominant image of Nature is that of the pre-eminently calculable and manipulable—Nature as object and machine. We stand off from it, manipulate and use it. This attitude prevails today in our actual practices and institutions, even after twentieth-century physics has, to a considerable extent, closed the gap felt to divide us from Nature.

In fact, of course, we never do cease to be participants in a vast whole of fellow beings, and never do cease longing, I think, to be confirmed by them as whole persons and as vital members of a Whole that is mysterious and marvelous beyond all manipulation and imagination. Most of us long for sustenance, affection, and respect beyond our ability to specify our need. But caught up in the glare of tremendous scientific accomplishment, this central human reality can be halfway forgotten. When atom smashers break down matter into its wispy constituents, or electron microscopes expose the genetic bases of life, and this knowledge, born through calculation and technology, used to remake the earth and ourselves, so stunning is the impact that it looks like the whole world has been opened by it.

But it has not. Ironically, the great area that has been opened has been so because of the highly constricted limitation of involvement necessary to do the science. What is concealed, and the concealment concealed, is our moody, immediate involvement as whole beings with fellow subjects, not just objects, in the whole earth. Given the dominant model of reality as precisely observable, objectifiable, and mechanical, this involvement must be ignored—ignored and tacitly devalued. But in fact it is only in this dilated involvement that key valuables in life are to be found, the great intrinsic valuables beyond all use-values and precise measurement: love, respect, awe, appreciation, the beautiful, the holy, the good, the sparkling experience of being a tiny but vital part of the universe.[1]

The task of the humanities is to intensify and clarify, to thematize and retrieve from forgetfulness, our whole involvements as whole beings in the whole world. There is knowledge to be gained all right, but it is knowledge of another order from science—though we must connect it with science at key points. It stems from dilation of focus and empathy, and may be found perhaps in art, in everyday but alerted perception and intuition, or in religious experiences of emancipatory, healing kinds.

As I've discussed before, our great science cannot know that only science can know. A claim to know this assumes that science's own methods and evidential bases are adequate to assess all other possible ways of knowing and to know they get us nowhere. But this begs the question of whether only science can really know. Claiming that only science can know is not a scientific but an ideological position: it is scientism, not science. And most great scientists seem to know this.

Even so-called pure science must constrict its focus to use-values, somewhat subtle ones: operational definitions. For example, a calorie of heat is what functions to raise a gram of water one degree centigrade, a neutrino is what will disturb an underground detector a certain amount within a probable time, the average life span of an American Black female is so and so many years and months.

But there are ways of knowing other than scientific. In order to know what *it* does of the world, theater—take this way, for example—must dilate its involvements beyond what fits into scientific predictions and measurements. What we know as theater derives from the most ancient human encampments and ceremonies, where the people gather together to mirror themselves for one another, and to confirm and empower themselves. Recall, for example, Black Elk's gathering his people together to participate in the enactment of his vision. Theater is a mode of involvement that knows human involvements themselves in all their amplitude, imprecision, power, and intrinsic value and disvalue.

More specifically, theater employs deliberate mimesis or imitation to disclose undeliberate imitation by persons of one another, as selves are built up for good or ill—particularly mimetic engulfment with authoritative others. And it discloses also attempts to individuate within this engulfment, with all the intrinsic values or disvalues attendant upon this: agonizing conflicts, say, between one's indebtedness and loyalty, on the one hand, and immediate personal interests, on the other—or between intrinsically valuable and buoying reconciliation, cooperation, and growth, on the one hand, and, on the other, the withering isolation of failures, alienations from both others and one's own self, with only one's anger as nurse. In theater the community gathers to get to know itself better and to share itself as a community of individuals.[2]

Let us look briefly at the dynamics of mimetic involvement and individuation within the theater that uncovers the dynamics of this sort of thing outside the theater. Take a production of Hamlet. As members of the audience in the theater house, we are involved in the enacted involvements, but at an aesthetic distance. Somewhat detached from both the involvements on stage and from our own involvements outside the theater, we gain a certain perspective and begin to be aware of affinities between the two involvements. We do not believe that any actual Prince is in the building with us, nor do we believe that a ghost of his father is there, too, but in this fiction the mimetic hold of fathers on sons is revealed just because we are not engulfed in the stress of personal survival in our own family. Theater is a universal language—though it takes somewhat different forms in different cultures.

Actors and audience do for each other what neither can do for themselves. The audience participates in the play's "world" from the side of the actual world, and in its relative passivity its mimetic engulfments in the actual world can be called forth through recognition of similar involvements in the play's "world." The actors, on the other hand, participate in the world from the side of fictional "world," and just because of the fictionality of their setting can initiate activity more daring, volatile, and free than the constraints and dangers of the *world* ordinarily allow. Theater can be understood in phenomenological terminology as free variations on the meaning of human involvements and acts, but *ambulando,* in act. That is, free variations conducted in full bodily action, not in the mind's eye while seated in an easy chair.[3]

Usually unsuspected by the audience (during rehearsals the director and others in the rehearsal space are the audience), the actors are listening to the sounds *they* make. They hear the sounds that slip from them—hear them on the margins of consciousness. The actor's mimetic tendencies are such only relative to other persons, but actors cannot see their own body and face when they are actively with and for others, and must rely upon the audience to signal them when they are on to something telling and essential. Nor can he or she hear his or her voice as it really is—a voice mimetically with and for others—unless others let the actor know what they hear. Not realizing that we in the audience are being heard and followed, and thinking that it is only a fiction to which we are responding, we are not on our guard, and so reveal ourselves deeply as beings who incorporate others mimetically and undeliberately. The goal of all involved is that rapt silence that discloses the habitually unspoken, or perhaps the unspeakable. It is that common life shared unwittingly and numinously. In theater the community gives birth to its own thematized meaning: it is a mimetic community of individuals.

I doubt if there has ever been a human community without theater, or something generically related to theater. Ritualized enactments are fundamental. Recall Black Elk's "The Horse Dance." His own private vision cannot be fully efficacious until he enacts it for the people. And when he and his company enact it—the horses arrayed in the four quarters, the virgins in their troupes, all on the earth, under the sky, and so forth—new dimensions of his vision reveal themselves. Indeed, without this participation and confirmation by the group, his vision is not fully real, not fully "objective"—a dangerous Western term, for it is accompanied by its opposite, the "merely subjective." But we want a level of reality more fundamental than the distinction objective/subjective.

Most theater today lacks the behavior-modifying mythic punch of a community bonded and aflame in one system of belief. And yet it retains vestiges of primal contact—humans in one another's actual, physical presence. It can never be completely outmoded by whatever dazzling technological innovations in communication come our way. A "chat room" on the Internet may facilitate initial contact between people—each at their console—but it is questionable how deep and revealing their relationship typically becomes.

For the Athenian Greeks, for example, theater was an educational institution essential for the state. Understanding how theater at its best is at all times educational illuminates the central role of the humanities in the university, its task for which it has ecstatic responsibility: the accommodation of knowing from all quarters—from the hard sciences to the fine arts (to focus only on what are commonly thought to be polar opposites)—and to provide forums in which the old and the young learn together with zest.[4] Without pursuing physical science as such, the humanities must grasp the sort of involvement and knowing of which these sciences are capable, and prize and protect it within the community of learners that is the university. Without pursuing the fine arts as such, the humanities must grasp the sort of involvement and knowing of which they are capable, and prize and protect it within the community of learners: Always open to sketching and resketching, appreciating and reappreciating, the big picture, the significance for human beings of the many ways of knowing.

Humanities are ways of knowing what is educational in the broadest sense, formative of self. Thus they occupy a key position in the university. How do we know what is profoundly valuable for the individual and the community? In the university today, we cannot repair to a set of doctrines authorized on high by a supramundane authority. In a certain sense there must be something broadly experimental about the humane inquiry into what is valuable for us. Socrates is the most appropriate model here. Following in a way in the footsteps of his mother, he thought of himself as a midwife. The midwife can only help draw forth what is already there, but unthematized, unavailable for integration and application, and probably half-forgotten. The true educator helps generate questions for us all to entertain and wrestle with: What matters most? Is the danger of choosing to do evil a danger worse than death? What is the heart of the self, the soul? For what can we hope when our immediate prospects are bleak? In the midst of immediate personal animosities and petty flare-ups, can we discover a deeper consensus that will develop ourselves as individuals in the very process of finding our most organic and fruitful role within community? Learning is conversational in the most serious sense. We feed out beliefs or suggestions and have them fed back to us from others, hopefully corrected or augmented, so that in this evolving circuit we better understand ourselves as simultaneously individual and communal beings. It is no accident that the Athenian Greeks thought of theater as the prime educational institution. Socrates brought the process of dialectical learning to the level of personal encounter in the streets of Athens that many found disturbing.

I know a university (and it is not atypical) in which the Provost charged a distinguished committee to devise more effective means "for the delivery of undergraduate education." One can only applaud greater attention given in research universities to the crying needs of undergraduate education. But the danger is that the whole process will be poisoned from the start unwittingly: *Education* cannot be *delivered.* Bread can be delivered, or cocaine; and instruction—say in certain computer techniques—can in a sense be delivered, and various forms of instruction do comprise some of the tasks of the university. But the very roots of the term *education* reveal the distinctive need that that word and concept were evolved to meet: To *educe,* to *draw out* or *lead out,* from us learners what most concerns us mortal individual beings in community, concerns that may have been halfway or wholly forgotten in the relentless press of everyday living. What in the end is important, what incidental?

The educator is one whose involvement in a joint project of learning is contagious: all take responsibility for learning. Education is making sense of things together. To enlarge the area of meaningful questions and discourse is valuable in itself, even if the meaning is not in every case formulated into beliefs and assertions that get verified. Discovery of meaning in its various forms is itself important knowledge. To expand horizons and imagined possibilities is to expand self and selves.

Education is a joint project of interpretation. I pool my interpretations about me and you with you, and you pool your interpretations with me. We supplement and correct each other. We help each other piece ourselves together. The point of education is to experience self-awareness as part and parcel of awareness of the world that holds us. Responsibility to meaning and truth wherever it obtains is simultaneously responsibility to ourselves, since the capacity to seek and to hold to meaning and truth is essential to who we are. Intellectual freedom is simultaneously ethical obligation. Knowing what to take responsibility for, and to take it, is an ecstatic experience. It is knowing—or at least beginning to learn—how to live as whole beings.

What is a meaningful life? I. A. Richards wrote *The Meaning of Meaning.* Meaning can mean many things. In our present context of assessing the role of the humanities in learning, meaning must involve the viscerally felt sense of our powers and limitations as small but vital members of the world, what the Greeks called cosmos, the "beautiful place"—in which we can be involved ecstatically in so many ways.

The greatest challenge to the integrating and involving powers of the humanities is the ecological crisis. Without a community of learners concerned about the community of all communities, Nature, the crisis will certainly be intractable, and all human life and institutions may collapse. As we have seen, in deft but broad strokes John Dewey located us better than most philosophers have in our century: Human cultures are transformations of Nature wrought by us unusual organisms, but always within Nature (despite our pretensions to transcend it). Amid the turbulence of ever-expanding scientific, technological, and commercial advance, and the evident need to appropriate if we can the ancient Earth wisdom of indigenous peoples, how can we knowers involve ourselves so as to better locate ourselves? Where have we come from? Where are we going? Where are we? What time is it?

We cannot spin the answer out of our heads as if we were gods. We can only listen, resonate to affinities, send out questions, listen for answers, send out more questions. We can only continuously echo-locate and re-locate ourselves. Calvin Martin writes,

> One of the great insights of hunter societies is that words and artifice of specific place and place-beings (animal and plant) constitute humanity's primary instruments of self-location . . . for mankind is fundamentally an echo-locator, like our distant relatives the porpoise and the bat. . . . Only by learning . . . true words and true artifice about these things can one hope to become . . . a genuine person. . . . To be mendacious about other-than-human persons springs back upon us to make us mendacious about ourselves.[5]

All learning and knowing that amounts to anything is dialectical and conversational in the broadest sense, a combining of daring initiative in questioning or suggesting with resonant receptiveness and responsiveness. The utterly necessary role of science in addressing the ecological crisis is fairly well known today: plant ecology, atmospheric chemistry, hydrology, and so on. Also somewhat known is the deep kinship between hypothesis formation in science and the artistic imagination: Niels Bohr believed that physics proceeds by image, parable, and metaphor.

But because it is not so well known how science's mode of progress requires it to limit itself to modes of involvement in Nature that can be calculated—Nature broken down into precisely enumerable units of functional value—it is not well known how even the most enlightened and advanced scientific thinking is not sufficient to produce an adequate ecology. For that must prize and preserve all that the environment does and can mean to us bodily and communal beings: we who can dilate as a whole to Nature as a whole, and who hunger for consummatory and intrinsically valuable experiences of vital belonging—not merely calculable, enumerable, and functional ones. Who hunger for all of what's valuable that all modes of echo-location can uncover, including indigenous modes enshrined and preserved in myth, ritual, shamanic healing. To become effective in our lives, the artistic aspect of scientific hypothesis formation must be integrated with explicitly artistic modes of making, involvement, knowing. And all this integrated into an art of life. Here the humanities are most needed and most taxed, for they verge on religious experiences that many of us no longer know how to imagine.

What happens when a painter, say, paints a scene? Years ago in the San Gabriel mountains of Southern California I gained a ridge and found a painter—easel, oils, and all—painting the crest of the range. I was fascinated but could barely contain my laughter. I was taking all that in, that vast scene and mood. Why try to reduce it to a square foot of canvas daubed with pigments, lumps of colored mud smeared into shapes? It was redundant, or worse than that, an insult somehow. As the painter worked, my fascination alternated with contempt. Are some people never happy? Then came a glimmering of why he was doing this. But I could not grasp it.[6]

Over the years I saw that by placing blank canvas, recalcitrant blobs of pigment, brushes between himself and the scene, he was becoming intensely aware of the feeling, touching, moving, coiling and uncoiling body itself. His feet planting him in the Earth, hand and brush darted out, flicked out, to deposit its load of pigment. Moving and intent head, molding and directing hands, viscera with their coiled intestines alive and alert, all this spontaneous activity was becoming aware of itself working-up materials.

Successful fine art reveals the conditions of sensuously meaningful experience, what makes it possible—our artist-artisan bodies world-involved. As we take from the surround and feed back into it, molding materials, we create some new thing. Fed back is awareness of what was fed in, prompting what we next do: A self-correcting and self-energizing circuit. Others can react to the art, identifying with it, experiencing themselves and the rest of the world through it. And their reactions—actual or anticipated—are fed back into the self, vastly augmenting the feedback, reflecting and confirming what the artist fed in, and how it was.

We are body-selves creating meaning in improvisatory concert with the world around us; ourselves-augmented-by-the-world replenishes us; and it is a world we cannot bound tightly within our comprehension. For there is always "the more" beyond any horizon—the domains of what we know we don't know and also what we don't know we don't know. We are magnetized by the unknown, and forged into one coherent, awestruck, vibrant being. Will integrated with desire—judgment with need, impulse, and intuition— there is no opening in the self for addictive fillers. We are not wildly hungry, for we are filled with awe. Painters give birth to paintings, but only as the world gives birth to themselves.

Artists are kin to shamans, creating in states of trance or semi-trance. Control lies outside the calculating ego-self. Adepts, they allow the larger world to move in and emerge through them oracularly. We find ourselves through the kindred that resonate to us—unpredictably gifting—vegetable, mineral, wild or domestic animal, serpents. Body-self and the rest of Nature circulate through one another in a womb-like way, but now the circulation is artistically articulated and explicitly prized and acknowledged.

Art and religion grow from a common root that is paved over and distorted by secular-commercial culture. Mythic forms of life: ways of participating in regenerative processes of Nature and disclosing them. Ways of drawing out fecund margins of awareness into regenerated foci, which feed again into the sustaining and probing margins.[7] Ways of thinking that are simultaneously ways of thanking and revering, perhaps worshiping. I think the superobjective of all learning is, in the end, to dilate to the whole and to praise and celebrate it. Fine art can be a springboard to the art of life, though by itself not sufficiently integrative and habitually involving. Here the humanities, linking the fine arts and the sciences, might play a visionary and integrative role. Here they might suggest ways of better using the monetary riches of the secular-commercial culture. In playing, stretching, and pointing beyond themselves, they are most themselves.

Notes

1. This is a dominant theme of my *Wild Hunger: The Primal Roots of Modern Addiction* (Lanham, Md., and New York: Rowman & Littlefield, 1998).

2. See my *Role Playing and Identity: The Limits of Theatre as Metaphor* (Bloomington: Indiana University Press, 1991 [1982]).

3. *Role Playing and Identity.* Also see my "Robert Wilson's Theatre as a De Facto Phenomenological Reduction," *Philosophy and Social Criticism* 5, 1 (1978). And "Theatre as Phenomenology: The Disclosure of Historical Life," *Annals of Scholarship*, special issue (Summer 1982).

4. See my *The Moral Collapse of the University: Professionalism, Purity, Alienation* (Albany: State University of New York Press, 1990). The old and the young learning together with zest is one of Whitehead's ideas.

5. *In the Spirit of the Earth: Rethinking Time and History* (Baltimore and London: Johns Hopkins University Press, 1992), 103.

6. See again my *Wild Hunger*, particularly chapter 10, "Art and Truth."

7. For a fine, integrative study of how James's notion of "fringe" of consciousness is germane to brain science and cognitive science, see, again, Bruce Mangan's "Taking Phenomenology Seriously: The 'Fringe' and Its Implications for Cognitive Research," *Consciousness and Cognition* 2 (1993): 89–108. See also *Naturalizing Phenomenology: Issues in Contemporary Phenomenology and Cognitive Science,* ed. J. Petitot et al. (Stanford: Stanford University Press, 1999). This concerns mainly Husserlian phenomenology—but Husserl owes a lot to James.

Pragmatism, Neopragmatism, and Phenomenology
The Richard Rorty Phenomenon

What was it that Nature would say?
—R. W. Emerson

The world does not speak. Only we do.
—Richard Rorty

Traditionally, the chief function of every civilization has been to orient its members in the world. Time-proven ways of getting about and surviving are imparted ritualistically, ways of avoiding confusion, damage, disaster, ways perchance of flourishing. Revolutions of all sorts in the last four hundred years have relentlessly disrupted or destroyed nearly all traditional maps of the world and modes of orientation. The very meaning of "civilization" has become problematical. As has "reason" and "reasonable."

To understand the emergence of pragmatic modes of thinking in the last half of the nineteenth century requires an understanding of the groundswell of crisis to which it is a creative response. Also required is a grasp of the connections between pragmatism and phenomenology. I now turn to a current literary phenomenon: Richard Rorty's so-called neopragmatism, and his assiduous avoidance of phenomenology. Finally, a note about the ecological crisis, and how a deeper attunement to the environment calls for a reappropriation of phenomenological impulses in the earlier pragmatism, along with a new appreciation of indigenous ways.

Every traditional civilization aims to orient its members within their immediate locality. This is true even when interpretations of local things and events are in terms of a "spirit realm" or "alternate reality"—construals fantastic to contemporary North Atlantic ears. Always a modicum of what we would call common sense is discernible; for example, a tree may be experienced as moving under certain conditions and for certain modes of numinous consciousness, but it is just *that* tree, the one that is always found in the workaday-world forty paces in front of the chief elder's house. Without commonsensical rootage in the local environment, elementary evaluations necessary for the orientation and conduct of everyday life are impossible.

Now it is just this rootage that four hundred years of revolutions of all sorts have disrupted. Western industrialization uprooted vast populations from agrarian—or earlier—forms of life in which time-proven routines and rituals integrated with Nature's regenerative cycles gave life energy, purpose, and direction. Euro-American science and technology produce marvels of aggressive movement that very quickly overrun the world, dislocating and destroying countless civilizations, and causing strain and dislocation within Euro-American civilization itself. Technological advances outpace structures of interpretation within which they can be evaluated.

Just a few examples of how traditional guidance systems, rules of thumb and proverbs, become obsolete: "As right as rain." But since the rain in many sections is so acidified from burning fossil fuels that it kills fish in lakes and streams, what is right about it? "Practice makes perfect." But if steroids injected in athletes allow them to outperform others who practice diligently but don't take them, what becomes of our maxim? A psychoactive pill may eliminate grief over the death of a loved one. But what if this also eliminates grieving and its traditional expressions, that closure that opens the way to new birth? Breaking out of the lifeways, the folkways, that allow us to evaluate them, our technological means of control may have gone permanently out of control.

The most cursory notice of the upsurge of modern European science and philosophy in the seventeenth century reveals the abrupt departure from traditional feelingful, orientation-laden, commonsensical local knowledge. For all his sophistication and intellectual power, even Aristotle presupposed the commonsensical life-world of the time. To learn about things is to make judgments about those characteristics commonly thought to be essential to them, and about those accidental traits that may be altered yet the beings remain themselves—these traits, for example: the location in geocultural space they happen to occupy at the time (if they are movable beings), or their mode of dress in given situations, or their more or less passing emotional states—but states typed, sorted, settled from time immemorial.

Contrast this to the skepticism of the seventeenth-century scientist-philosopher Descartes. He assumes that the world is not as common sense describes its traditional, myth-laden sensorial richness. As previously pointed out, Descartes doubts the trustworthiness of the senses. Only when they are employed with the aid of scientific instruments are they trustworthy. For him the physical world is only as mechanistic mathematical physics describes it: a vast collection of contiguous objects exhibiting only such clinical and feelingless properties as extension, shape, mass, acceleration, force.[1]

Having thus reduced and objectified the "outer world," he turns "within" and objectifies a nonextended domain that he thinks is mind: private and personal consciousness, floating and transient "inner" feelings, tones, colors, smells, sensations of various kinds, mere appearances.[2] No longer the moral, aesthetic, or spiritual qualities of things in the immediately apparent world, they are reduced to being psychical qualities merely. The gain from this caustic way of thinking repays the loss, he thinks: one certitude remains: I think therefore I am. At least he can know he is a thing that thinks.

On every level—from the most abstruse domain of philosophical and scientific theory to revolutionary political, economic, and world-historical events—modern European civilization shifts off its basis in local, sensuous knowledge and traditional modes of feeling and evaluation. Kant noted with alarm that two essential, intertwining strands of civilization—science and morality—unraveled. If only the observations of mechanistic science reveal the "external" world reliably, and badness or evil is not an observable property of things, then the judgment, say, *Rape is bad*, is not really knowledge. It reveals nothing about who we essentially are as beings-human who must find our way and survive and perchance flourish in the vast world, but is merely a venting of our subjective negative sentiments—feelings and preferences we have been conditioned to feel in a particular culture, but that we might not have been.

Try to imagine the inception of the nineteenth century: the French Revolution reducing itself to chaos and despotism is just the most obvious disruption of traditional local ways. That century opens with titanic efforts to reweave the fabric of civilization, to conceive the world at such a primal, originative level that science and technology and every other revolution can be reintegrated with local knowledge and normative emotional-evaluational life—ways of living deeply rooted in the history, even prehistory, of human survival and flourishing on earth. This is the matrix within which pragmatic modes of thought emerged in the second half of the last century.

Earlier in the century, Schelling and Hegel launch a vast critique of European philosophy. They realize that they root within its floodplain; but its channel must be radically deepened if its wandering currents are to be collected into one sustaining flow. We must, they think, get beyond seventeenth-century "scientific realisms" that take for granted bases of judgment that should be thematized and superseded through reflection. Without this, civilization will continue to disintegrate—facts coming unhinged from values in endless future-shock—for we will not grasp intertwining principles of thought, action, feeling, and being that are sustaining and orienting in any local environment. (Recall Bugbee's insight that the very birth of awareness is the birth of deep, fulfilling action.)

Where does Descartes stand, what does he assume, when he objectifies the "outer" world in terms of mechanistic physics, takes an aspect of the world for the whole? And where does he stand when he objectifies mind as a private field full of ephemeral psychical entities merely, takes the psychical aspect of mental life in the world for the whole? Answer: he stands on the whole processual natural and cultural world, and the whole communal minding and knowing of it within which he was born, and in which he participates every instant, whether he acknowledges it or not. Only this allows him to make the objectifications, individuations, abstractions, and reductions that he makes. He assumes the ordinary world in which we live, and this he does not acknowledge.

Also, as we have seen, Hegel in the nineteenth century writes that mind is not like a lens that might fatally distort an "external world"; Descartes' doubts are concocted, artificial. For to imagine a world external to mind is already to use the mind.[3] No, for a world to be a world, an intelligible whole, minding must be something that the world does. The world's evolution is the development of its ever-deepening coming home to itself, its self-comprehension, as that energy that is mind or spirit (*Geist*). As Schelling writes in "The Relation of Plastic Art to Nature" (1807), it is "the holy and continuously creative energy of the world which generates and busily evolves all things out of itself," comprehending them in the very process of evolving them.[4] It follows that truths, facts, concerning what satisfies the deepest human potentialities and hungers, given our place in the evolving whole, are simultaneously values. With Schelling and Hegel, local, rooted, sense experience and evaluation seem to be rewoven with scientific

research and cosmic speculation and reverence; reason achieves a new flex-
ibility, resourcefulness, and daring, and civilization seems on the verge of
recovery (at least in thought). In a sanguine moment we might even imagine
rapprochement with certain indigenous modes of thought and action.

Charles Peirce, William James, and John Dewey—the paradigmatic
American pragmatists—are inundated and deeply rooted in this so-called
idealist tradition. They cannot accept the notion of Absolute Mind or Spirit,
particularly as Hegel left it: the belief that since the universe is One, there
must be one Mind working in and through it all, and that we can enter into
this working and discover its continuously world-creating dialectical logic—
philosophizing a reverential act in which we think God's thoughts. But—
but—the idealists' critiques of most modern "realisms" are accepted. To
allow philosophical thought to make unexamined assumptions in order to
begin is to countenance partial views, aspects, and abstractions to pass as the
whole, and this is to abet fragmentation, disorientation, frightened and aggressive restlessness. Particularly damaging is Cartesian dualism, which pictures
Nature as a machine. How could we feeling beings, capable of tradition, ever
fit into this? The very time in which Europeans used their mechanical model
and their tools to overwhelm the globe, they lost all sense of being rooted
sustainingly in Nature, and all appreciation of indigenous peoples' profound
contentments.

How is philosophical thought to begin authentically? It must somehow
be self-starting and self-validating. This can only mean that we must start
with where we actually find ourselves here and now in the local environment.
We find ourselves within the circumpressure of things as they appear to us.
Appearing things that can no longer be denigrated as mere appearances, for
they compose the primal tissue of meaning without which no other meaning
can be made, without which all deliberate inquiry, analysis, reflection, research,
and technology are impossible. And when we describe these appearances
closely, we see they hold within themselves connective tissue. Any local
environment presents itself within a horizon of the immediately sensible—
audible, visible, smellable, touchable—and every horizon points both inward
at this and beyond itself to *everything else*—whatever exactly the universe
might be. The earlier pragmatism retained in broad outline organicist assumptions: at all levels of analysis parts are parts-of-wholes, organs of the whole
organism, and their well functioning is for the sake of the whole. And
organisms at all levels are wholes-of-parts that feed back into the parts,
feeding and sustaining them for their allotted time within the whole.

That is, nineteenth- and early twentieth-century pragmatisms are simultaneously phenomenologies, attempts to describe the primal birth of phenomena or appearances within our experience in such a way that the basic categories for weaving together and interpreting the whole world are discerned. For the original pragmatists, meaning and truth are "what works" in the sense that they function to weave together a world in our experience. We must believe whatever is necessary to have a world. Pragmatists' idea of what works has been, and in many quarters still is, misunderstood, because of a scandalous ignorance of the history of philosophy, of the matrix within which their ideas grow. The misunderstanding at its crassest goes like this: "Pragmatists believe that meaning and truth are whatever makes you happy to believe."

No, ideas have a life of their own; they are strands of activity that either interweave with the rest of the world as they predict in their very meaning they will, or they do not. How this happens to make us feel as individuals is irrelevant (unless the ideas are about our feelings themselves). Misunderstandings of original pragmatism typically spring from Cartesian abstractions from the whole experienceable world that forget this experienceable whole, and, without grasping how any objectification is possible, objectify and demarcate minds as private individual containers with ideas and other mental contents—like feelings of satisfaction—floating inside them. This is cheating.

Let us note briefly categories of world-interpretation generated in nineteenth-century pragmatists' phenomenological descriptions of every situation of sensuous experience, every one a womb of meaning; without this understanding, we cannot evaluate Richard Rorty's neopragmatic departures from what he takes to be an outmoded way of thinking, the categorial way.

Categories are generated when shown to be presupposed as the abiding conditions of sensuous perception. After trying and failing to come up with a long list of categories in the manner of Hegel, Peirce settles on three, firstness, secondness, thirdness. Firstness is the possibility of irreducible, spontaneous, freshly felt quality: redness, say, or a heard tone; to say these are subjective or merely mental is to operate on unexamined Cartesian assumptions. Secondness is the brute, contingent, resistance of things, like running blindfolded into a post. Thirdness is the way one thing is mediated by others to become other than it was; it is development as habit taking: the emergence of lawfulness out of brute encounters. (Thinking as the use of signs is a paradigmatic case of thirdness: a mere thing or event comes to signify something when emerging within a context that mediates its relationship to the rest of the world so that it becomes a sign with an interpretation. Insofar as Peirce thinks the universe has the master habit of taking habits, of becoming ever more mediated and "thirded," we hear echoes of Hegel's idea that the universe's evolution is its developing self-interpretation.) For Peirce, innovative interpretation can occur only because of the stability and continuity of the funded habits that compose every meaningful situation, and within which we live, move, and have our being.[5]

Dewey's categorial scheme resembles Peirce's to some extent. We are cultural beings, and culture is habitual modes of interpretation and transformation of Nature, but always within Nature. Every situation for us thinking organisms has an irreducible lived quality that gives it its ambience and possibilities, the meaning without which all deliberate interpretations, analyses, and technical projects would be impossible. Situations can be really dangerous, calm, shockingly disrupted, inviting, repulsive, challenging. Categorial features of the world emerge through commonsensical or instinctual phenomenological readings of situations: for example, the paired categories of the stable and the precarious.[6] When we come home to ourselves reflectively, we find ourselves already within a circle of categories. When we reflect, we can start anywhere we like within the circle, but we are unable to justify the circle itself, because all justification is in terms of it.[7]

William James is least explicitly categorial, but his emphasis on stable adaptational habits and involuntary attention as the pre-given matrix for all innovative action and interpretation plays a categorial role. He pursues assumptions relentlessly, demanding they be "cashed" or clarified in terms of their concrete experienceability. For example, how is truth actually experienced, what is it known-as? This: we navigate through the world, orient ourselves, get where we think we will get (though that may not always please us). True thinking grafts itself fruitfully into the rest of the world. Evolved organisms think; there is no gulf between the mental and the physical that is spanned in a "truth relation." Truth is a species of goodness. He could never be satisfied with reifying an abstraction like *proposition* or *sentence* and saying it has the property of truth when it corresponds to what it purports to be about. Since we define "proposition" as being either true or false, then *of course* it must be one or the other; but this trivializes truth. This refusal to reify either propositions or sentences contrasts starkly to what we will see develop in Rorty's neopragmatism (and recall Chapter 5 above).

James's conception of an authentic beginning for thought, a self-validating starting point, penetrates to a primal level of experiencing in Nature. Phenomena immediately experienced, "hot off the griddle of the world," are pure or neutral, as we have seen. Reflection, however rapid, has not yet assigned them to either the first-person immediacy of a personal history, or to the history of the world at large. The example we have used is the blue of the sky as we happen to look up into it. We are absorbed in it entrancedly. We haven't reflected and thought "It would be good to look up and achieve the sight of blue" (see Chapter 4 above).

Prereflective experience is a "much at once," but we need concepts to fill out our sense of *world, the everything else* beyond the sensory horizon. But no conception, no matter how essential or breathtaking, can substitute for the world's concrete sensorial richness. As we have seen, James at the end of his life aims to supply the ultimate connective tissue: Science is to be accommodated, also religious experience, indeed the most primal religious experience—shamanic—in which distinctions are not yet drawn between self and other. In which we fuse, at least for a time, with powerful "medicine animals," say, regenerative presences such as bears, dolphins, snakes, or become one with trees that nod familiarly to us (Emerson's phrase). The very same bear that carves out its history in the world also figures in my history—and if deeply enough I shape-shift and become the bear (in a sense that challenges phenomenological description). The very same tree that, for certain purposes, we regard as rooted and immobile, may, for other purposes, be regarded as flooding our lives with its presence and moving with us through the day.

As we saw, James flirts seriously with Gustav Fechner's idea of plant or animal souls, or even the Earth soul—the animating principle of a strangely animate cultural-natural world.

Richard Rorty's neopragmatism is a current (or is it now recent?) literary phenomenon. A collection of his reshaped papers and lectures published in 1989 has been reprinted at least eight times, a collection from 1991 at least four.[8] Not since Dewey has an academic philosopher exerted significant immediate influence on the culture at large. He is mentioned in some segments of the popular press; newsworthy and significant figures (for example, the feminist legal scholar Catherine McKinnon) regard him as a kind of guru; many professors in English and literature departments vie to see who quotes him most. He is cited in some Landmark Education programs, a remarkable educational venture in sixteen nations, forty-seven cities, five languages. Not since William James lectured on pragmatism to a thousand at Columbia nearly a hundred years ago have we seen anything quite like it.

The reasons are not far to seek. Many know that there's something about pragmatism that's distinctly American and somehow important. Why not get the latest word on a great quantity of greatly ignored and difficult work done long ago? Related is Rorty's facile and brilliant intelligence and engaging, straightforward style. And beyond this is a voracious but difficult-to-articulate kind of spiritual hunger to which Rorty seems to minister. In an age that for many is a completely desacralized world, one where even the most elementary distinctions between right and wrong are toppling, to find a brilliant and courageous thinker who will face the grim reality and still offer *something* to believe in, that's welcome nourishment! (I mean his tenacious and blunt liberalism.)

Finally, another facet of this dazzling and attractive figure: his delicious ridicule of academic philosophers still caught up in the unexamined assumptions and artificial problems posed by dualizing Descartes and Company over the last four centuries. For the general public, including the undergraduates (ever decreasing in number) who take philosophy courses, most professors of philosophy must seem a quaint and perverse lot.

One of the most obvious and exciting themes of the earlier pragmatism Rorty retrieves is the connection between democracy and truth. Truth is not some occult relation that bridges "a mental domain" and an "outer world," but rather the honorific term we apply to those beliefs that win out in the marketplace of ideas and the tough competition of finding our way about in the world. As Dewey said, the conditions for truth and the conditions for democracy are essentially the same: every idea, no matter how humble its origin, has the prima facie right to be considered and tested. The only nobility in America is that of accomplishment. Rorty puts it tersely: if the conditions of respect for individuals are established, a truly democratic liberalism set in place, truth will take care of itself.

Another salient feature of the earlier pragmatism retrieved excitingly by Rorty is what *they* called the categorial feature of chance, precariousness, contingency. Talk about return to the local and never fully predictable environments we all occupy each second of the day, and the need for solace and some kind of guidance within them! Even more eloquently than the earlier thinkers—if that is possible—Rorty discourses on the blind impress of events that all our behaviors bear. Our vulnerability, our capacity for humiliation and pain, our huddling to a few others in the darkness, are brought home with tremendous poignancy—the impress of events very like the crucifixion some feel the events to be. With great finesse and delicacy, Rorty alludes to Freud's analyses of the defense mechanisms of dissociation, fusion, or reaction-formation, subvocal symbolisms we engage in to soften or deflect the impact of a blind and obdurate contingent world. Modes of self-deception they may be, but also they are tactics employed by poets, and Rorty writes endearingly of the spontaneous poetry of the common man and woman.

Carried along in this surging and sparkling stream of words—this ingenious unleashing of communication—many perhaps never realize that vast tracts of the earlier pragmatism are ignored or occluded. Essential, of course, to the earlier thought's grasp of the local environment is the body—the human organism's need to cope with the world around it. Now, to be sure, Rorty's talk of pain and humiliation implies that we are indeed bodily beings, but he does not address the body as we immediately live it each moment, the body that each of us is, the body-self (as I call it) capable of more than pain. As far as I can tell, only the body objectified by science, or by analytic philosophers speculating about "the mind-body problem," is addressed typically by Rorty.

But then, ironically, he is left in the Cartesian position he has instructed us to despise: of having to account for the point of view from which he makes the objectifications—immediate ongoing bodily experiencing in the world around us—and he does not do this, no more than does the philosopher he ridicules, Descartes. In other words, Rorty completely ignores phenomenology (and the decades of work by phenomenologically oriented philosophers on the American pragmatists), and how phenomenology of one sort or other is the taproot of the categorially structured worldviews of the earlier philosophers that situated us as body-selves, locally and cosmically. Ignoring phenomenology, it follows almost inevitably that he has little or nothing to say that would jibe with indigenous peoples' experiencing of Nature and their place in it. His departure from the earlier American thinkers is profound and irreversible.

At times Rorty's naive objectification of the body (posing as scientific) virtually reduces itself to absurdity. Following the tack of certain analytic philosophers, he refers to "neural states of the brain," which somehow correlate to "beliefs and desires," and these beliefs and desires "in continual interaction redistributing truth values among statements" [ORT, 123]. Is he saying that minds are composed of statements, or that statements just float in the blue and get their truth values determined by beliefs and desires in the mind? But either way, that is only a fraction of mind or minding. Moreover, "beliefs and desires" are abstractions that have been reified. What we actually experience moment by moment as bodily beings in environments are believings in states of affairs believed-in, and desirings of things desired. Experience is "double-barrelled," as James and Dewey said. Moreover, Rorty, following a great crowd of analytic philosophers, limits truth to some (adulatory) property assigned to sentences or statements. In the earlier tradition's light, this appears artificial and thoughtless. It deprives truth of its existential reference, as Dewey put it, and masks out the palpable fact that it is not just true sentences or statements that navigate us through the world. Silences of certain kinds, images, icons, bodies, faces, scenes, artworks, music, perhaps mystical experiences amplify, clarify, and reveal the world, and are true, in their own ways.

Praising poetry, and at the same time exhibiting a bald literal-mindedness, Rorty declares that only humans speak [*CIS*, 6]. Immediately Emerson's words obtrude and contrast: Nature speaks, and this speech is the first teacher of the American scholar.[9] Of course, Rorty can object that "speak" is equivocal, and that Emerson is using it in a metaphorical sense, and he in a literal. But that he has so little to say about Nature speaking in Emerson's sense is a telltale fact.

The Emersonian tradition in some form lies behind all the earlier pragmatists, and of course also behind Hocking and Bugbee. Nature as we immediately live, suffer, enjoy it, and are sustained by it, is silent in Rorty, and it is a silence that does not reveal but conceals. Moreover, it is a silence that, for many urban readers today, probably conceals that it is concealing anything. A concealing of the primal, and a concealing of the concealing, is a hobbling of mind and imagination, a baffled rootlessness, a loss of possibilities. What could Rorty possibly make of Dewey's advice that we emulate animal grace?[10]

For all his courage, Rorty fearfully over-reacts to the dangers of talking about Nature in the way that some traditional rationalistic or empiricistic philosophers talked about it. That is, as a domain of things with fixed essential characteristics (essences) that determine and limit our behavior. This way of talking, he thinks, obscures our freedom: the power of individuals and cultures to freshly interpret the world.

Now no doubt this power is great, but he exaggerates it, I think, not only revealing the uprootedness of ever-spreading North Atlantic civilization, but contributing to it. Socialization goes all the way down, he writes. The old pragmatists never said anything like that! They perpetually stressed the interactive, interfusing, reciprocal organism-rest-of-Nature weaving of influences. Culture is not made out of whole cloth, but as Dewey for one maintained, culture is human organisms' distinctive alteration of Nature, but always within Nature. Rorty is a self-styled ironist: "Anything can be made to look good or bad by being redescribed" [*CIS*, 73]. Maybe. But that won't make it *true* that it is really good or bad, or that, if good, it really promotes growth in the long run for beings essentially culture-and-Nature involved, human beings.

Ungrounded in any description of life as we immediately live it in actual interactions in various environments, devoid of any phenomenology, Rorty writes in a kind of feverish reaction-formation to any notion of a determinate physical universe. Lacking any sense of matrix, of connective tissue beyond human associations for purposes of liberal agendas, he is thrown into a series of unmediated distinctions and oppositions. These help hurried readers catch hold, but they produce a partial, uprooted, eccentric, and unnecessarily lonely and anxiety-producing interpretation of the world. For example, the slogan, "Truth is made, not found" [*CIS*, 3]. But the truth plainly is: Truth is co-created, co-made by humans and the rest of the world. Following Bugbee, we should say that we participate in creation, not simply that we create.

Contrasts and oppositions are helpful only when mediated, and they are this only when emerging in systematic descriptions of our lived situations. Lacking the connective tissue of phenomenological insight—any feel for the kinship any meaningful contrast presupposes and partially conceals— Rorty's picture of the world fractures. Of course, he lacks affinity to indigenous ways of thought and being, ways bound up in a vivid picture of the world and our place in it.

Rorty treats us to a diaeresis of unmediated distinctions, for example, knowledge as either "a useful tool" or as "fitting the world" [*CIS*, 19]. But useful tools fit the world in some sense or they wouldn't be useful. Or, self-knowledge is not "discovery" but "self-creation" [20]. But self-creation that amounts to anything must discover body-self's tendencies or potentials for fruitful growth. Or again, the "universal" or the "concrete" [34]. But where is the "concrete universal," as Hegel put it, the actual nexus of habitual or institutional practices in particular situations? Yet again, philosophers, we are told, are either "foundationalists" or "conventionalists" [28]. But the earlier pragmatists he is supposed to be reviving or refurbishing can be fitted into neither side of the dichotomy.

Now look again at his poignant allusions to the blind impress of events that all our behaviors bear, and to "sheer contingency." But "sheer contingency" is no guide for living, because it is unmediated, that is, simplistically opposed to something like "blind mechanical necessity." Peirce, his three categories phenomenologically grounded, gives a much better idea of contingency. Certainly it exists—secondness exists. Part of what we mean by categorial thinking is that we must find the categorial trait in our experience of the world—at least as long as the present epoch of the world lasts. But firstness, sheer sensed quality also exists, as does thirdness, habits of interaction and interpretation that are relatively stable, and may allow us to cope with and bear (or fruitfully enjoy) the element of contingency.

Rorty dismisses categorial thinking as a regressive or atavistic element in otherwise valuable bodies of thought.[11] But Rorty inadequately grasps the metaphysics of *pragmatism*.[12] It is just, for example, Dewey's "commonsensical metaphysical" paired categories of the stable and the precarious that could save Rorty's thought from chronic instability and eccentricity. For perhaps the prime example, Dewey's category of stability turns our attention to the stabilities of Nature. Our instincts, for example, and I don't mean necessarily some phony contrast to something like "fundamental immobility" [*CIS*, 25, n.], but just the habits we are born with. Even if we mean, for instance, the genetic structure that determines that normal females can conceive, bear, and give birth to new human beings, and that given cultural or personal factors a particular woman may be disgusted or frightened by her reproductive powers, still she will have to deal with the actuality of this capacity in a way a man will not. Yes, and given personal or cultural factors particular men may be more nurturing than many women, but they will not lactate when the baby cries. Which is a not-insignificant element in the mix of our lives.

Tellingly, Rorty ends his *Contingency, Irony, and Solidarity* with his version of liberal "ethnocentrism": "What takes the curse off this ethnocentrism is not that the largest such group is 'humanity' or 'all rational beings'— none, I have been claiming, *can* make *that* identification—but, rather, that it is the ethnocentrism of a 'we' ('we liberals') which is dedicated to enlarging itself, to creating an ever larger and more variegated *ethnos*. It is the 'we' of the people who have been brought up to distrust ethnocentrism." There is something tragic or at least pathetic in this eloquent meta-ethnocentrism. For he is so excessively wary of anything suggesting an "essence" of humanity that he bereaves himself of auxiliaries, as Emerson put it—auxiliaries, allies, for his challenging quest. Rorty sees no need of bonding with far-flung living kindred of earth, human or not. The heroic contemporary corporate individual, "we liberals," will stand alone.

I believe what Dewey believed: that, if one looks with a sufficiently synoptic eye, one can discern universal human needs. One of these is to be a respected member of one's group, and this involves the correlative need to empathize profoundly with others, to introject their bodies mimetically into one's own. But we need an existential phenomenology to really understand this bonding, and here Rorty is empty-handed.

Certainly, this capacity to identify empathically with others can be over-ridden or limited by contingent factors; that people, say, have not been prepared to cope with strangers. But the mimetic capacity exists, is a stable inheritance within Nature, and it is just its enlightened development that will probably make the difference between Rorty's closing vision being a pipe dream and being a lure to approximate in practice.

The most lamentable element in Rorty's thought is his failure to address the reality of Nature (if the reader prefers, give it a lower case "n"). This means Rorty cannot enlist whatever aids there are in our instinctual, archetypal-communal, or artistic nature to convert marketplace commerce—at its present rate environmentally disastrous—to an ecological commerce.[13] If the environment disintegrates, all liberal visions of a community of humankind will disintegrate along with it.

In the end, Richard Rorty spends too much time conversing with philosophers molded in the very analytical tradition he so severely criticizes—Willard Quine, Donald Davidson, Wilfrid Sellars, among others. He may be appreciated by some of them, but he could do much more to develop the fundamental thinking of the original pragmatists, who were able at crucial junctures to combine the primal and the pragmatic. Indeed, Richard Rorty distorts this tradition. His sparkling vision is contorted by an ethnocentrism that he perhaps cannot acknowledge: his professional academic specialty, his plainly ethnocentric specialty, as a constructivist master of words and logical analysis.

Rorty leaves us very hungry indeed.

Postscript

As I reread this essay just before publication, I have misgivings. Perhaps I have been so single-minded I have missed something. Perhaps I have refused to dilate and to discern the more immediately involving human aspects of what Rorty emphasizes. And after all I've written in this book!

I think I have missed something intrinsically valuable, and that accounts as well for the great response Rorty has got. It is what Bugbee calls the depth of true affirmation. It ties in also with Kierkegaard's aphorism, We live forward but understand backward, which James quotes admiringly at least three times in the last years of his life. Or as Bugbee has it, we stand forth beyond knowledge, beyond where we have been.

That is, we can create possibility. Understanding easily misses this, because we understand backward, and in two related senses: (1) We must understand by using concepts like causation, which have been built up over the past, and (2) In searching for understanding we lose touch with the instant of encounter with things or events, in which the future opens up for a dazzling moment, and all too often closes just as fast. We lose touch with the very reality of possibility.

I think Rorty is affirming the dazzling power of possibility when he asserts "we liberals!" We liberals whose "ethnocentrism . . . is dedicated to enlarging itself, to creating an ever larger and more variegated ethnos . . . [we] who have been brought up to distrust ethnocentrism." I have inadequately appreciated this.

However, I continue to believe that Rorty lacks elements of what Bugbee calls the depth of true affirmation. His affirmation excites some readers— and for good reason—but it is thin, I am afraid.[14] I wonder about its staying power. I think it lacks the full force of the body caught up in a *communitas* much broader and deeper than the human typically construed. And his phrase, "who have been brought up," is too abstract. It leaves out ritualized readiness to be caught up together in the mysterious sensorial and communal life. And it misses the instant—say the one in which Bugbee beholds the leaping, gleaming fish, and is instantly reborn. Here and now he and we can tap into energy new as on the first day.

We must be explicit about all this and work out graphically the implications of it. Can't we be fully primal and fully pragmatic!?

Notes

1. *Meditations on First Philosophy: In Which the Existence of God and the Distinction of Soul from the Body Are Demonstrated,* 3d ed., trans. D. A. Cross (New York: Hackett Publishing Co., 1993).

2. I say mind is "a kind of container" for Descartes. But I get no clear idea of what he thinks mind is. He seems to me greatly confused.

3. *Phenomenology of Mind* (New York: Harper Torch Books, 1967 [1807]). This is the abiding premise of Hegel's book.

4. This quotation is from the opening pages of that work. The translation is found in my *Romanticism and Evolution* (New York: G. P. Putnam's Sons, 1968), 128–30 (reprinted Lanham, Md.: University Press of America, 1985).

5. See particularly "The Architecture of Theories," in *The Monist* series of articles, 1891–93, in, of course, *The Collected Works of C. S. Peirce* (Cambridge, Mass.: Harvard

University Press, 1931–35, 1958), but also in *Charles S. Peirce: The Essential Writings,* ed. E. C. Moore (New York: Harper & Row, 1972).

6. See the second chapter of *Experience and Nature* (New York: Dover Books, 1958 [1929]). *John Dewey, the Late Works, 1925–1953,* vol. 1 (Carbondale; Southern Illinois University Press, 1983) (hereafter cited as "critical edition").

7. See *Logic: The Theory of Inquiry* (New York: Holt, Rinehart & Winston, 1938), opening chapters. Part i is aptly titled "The Matrix of Inquiry." John Dewey, *Logic: The Theory of Inquiry, The Late Works, 1925–1953,* vol. 12 (Carbondale: Southern Illinois University Press, 1986).

8. The first is *Contingency, Irony, and Solidarity* (New York: Cambridge University Press, 1989); the second is *Objectivity, Relativism, and Truth* (New York: Cambridge University Press, 1991). *I typically abbreviate these as CIS and ORT, and page references are placed in brackets in the body of my text.*

9. See "Nature," in, for example, *R. W. Emerson: Selected Essays,* ed. Larzer Ziff (New York: Penguin Books, 1982), 43, and all of "The American Scholar."

10. *Art as Experience* (New York: G. P. Putnam's Sons, 1980 [1934]), for instance, 25, 33. *Art and Experience, John Dewey, the Late Works, 1925–1953* (Carbondale: Southern Illinois University Press, 1987) (hereafter cited as "critical edition"), 10:31, 40–41.

11. *Consequences of Pragmatism,* for example, "Dewey's Metaphysics" (Minneapolis: University of Minnesota Press, 1982).

12. Compare Sidney Hook, *The Metaphysics of Pragmatism* (Amherst, N.Y.: Prometheus Books, 1996 [1927]).

13. Paul Hawken, *The Ecology of Commerce* (New York: Harper Business, 1993).

14. I myself am excited by it. Perhaps the NATO attack on Yugoslavia in the Kosovo war signals a sea change in world consciousness: genocide anywhere will not be tolerated.

William James's Prophetic Grasp of the Failures of Academic Professionalism

Nearly a hundred years ago, William James was ahead of most of us. In "The Ph.D. Octopus" (1903), he foresaw the existential crisis into which the professionalization of disciplines and the segmentation and bureaucratization of the university were leading us. "America is . . . rapidly drifting towards a state of things in which no man of science or letters will be accounted respectable unless some kind of badge or diploma is stamped upon him, and in which bare personality will be a mark of outcast estate. It seems to me high time to rouse ourselves to consciousness, and to cast a critical eye upon this decidedly grotesque tendency. Other nations suffer terribly from the Mandarin disease. Are we doomed to suffer like the rest?"[1]

What happens to our sense of ourselves—our cemented sense of our significance and worth—when to establish our identity we must display certificates stamped by institutions? Particularly by ones to which we have never wholeheartedly bonded? James fears that our identity will crumble, in spite of all the shiny facades erected around it.

James's voice intermixes with other prophetic ones: Kierkegaard's—that lampooning of learned professors who build a mansion of world-historical thought but live in a shack out back; Nietzsche's—"The proficiency of our finest scholars, their heedless industry, their heads smoking day and night, their very craftsmanship: how often the real meaning of all this lies in the desire to keep something hidden from oneself!" Dostoyevsky's—"Ah . . . nowadays everything's all mixed up . . . we don't have any especially sacred traditions in our educated society; it's as if somebody patched something together the best he could out of books . . . or extracted it out of the ancient chronicles. But those would be the scholars, and they're all blockheads." And we can't leave Dostoyevsky without hearing the spiteful voice of The Underground Man who complains of his inability to become, to *be*, anything—even an insect.[2]

Finally, let us hear for a moment that balked and despairing but persevering giant, Max Weber, who details in *Economy and Society* "the iron cage of bureaucracy."[3]

What is it that all these voices lament? It's simply stated but difficult to unpack the meaning: To be, we must be validated by the universe that evolved us and holds us. When our place within the universe is no longer guaranteed by ages-old religions, or by settled modes of ethical thought, the vacuum draws into itself untested institutions, turned obsessively within themselves, to stamp us with a putative identity. Lost, one might say, is our ability to *vow* to be this or that, a vow coordinated with the wheeling universe itself through our people's rituals and enduring customs.

Joseph, defeated chief of the Nez Perce people—"From where the sun now stands, I will fight no more forever."[4]

James detected that sore, that wound, that all our science and quasi-science, technology and methodology, scientific linguistics and semantics can conceal but cannot heal: the inability to be firm, centered, confident in our inherently expansive and ecstatic being.

Let us focus on that academic field that some might expect to pursue the question of being—philosophy. Aristotle declared that it is this question that has always been, and will always be, asked. But enlightened "scientific" thinkers, authorized now by a national professional association, seem to know better. Only a few philosophers have raised it in this century, for instance, James in *Some Problems of Philosophy*, Heidegger in many places, and, implicitly, Dewey and the later Wittgenstein.

Most of the rest just assume that the question of being is too vague or abstract. It must be replaced with specific questions that can be handled by specific methodologies. Lacking a centered sense of themselves as vital members of the whole, they fail to see that Aristotle's question applied to our times might allow a coordinated view, which, gathering things together, would encourage *coherence and concreteness.*

Whereas in Aristotle's vision quantity and quality are essential aspects of the ground of being, in the scientist-philosophers from the seventeenth century on they fly apart. When universities were professionalized in the last decades of the last century, they were partitioned and constituted along the lines of dualisms or polar oppositions.[5] These are eccentric bifurcations in which one side or the other is given precedence as a result of whatever wind of doctrine or individual whim is blowing at the moment: subjective/objective—which matches qualitative/quantitative—and self/other, individual/group, mind/matter, rational/irrational, present/past, male/female, and so on. Professors live embedded in these mental-institutional structures. No fiddling with managerial arrangements in the university moves them out of this trance.

I have just concluded a course called Philosophy in Literature. Both students majoring in philosophy and those in English complained of their experience in the university over several years: each field was obsessed with the technical apparatus and glossary of terms distinctive to it. Subject matter of the greatest human concern was peripheralized or eclipsed by the shiny tools that ought to have revealed it. The students' experience fell to pieces.

This must happen when an organic sense of the whole falls away, leaving the quantitative and the qualitative disconnected, and when inquirers lose a sense of their own centers as existing beings. Individuation cannot be a vital matter of responsibly placing and conducting ourselves as whole living things in the world, but must be decided by externals: the current methodologies of professional-academic disciplines that define and individuate themselves nationally and internationally in the information business, and by which young professionals must be certified if they would advance in the business. For a prime example, anthropologists arrive uninvited in the front yards of indigenous peoples and expect them to submit themselves as objects for scientific investigation. The researchers assume superior knowledge and a kind of divine right—indeed, obligation—to understand these others.[6]

Across academia it is assumed that all issues are questions formulable in some specialized vocabulary or other, and that the only responsible way to get "the big picture" is to add up the results from each field. But the summing somehow never takes place. The possibility of other questions, perhaps better questions, is concealed, and the concealment concealed.

When this kind of presumption reigns in the field of philosophy, the results are particularly fatuous and absurd. A kind of scientism pervades the seemingly most various philosophical coteries. To reiterate: this is the view, insupportable by science, that only science can know (or some conceptual activities somehow associated with science or appearing sharp and precise and "scientific").[7] When it presumes hegemony, it just assumes that art, religion, "literary" history, common sense, and everyday intuition cannot know essential aspects of reality. This is fanaticism and dogmatism every bit as rank and brash as ever religious organization exhibited, and, indeed, without the religion's cover story about the ultimate mystery of things.

Professional philosophers today commonly assume that logical positivism, with its uncritical reliance upon the science of the day, is dead. This is self-congratulatory delusion, the fruit of a scientist faith in progress. For example, the positivistic opposition between the emotive and the cognitive informs at a subterranean level much of the crossover work of philosophers and cognitive scientists. Take Steven Pinker's *How the Mind Works*. He advances interesting ideas about understanding human mind in terms of "reverse engineering": we see that adaptations to environments have been achieved, and define our task as explaining the means by which these have come about. And certain computer models of information processing are provided that have some value.

But Pinker finds music making—universal and fundamental in all cultures—to be anomalous.[8] Which means there must be something basically wrong or missing in his view. James could have told him what it is: To miss the joy is to miss all. Pinker's work exhibits the haunting unreality of "realistic" books.[9] The fusion of reality and ideal novelty excites and empowers us, and does so because we are organisms that, to be vital, must celebrate our being. On this level we are not all that different from chimpanzees who—I have heard—feel a storm coming on, resonate to it, and do their marvelous rain dance in which, perhaps, they celebrate the bare fact of just being in a universe of such power.

The rhythms, melodies, harmonies, phrasings of our music are part and parcel of this celebration of bodily and personal being within a processual, rhythmic, engaging universe. Intensifying, clarifying, confirming our feeling-experiencing in typical situations, music develops our capacities for adaptation. Not to see it as biologically significant is to artificially encapsulate the so-called hard sciences. Only thinkers lost in scientism and the information business could fail to see it, or glimpsing it, find it anomalous. They've read too much in *Mind* perhaps and not lived enough in mindful and grateful celebration. Dostoyevsky defined the modern human as the ungrateful animal, and Heidegger tr:- l to cultivate *denken als danken,* thinking as thanking. But they no more than James are mainstream philosophers today. What passes as education is not the *educing (educare)* of our needs, yearnings, questionings as beings who must develop ourselves or rot in boredom—or spin out of orbit in futile eccentricity. But it is rather instruction in data and the methods for amassing more of them: instruction, *instruere,* structuring-into. Such has a place, of course, but without a vital sense of the organic whole we don't know what that place is.

Or take the old positivist cut dividing "doing philosophy" from "doing the history of philosophy." The latter has a place within "scientific" philosophy, for it is construed as the scientific study of the past: scholarly antiquarianism with its apparatus of relevant languages and literature searches, and so on. This cut is still commonly made, and historians in the field of philosophy stand firm for the paltry degree of respectability still possible for them.

For William James this division is artificial and stultifying. As we saw, all meaning and truth are a species of goodness, and this is the fruitful building out of the past into the present and future. Meaning-making and truth are essential features of being vitally alive and centered, of fully being, and philosophy is meant to nurture and feed us ecstatic body-minds.

Professionalized philosophy has done exactly what James said in 1903 it would do: it distends and dissociates us from our moral and psychical centers as persons. Endless ill-formed and fruitless debates, for instance, over "determinism or freedom," have sapped human energies and burdened library shelves. James responds to the existential crisis that is upon us. If we would grasp the question of freedom—as many of our undergraduates want us and need us to do, afflicted as they frequently are with addictions and despair—it cannot be within some concocted framework that passes as scientific detachment and objectivity. That way we have already gone out of touch with our immediate experience of ourselves. We must pose the question in a way that doesn't beg it against freedom. In his *Talks to Teachers* ("The Will"), James argues in the fitting way, and let us touch on it again: logically and scientifically speaking—really scientifically speaking—to *wait* for evidence for *freedom* is nonsensical. *If* we are free, the first act of freedom should be to freely believe in free will!

This is the heart of what Ralph Barton Perry happily meant in his title, *In the Spirit of William James.* It's thinking charged with the spirit of adventure that refuses to be trapped in dualisms or in hypostatized abstractions or noun phrases like "the mind." That refuses to get caught in a verbalism like "the mind turning in upon itself." That escapes the self-deception of an act of reflection and analysis unaware of itself that mistakes its artifacts for building blocks of knowledge and life. I mean, of course, putative sense data, images, sensations that act like a screen that divides us from the world that formed us over millions of years.

As we saw in the earlier essays on James, his notion of pure or neutral experience is no mere academic-intellectual exercise but a vital stage of learning, knowing, and being—education. He reintroduces us to the oldest forms of religious and healing orientation within the world.

Education today must be ecological. This is not because it is fashionable to be this, but because it is physically and spiritually necessary for our lives. In 1998 a marvelous book appeared: *The Spirit of Regeneration: Andean Culture Confronting Western Notions of Development*.[10] It offers articles by Peruvian intellectuals who are returning to their Andean roots after discovering the limitations—or worse—of Western notions of development: sweeping formulae of agribusiness and international trade that ride roughshod over the local knowledge of growing, nurturing, and living that has funded itself over 10,000 years in the Andes. There is a web of life, of concrete coherence, in which everything converses with and nourishes everything else: greatly various gods, goddesses, animals, climatic regions and altitudes, seasons, stars, the sun and moon—or the color, taste, texture of soils and the two thousand plus species of potatoes that the people nourish and that nourish the people and that outnumber the pestilences or climatic anomalies that might strike any particular species. Talk of Clifford Geertz's idea of local knowledge! These Peruvian intellectuals are deprofessionalizing themselves.

I am inspired by this. Along with Ivan Illich, for another example, I think we must both deprofessionalize and de-school ourselves if we would break out of a mindless secular catechism.

Before making any proposals for restructuring the university, we should be sure that the heart of James's vision is securely in place. Otherwise the status quo perpetuates itself furtively, that is, the managing mania, what Mary Daly calls methodolatry. James's is the vision of human life as freedom, of human life as ecstatic.

In that impossible book that somehow did get written, *Varieties of Religious Experience*, James wonders what we contact in religious or mystical experience. He thinks that on its "hither side" it is our own subconscious minds (whatever that means exactly). On its "farther side"? He echoes Emerson's notion of the horizon and the beyond it entails. James can only say it is "the more." That is all that can honestly be described. To attempt to follow the flow of our feeling into this more, into its richness, depths, and shadowy surroundings, is to be free. It cannot be followed in our everyday mode of awareness for it does not present itself as an action-oriented movement. It is a kind of abandonment, a way of being that is allowing, a choice that would encompass and facilitate all further choice.

James's student, William Ernest Hocking, asserted that the original sin is the failure of awareness. The language is not too strong. For the difficulty, the failure of awareness, cannot be attacked by individuals, no matter how sharp and sincere and responsible they might be. A lack of awareness cannot be remedied on command: when awareness is lacking, we cannot know just what is missing, just what must be achieved by just what means. We face the essential finitude of human being—how we conceal the fact of concealment itself, and how we typically overlook the very possibility of our self-deceptions and our lacks.

Like Socrates, James stings us into wakefulness with respect to our tedious hungers and our mind games. He italicizes situations in which we cannot escape choice, in which opportunities will never come again, and in which not to choose is to choose. The ultimate forced option is, Will we choose to wake up?

But, again, it is not a choice to achieve an end by such and such means. It must be a kind of strange choice, a meta-choice, to be trusting and vulnerable, to be open to the unexpectable, to inarticulable possibilities of nonbeing and to unimaginable possibilities of being, and to the possibility that ends all the others, death. Only open this far can we be willing to give up stupid habits and be open to transformatively new possibilities.

James suggests that we exist most of the time in profound, stupefying self-deception, and without awareness of this viscous state, all talk of education is syllabub, flattery, and spongecake. The world is meaningful, his philosophy of pure experience teaches us, because it is experienceable in various ways. But as meaningful, as experienced and experienceable by me, the world has always had me in it! How can *I* die, *not* be!?

The good teacher and learner is always prodding us out of this deadening self-deception, this dribbling out of our lives. The prodding cannot be direct, for then we, the prodded, raise our defenses and fearfully block the dilation of consciousness into "the more." This holds the dim and dreaded real possibility (focal at some moments) that we are incredibly fragile and ephemeral, existing for a few moments within the vast ongoing universe that spawned us, generation after generation, over millions of years—existing for a few moments and then gone.

James sidles up beside us and nudges us toward awareness. His "On a Certain Blindness in Human Beings" is mainly stories—by R. L. Stephenson, W. H. Hudson, Walt Whitman, and others. As if only stories, not our desiccating Cartesian epistemologies, could put us in touch with what most needs to be known, ourselves. But in his own gnomic—better, shamanic—voice he sometimes meets us:

> When your ordinary Brooklynite or New Yorker, leading a life replete with too much luxury, or tired and careworn about his personal affairs, crosses the ferry or goes up Broadway, his fancy does not "soar away into the sunset" as did Whitman's, nor does he inwardly realize at all the indisputable fact that this world never did anywhere or at any time contain more of essential divinity, or of eternal meaning, than is embodied in the field of vision over which his eyes so carelessly pass. There is life; and there, a step away, is death.[11]

To acknowledge death, to acknowledge it in one's body, is to be freed to the preciousness of each moment of life. If we are aware, just to be is joyous. "For to miss the joy is to miss all. In the joy of the actors lies the sense of any action." James is drawing from Stephenson: "His life from without may seem but a rude mound of mud: there will be some golden chamber at the heart of it, in which he dwells delighted."

Any proposals to reorganize the university not predicated on the principle that to miss the joy is to miss all perpetuate the iron cage of bureaucracy, business as usual: finding tenure-track jobs for bright young Ph.D. students, the unreeling of technical expertise to lure approval from authorities in the professional association, all the ephemeral pleasures of the engineering mentality that has lost touch with poetical and musical sensibility, with real, troubling, human concerns, and with ecstatic transports and joys.

Professional attitudes are incarnated in, and controlled by, national academic associations, for example, The American Philosophical Association. It is a rigid pecking order that controls nearly all the prestigious jobs (in an ever-shrinking pool) and nearly all grant money, because referees for all occasions are picked from the top of the hierarchy. Those outside it are invisible. It is not too much to say they are untouchable. Each academic field, from English to physics, has its own professional association and is pretty well defined by it.

The academic world is segmented into departments-bureaus. This stifles creativity, even minimal general education. A graduate student properly professionalized in philosophy, say, will tend nearly always to miss the philosophical content in both the literary and scientific domains (although given the ruling "analytic" philosophy, which fancies itself to be scientific, there is slightly less chance of missing philosophical content and issues in the sciences).

It is hard for generally informed citizens to believe, but it is true: Figures whom they themselves probably recognize to be philosophers may not be recognized to be such by the best and the brightest Ph.D. products of the best and the brightest philosophy departments. I mean household names like R. W. Emerson and Henry Thoreau, not to mention "merely literary" figures such as Dostoyevsky or Tolstoy or Melville, or "religious figures" like Kierkegaard, or "sociologists" such as Max Weber. Preening, shameless, unabashed parochialism parading as clarity, science, and enlightenment presents a nearly incredible spectacle. Everyone suffers, most obviously students who hunger for ecstatic connectedness, the creation of meaning. Dominant analytic philosophers betray the trust the public places in them.

To miss the joy is to miss all. By joy I mean specifically the moral-ecstatic energy of the creation of meaning across received boundaries. To leave out of account this missing joy as one tries to reconstruct the university is to be caught up in flailings and fumblings and exhaustions that miss the central point, the heart of education itself: the creative eliciting and forming of self. It is idolatry shrouded in good intentions—methodolatry.

We should not proceed further without mentioning a cautionary historical fact. When the American Philosophical Association was being organized in 1901, an invitation to join (and to probably be elected president) was issued to James. He replied that he expected little to come from professionalizing what should be the patient conversation between trusted friends and colleagues. "Count me out," he replied curtly. Very soon, however, two younger philosophers—John Dewey and Josiah Royce—were elected president. James promptly changed his mind about joining, and was elected president.

Well, well, what does this prove? What we should know and remember all along: Human all too human. There is no underestimating human vanity, or the fear of being unrecognized and erased and deprived of power to resist a world in which we dimly but really apprehend ourselves to exist precariously every moment. Not even a famous Harvard professor from a famous family is immune. (James was particularly prone to jealousy with regard to accomplished younger men, as his ambivalent attitude toward his brother, the novelist and dramatist Henry Jr., amply attests. Consult Leon Edel's massive biography of Henry.[12])

I will sketch some steps we might take to reorganize the university to bring it closer to what the public thinks it is already, an educational institution. Each step presupposes a new attitude toward the University. The birthright of all humans should be the opportunity to develop each's capacities to the utmost, to experience the joy of having these capacities touched, educed, drawn out (*educare*). Just by virtue of being human, everyone has a stake in the University, an idea beautifully elaborated in Henry Rosovsky's *The University: An Owner's Manual*.[13] From the most frightened freshman to the most exalted dean, everyone's voice must contribute to the drama of what we are to make of ourselves.

Once the first seeds of a new attitude and its new expectations sprout, perhaps the first "structural" move should be to eliminate the philosophy department. All fields, pursued to their conceptual foundations, involve philosophical assumptions and commitments, however implicit. This was the original rationale for the Doctor of Philosophy degree: anyone who does any creative work in the foundations of any discipline should receive the ultimate recognition of intellectual distinction. And in fact some of the most important intellectual work in the last centuries has been done by people who would not be employed in philosophy departments. Just a few: Darwin, Freud, Jung, Einstein, Bohr, Pauli, Heisenberg, Mann, Borges. And, especially more recently, an emerging group of women, to mention a few: Elizabeth Cady Stanton, Jane Ellen Harrison, Willa Cather, Marija Gimbutas, Julia Kristeva, Luce Irigaray, Toni Morrison, Leslie Marmon Silko.

To eliminate philosophy departments would not entail eliminating the members of the department. They should be left free to associate themselves with whatever departments are closest to their interests and accomplishments, and they would, presumably, associate themselves with members whose interests are closest to theirs. In some cases, adroit administrators would be needed to find a proper home for some philosophers.

I would also suggest that each member of the university, tenured and untenured, be required to deliver a presentation every five years to the intellectual community of the university at large. Inevitably, in speaking across departmental lines, thinkers would dwell on assumptions and issues relevant to all fields, that is, on philosophical matters.

In the end, we should proceed to a completely decompartmentalized and deprofessionalized university as rapidly as we wisely can. That is, to a *university* that lives up to the literal meaning of the name: that which has a center and turns around it—the creation of meaning, the discovery and husbanding of truth, and the development of centered and expansive persons. All that would remain would be a very few general fields, defined in greatly overlapping terms, and headed by universal minds who appear now and again in the strangest places. Consider Isaiah Berlin, Albert Einstein, James Conant, Susanne Langer, or William James himself.

The present situation has reduced itself to absurdity. Yes, there is overlap today between philosophy departments and cognitive science departments, say. But this itself is eccentric, and produces grossly incomplete views of "mind," such as Steven Pinker's. Beyond this is the patently absurd: fairly recently the Leiter Report appeared, ranking analytic philosophy departments. In itself it might be considered trivial, the work of a recent Ph.D. from Michigan State, a one-man gang, so to say. But nothing exists merely in itself. The Report has had considerable impact—given the vanity and fear of human beings—and it is symptomatic of a larger reality, laughable though some might think it. Each year it ranks departments contending for the top spots. In detailed footnotes, the analytic "stars" are tracked from school to school as they fly to ever-brighter lights, or as rumors circulate that they might be contemplating a move. Or, perhaps they might not move, as a spouse might not be movable, or they might retire, and so forth. The Report reminds one of gossip columnists peddling news of Hollywood stars, or of how the moves, pranks, and peccadilloes of royalty were watched intensely and reported at the turn of the century—and still are.[14]

The Report includes the judgment that the best training in nonanalytic approaches to philosophy is, nevertheless, obtained in the best analytic departments.[15] Fatuous in the extreme, fatuous on its face, The Report nevertheless has had impact. Nothing better indicates, I think, the lack of confidence in one's own judgment, particularly analytic philosophers' lack of centeredness in their own situated, bodily, and feelingful existence, and, concomitantly, their inability to ground their evaluations in intellectual history.

But it is not only their failure, but of university personnel in positions of power. How can deans, for example, allocating funds and professorial positions to their colleges, and themselves trained very often in the "best" multiversities today, be expected to know what is happening in the various professional-academic "worlds"? Evaluations, however, must be made, and they will be—within whatever flimsy frameworks for ranking are available, and however incredibly short is the time given them to evaluate.

The slightest knowledge of intellectual history, and the barest confidence in one's own judgment, shows that the most creative advances in knowledge and appreciation occur not in "mainstream" departments, but in the foggy overlap areas between disciplines, or in areas that have not yet been mapped and given a name, but in which individuals exercise their intuition, invention, perseverance. (I think, for example, of the recent discovery by Francine Shapiro of eye-movement therapy for emotional trauma.[16])

It is time that the iron cage of academic bureaucracy be dismantled. The progress of knowledge itself requires it. Even more obviously, students' hunger for meaning, and the whole society's call for integration and council, are too urgent to allow dawdling. As Emerson prophesied would be increasingly the case, "The state of society is one in which the members have suffered amputation from the trunk, and strut about so many walking monsters—a good finger, a neck, stomach, an elbow, but never a man."[17]

William James is closer to us than is Emerson. It is his warnings—as a man of science, of common sense, and of wide and humane learning—that we should most directly heed.

I have written centrally about the degeneration of academic philosophy in the university. But this is a bellwether discipline: mandarinism and vitiation here reflect hyperspecialization, frivolousness, and flaccidness across the culture. A necessary condition for recovery is to place as much stress on rebuilding education and educators as was placed on rebuilding Japan and Germany after World War II, or now on spending billions to bail out nations that have collapsed economically. We should send a vast Peace Corps into the public schools, reward persons with compassionate hearts and good minds and the toughness of Green Berets, and give master teachers their economic and social due. We should pay the tired, weary, and demoralized—many of them tired, weary, and demoralized for good reason—to retire early. The present situation is an insult to us all.

I agree with Jim Garrison, who has written in a personal communication: "What I found in education was a world of wonderfully dedicated kindergarten through twelfth grade teachers controlled by bureaucracy, downtrodden by dead but dominant versions of technocratically applied positivism, . . . and scape-goated for their efforts in ameliorating social ills."

The notion of "social ills" should be unpacked. Both William James and John Dewey knew that science and technology must inevitably develop, but that there was much more required for a fulfilled life than they could supply. Despite all our interventions, inventions, conventions, we still belong to Nature. Despite all our clever turnings of attention and employment of technological fixes, the vast matrix of our lives is involuntary. As things are going, the malcoordination of the voluntary and the involuntary only increases.

In their somewhat different styles, both James and Dewey see that for thought to be effective it must be both pragmatic and primal. The tragic feature of Dewey's thought is that he knew that modern life had introduced dissociations on the subconscious level of minding, but his deployment of critical thought penetrates to this level only sporadically. Art can do some important knitting together here, Dewey saw. Body-work of the Alexander variety, say, can do some more. But Dewey could not supply a wholly viable alternative to ages-old myth and ritual, could not suture together science, technology, and "individual fate lore," could not reintegrate Father Sky and Mother Earth, as Black Elk would have put it.[18] Dewey quotes Matthew Arnold on contemporary persons as "wandering between two worlds, one dead, / The other powerless to be born." Perhaps the old world is not as dead as Dewey and Arnold thought, and perhaps the Socratic job of midwifery to the new world that Dewey calls for should take this question into consideration.

James's tragedy is several faceted. He saw that belief—indeed, belief beyond presently available evidence, overbelief—is essential for a sound and coherent life. But he himself had great difficulty believing. It took a tremendous effort of will to sustain himself in what he called the strenuous life, particularly as life ebbed out of him in sickness and advancing age. Some of us understand this only too well.

A reader of this essay complained that it goes way beyond what is supported by James. Since some—probably not well acquainted with James—might agree, I will add a few final words.

No. I imagine that if James could see what has happened to "education" at the end of this century he would denounce it more eloquently and damningly than I ever could. This is exactly how he responded in 1901 to the invitation to join the fledgling American Philosophical Association: "I don't foresee much good from a philosophical society. Philosophy discussion proper only succeeds between intimates who have learned how to converse by months of weary trial and failure. The philosopher is a beast dwelling in his individual burrow. Count me *out!*"[19] True, as I've noted, James joined the APA and was elected president in 1905. But his better self is evident in his initial refusal. He knew from long experience with the likes of Charles Peirce and Josiah Royce that philosophers best converse with intimates through months of weary trial and failure. This is so because we grope for meaning, and we must be able to trust others to patiently show where we are going wrong and to help us to go right. How would James react to the greatly impersonal and rushed atmosphere of philosophy today? I think he would be appalled.

There is a profound difficulty here for professionalized thought of all kinds. Professionalization sets up a vast machinery of evaluation of submitted work. It seems self-evident today that work should be blind reviewed, and by more than one person.

But probably not everyone judged to be a competent reviewer will detect very creative work the first time through it. Maybe one or two readers will reject it. And this will very probably kill it. For most editors of the "best" publications, it seems obvious that one black ball in the urn is like a fly in the ointment—"we publish only the best!"

Despite a surface show of innovation and adventure, built into most of our academic institutions today is a stupefying conservatism. It was evident to Emerson before James was born. "The American Scholar:" "[The scholar] must relinquish display and immediate fame [and in creating and discovering endure] the self-accusation . . . the frequent uncertainty and loss of time . . . the state of virtual hostility in which he seems to stand to society, especially to educated society."[20] To use a distinction made famous by Thomas Kuhn, academia on all levels tends to reward competent but conventional thought and tends to discourage revolutionary thought—what we desperately need to survive as individuals and as a species.

All this is hard to stomach for academics who, for the most part, have been rewarded for competent but conventional work. But if we want change we will have to bite the bullet, maybe swallow it. I will close with the most notorious case of discrimination against regenerative and revolutionary thought I know of: the persecution and exclusion of C. S. Peirce, probably the most brilliant mind (along with Jefferson) that the United States has produced. Good biographies have finally appeared to the point at which only a few of the most salient facts need be recounted: the vengeful pursuit of Peirce over forty years by the president of Harvard, Charles Eliot; his betrayal by the now nearly forgotten astronomer Simon Newcomb (who, among other things, scuttled Peirce's application for a desperately needed Smithsonian fellowship); his dismissal as assistant professor at Johns Hopkins on vague grounds of impropriety.

I'll close with lines from the obituary of Peirce by Joseph Jastrow, ninth president of the American Psychological Association (!). I wish it could serve as an obituary for education as we know it.

It cannot but remain a sad reflection upon the organization of our academic interest that we find it difficult, or make it so, to provide places for exceptional men within the academic fold. Politically as educationally, we prefer the safe men to the brilliant men, and exact a versatile mediocrity of qualities that make the individual organizable.... Certainly it remains true for all times that no more effective stimulus to promising young minds can be found than to give them the opportunity of contact with master minds in action. The service that a small group of such men can perform is too fine, too imponderable, to be measured; and likewise too intangible to impress its value upon the judgment of those with whom these issues commonly lie.[21]

Notes

1. "The Phd Octopus," *Essays, Comments, and Reviews, The Works of William James* (Cambridge Mass.: Harvard University Press, 1987), 69. The essay is included in the main in my anthology, *The Essential Writings of William James* (Albany: State University of New York Press, 1984).

2. These quotations from Kierkegaard, Nietzsche, Dostoevsky are, respectively, *Journals* (February 7, 1846); "Schopenhauer as Educator" (in *Untimely Meditations*); *Crime and Punishment* (from the mouth of Svidrigailov, part 5, sec. 5), and, of course, *The Underground Man* (the first pages). I trust the reader will pardon me for not giving more detailed annotation. These are famous books, each in a number of editions. But in an article of this bent, to give detailed annotation? These writers would have loved the irony: an essay encumbered with heavy scholarly apparatus critical of scholarly inertia and apparatus!

3. See, for example, *From Max Weber: Essays in Sociology* (New York: Oxford University Press, 1946), sec. VIII, "Bureaucracy."

4. This justly famous vow can be found in many sources, for example, H. A. Howard and D. L. McGrath, *War Chief Joseph* (Lincoln: University of Nebraska Press, 1964 [1941]), 282.

5. See my *The Moral Collapse of the University: Professionalism, Purity, Alienation* (Albany: State University of New York Press, 1990), esp. 37 ff.

6. Recently certain anthropologists have exhibited greater sensitivity to their research "subjects." But even if culturally disruptive trade goods—gifts to elicit information from informants—are discontinued, the very act of studying and objectifying cultures is alienating for them (and also for the Westerners doing the studying). However, given the ever-encroaching commercial interests of North Atlantic culture, there is little even the best-intentioned anthropologists can do to protect indigenous peoples.

7. See my *Wild Hunger: The Primal Roots of Modern Addiction*, (Lanham, Md., and New York: Rowman & Littlefield, 1998), indexed under "scientism."

8. (New York: Norton, 1997), 534–37. I believe music is a primal adaptation. When normal body-selves respond to the "outer" environment, or take initiatives with respect to it, the body

resounds fittingly within itself. Music is feed-out-feedback that conducts, confirms, orients body-self—underwrites its identity through time. It has done this from time immemorial. Pinker's dualistic talk about "the mind" renders him incapable of grasping how music is primally adaptive, a motor of evolution: he generates a pseudo-problem of identity. As thinkers, we are left not fully engaged with our bodies, not fully engaged with our capacities for ecstatic life. This furthers contemporary alienation and disintegration of identity. How ironical for an evolutionary approach to self! Despite some interesting science, the overall effect of Pinker's work is scientism. It is all the more significant that Pinker can't find a place for music, when the latest work in physics—superstring theory—is a kind of neo-Pythagorean envisioning of the interweaving of music, mathematics, and physics (see Brian Greene, *The Elegant Universe: Superstrings, Hidden Dimensions, and the Quest for the Ultimate Theory* [New York: Vintage Books, 2000]).

9. See James, "On a Certain Blindness in Human Beings," *Talks to Teachers on Psychology and to Students on Some of Life's Ideals* (Cambridge, Mass.: Harvard University Press, 1983).

10. Edited and introduced by Frederique Apffel-Marglin (London and New York: Zed Books).

11. *Talks to Teachers on Psychology and to Students on Some of Life's Ideals*, 252. Also to be found in my anthology, cited note 1 above. *Talks to Teachers on Psychology and to Students on Some of Life's Ideals* (Cambridge, Mass.: Harvard University Press, 1983), 144.

12. *Henry James: The Conquest of London, The Middle Years, The Treacherous Years*, 3 vols. (New York: Avon Books, 1976). A strand through these volumes traces the brothers' relationship.

13. New York: Norton, 1991.

14. A frothy article by Christopher Shea details the controversy that has finally arisen over the report, in *Linguafranca: The Review of Academic Life* (July–August 1999). My opinion of the report is rendered exactly by Shea: "A fatuous piece of bullshit."

15. Nonanalytic approaches are lumped under the heading, Continental. This apparently exhaustive set of alternatives completely occludes the whole tradition of American philosophy—a third alternative—in other words, what concerns the present book.

16. Francine Shapiro with Margot Silk Forrest, *EMDR: Eye Movement Desensitization and Reprocessing* (New York: Basic Books, 1997).

17. "The American Scholar," in *R. W. Emerson, Selected Essays*, ed. Larzar Ziff (New York: Penguin Books, 1982), 84.

18. See Dewey's *The Problems of Men* (1946), especially the articles on William James (where Dewey uses the phrase "individual fate lore") and the Introduction. The Introduction to *The Problems of Men* is found in the critical edition, *John Dewey, The Late Works, 1925–1953* (Carbondale: Southern Illinois University Press, 1989), 15:154. Dewey contrasts "the secular" to "the theological" and "the supernatural." But there is a meaning of "religion" that falls into neither camp, and it is just this meaning that is relevant for understanding the native American, Black Elk, as well as Thoreau, Emerson, and James. "The Philosophy of William James" (written originally as a review in 1937) can (with effort) be found in the critical edition, *John Dewey, the Late Works, 1925–1953* (Carbondale: Southern Illinois University Press, 1935–37), 11:464–78. I thank John McDermott for help in finding my way in the critical editions of James and Dewey. (The critical edition of James does not include a general index to the series; the Dewey does, but in listing works chronologically it breaks up materials included together in previous editions.)

19. See my *The Moral Collapse of the University*, 106–7.

20. Again, in *R. W. Emerson, Selected Essays*, 95–96, and quoted in my *The Moral Collapse of the University*, 88.

21. Quoted in K. L. Ketner, *His Glassy Essence: An Autobiography of Charles Sanders Peirce* (Nashville: Vanderbilt University Press, 1998), 29.

13

Charles Peirce on the Pre-Rational Ground of Reason

I should not be quite silent as to this magnificent prologue to the, as yet, unknown drama. Yet I, like others, have little to say where the spectacle is, for once, great enough to fill the whole life, and supersede thought, giving us only its own presence.
—Margaret Fuller at Niagara Falls, June 10, 1843

Probably many have noticed what may appear to be a contradiction in Charles Peirce's early "Some Consequences of Four Incapacities." The heading for the fourth incapacity reads: "We have no conception of the absolutely incognizable." Yet just a few pages later we find "the Immediate (and therefore in itself unsusceptible of mediation—the Unanalyzable, the Inexplicable, the Unintellectual) runs in a continuous stream through our lives."[1]

But a little digging reveals that this is not a contradiction. Rather, distinctions are being made that open up a vast vista of phenomena. Already Peirce clues us: We have no *conception* of the absolutely incognizable. Might there be ways of being in touch with the world that are nonconceptual? As it turns out, there are. And he clues us to how fundamental they are in his capitalizing of the words, Unanalyzable, Inexplicable, Unintellectual. Is he suggesting these have portentous importance, perhaps mythic importance, as in "unqualifiedly powerful and valuable"? I think this may be so, but let us wait a bit.

Peirce the scientist is greatly concerned with concepts. In his famous elucidation of meaning in "How to Make our Ideas Clear," he repeatedly uses "concept" and "conception." Roughly: the sum total of our conception of anything is the sum total of our conception of its effects or consequences for our experience. Without clearly defined concepts, science cannot do its work. Nor can it do it without clearly defined hypotheses. And the very essence, purpose, of hypotheses is to explain. So to say that as scientific thinkers we have formed a hypothesis about an inexplicable reality is to contradict ourselves—it is absurd. It is to say this: We hypothesize that A, B, C are the causes of . . . we know not what.

But Peirce was not only a scientist and logician but also a philosopher and a phenomenologist—and, indeed, a religiously inclined thinker. He was a keen critic (but also appreciator) of Kant's idea of the unknowable thing-in-itself: To claim to know there's an unknowable is absurd *if* we mean we claim to know *what* the unknowable *what* is—if we claim to have a concept of it. But Peirce the phenomenologist and philosopher knew (as did William James) that we primally encounter realities that resist or support us, but that we can only denominate *thats*. They may—or may not—be ready to become all kinds of *whats*, but in the primal encounter they are *thats only*.

But not unimportantly! Again, Peirce the scientist-logician is also the phenomenologist-philosopher. The vagueness of something is not a reason to try to precise it into clarity, and failing to do this, to jettison it. No, no! Peirce discovers the ineliminably vague, the pre-rational, and discovers that *that* is the foundation, matrix, orientation of our existence. The logician encounters the limits of logic, and of reason in general; as philosopher he builds on ground beyond them.

Story has it that Peirce read his copy of Kant's *The Critique of Pure Reason* so many times that it disintegrated (and it was not a paperback). It helps to remember this. In an oft-quoted comment, Kant tells us that reading Hume awakened him—rudely it must have been—from his dogmatic slumbers. The dogmatism was the Leibnizian-Wolffian rationalism that stressed the principle of sufficient reason: very roughly, there's a reason for everything, and humans' powers of reason must discern it. An abyss looks out at us through Hume's skepticism concerning our ability to know fundamentals such as causation and the nature of self.

Well into middle age, and no longer content to be a Newtonian astrophysicist, Kant girded up his loins to try to preserve some sanity, some place for civilized life in the face of death, and God only knows what. His strategy for regrounding reason was both ingenious and, it might appear, desperate: *Begrunden ist begrenzen*—to ground is to limit. Briefly: it's absurd to claim to know that we cannot know anything, and, besides it's evident that we do know some things—Euclid's and Newton's stellar achievements attest to this. So, given that knowledge is actual, the question becomes How is it possible? Again briefly, Conceptions are essential for knowledge, and they are meaningful just because each is a distinctive weaving within sensuous experiencing of the world. Our concepts apply because they apply to this sense experience. And the corollary: our concepts apply *only* to our sense experience (aided or unaided senses). Reason is grounded in the very act of being limited.

Peirce is deeply impressed by this, as are many of us. But he knew that Kant's idea of sense experience is badly flawed. It owes far too much to Hume and the whole Cartesian-Lockian tradition that stems from the seventeenth-century mechanistic ideal of building up wholes out of simples, building blocks. So their project becomes: build up "the mind" out of the elements that compose it—discrete, atomic sensations, images, representations, etc. But these elements don't exist; they can't be made evident in even a halfway-unbiased inspection. The Cartesian-Lockian-Humian tradition commits itself to a view of reality—either physical or mental reality or a combination of both—before grasping the meaning of what it's asserting. Their phenomenology is hopelessly tainted. There are no mental elements or building blocks evident on the primal level of immediate involvement in the world. Such "elements" are the by-products of an analysis that forgets itself, that's been smuggled into the account unwittingly.

This is not a mere scholarly flaw—it's at the farthest remove from that. The Cartesian-empiricist tradition conceives of "mind" as some "inner domain" that has "contents." Since sensations *are* felt to be in us, it is they that become paradigmatic for "the mental." But then our account of emotions and moods, and indeed of thinking, becomes an account of something internal: it gets hopelessly warped. For we immediately experience this vast remainder of minding as *of* or *about* the world around us. That is, our pre-reflective integrity as worldly beings is destroyed, our intimate participation in the world obscured. The world appears to be something "out there": a feeling of alienation and loneliness—and ego-centrism—is inevitable. The door is wide open to nihilism.

Hence the utterly crucial role that Peirce's phenomenology plays in his thought as a whole—phenomenology, what he assigns as the first business of philosophy (regardless of terminological variants, James, Dewey, Hocking, and Bugbee follow suit). Once this is seen, we can easily detect how Peirce appropriates Kant, supersedes him, and opens the way for the next generation of philosophers, e.g., for Edmund Husserl. Peirce's way of grounding reason by limiting it is at least as ingenious as Kant's, and much more fruitful for us today, I believe.

Note well Peirce's incredibly brilliant and creative article, "Critical Commonsensism."[2] He touches base with the Scottish commonsensists—for example, Thomas Reid and Dugald Stewart—those thinkers who reacted at the time so gallantly against the nihilism implicit in Descartes and Locke and fairly explicit in Hume. They knew there were beliefs we cannot live without, hence cannot think without, so why pretend to doubt them?

But Peirce is a *critical* commonsensist. That is, he does not precede Kant; he appears after that "critical" philosopher's momentous career. And Peirce is critical in another sense. He spied things across the divide of the nineteenth and twentieth centuries that were so far ahead of most of his contemporaries that they had no idea what he was talking about. I mean he caught sight of some lineaments of relativity theory, gained a glimpse of indeterminacy, which was to appear in quantum theory, and he saw as well the corrosive affect of dividing mind from body, thinking from emotion, facts from values. He saw the specter of nihilism—now more boldly apparent than it could ever have appeared to Kant—and it shuddered and shook in his own person in a way that had to be massively counteracted by the chastened power of his intellect and his character.

That is, Peirce knew that we cannot just repeat the line taken by the Scottish commonsensists. We cannot simply affirm that our selves are substances and that we just know what causation is. We've learned too much through science. His moves are remarkable. Yes, there are fundamental background beliefs that ground, orient, and stabilize us, and essential to them is their very vagueness. And we can't just decide to doubt them all, as did Descartes, who gives us only "paper doubts." If we would effectively doubt some of the beliefs, we must hold the remainder constant; otherwise there is no stable platform, so to speak, upon which to stand and orient ourselves and focus on what is to be doubted. We can no more decide to doubt all our beliefs than we can decide to surprise ourselves.

Nevertheless, as logicians and scientists we can make each belief more precise—so it would seem—and when we do so each ceases to be indubitable in the sense of habitually undoubted; each becomes dubitable. So the inference seems irresistible to the logical mind: why not doubt them one or two at a time until we've doubted them all? After all, the argument seems overwhelming, necessarily true: If we doubt each belief in a set, we doubt them all. Not to believe the conclusion is to contradict ourselves.

But Peirce finds no simple set of beliefs that he can doubt one or two at a time until he has exhausted the set. And in a momentous move he writes that contradictions at this point become meaningless. I quote the pivotal lines in "Critical Common-sensism":

> The Critical Common-sensist's personal experience is that a suitable line of reflection, accompanied by imaginary experimentation, always excites doubt of any very broad proposition if it is defined with precision. Yet there are beliefs of which such a critical sifting leaves a certain vague residuum unaffected. . . . He quite acknowledges that what has been indubitable one day has often been proved on the morrow to be false. He grants the precis proposition that it may be so with any of the beliefs he holds. He really cannot admit that it may be so with all of them; but here he loses himself in vague unmeaning contradictions. [295, 297]

For a logician to regard contradictions as "unmeaning" is to give away the store, isn't it? But what he gets is something beyond logic! Here Peirce—logician, phenomenologist, philosopher—has made an astonishing move. Through "imaginary experimentation" and "critical sifting" he has pushed to the limits of logic and science, and finds that only by looking beyond these limits can he ground logic and science and also ground—intellectually—our own existence. At this point, contradictions become "meaningless." This is his version of the Kantian dictum: To ground is to limit. He is saying, I think, that the sense of the world's presence is the ineliminable condition of all life and thought. We cannot reduce this to a neat set of beliefs. He is saying—following Margaret Fuller at Niagara—that he has little to say "where the spectacle is, for once, great enough to fill the whole life, and supersede thought, giving us only its own presence."

World as presence! There are depths to be explored here.

Phenomenologists try to uncover what is hidden and presupposed in everyday experiencing. Things can be hidden in two senses of that term: (1) As what is so momentary and fleeting, flitting, that it can only be touched on perhaps but not grasped decisively as *what* it is; and (2) As that which is present in every moment—present as the ever-present conditions of all possible experience—and is so constant and contrastless as to be detectable with only the greatest difficulty. We can however find some halting "what" for it—the sense of the world's presence and of ourselves as tiny but vital members of it. This, in rough outline, is Peirce's version of Kant's transcendental investigation of the possibility of any experience.

Let us expand on this. "The Immediate (and therefore in itself unsusceptible of mediation—Unanalyzable, the Inexplicable, the Unintellectual)" that "runs in a continuous stream through our lives" can be taken to mean two things. First—and again—it can mean the immediate, flowing, sensuous core of our continuity and identity—a too fleeting and immediate *that* to be mediated by any concepts, any *whats*—only hinted at (or grasped to some extent in art): I mean the momentum of our experiencing bodies uncoiling in time, lived from within, encountering the turbulence of the unexpected and the chaotic, but that we must trust without needing to specify our need.

And the second, overarching meaning of "hidden" is, to further elaborate, that which is present in every moment as the constant and contrastless conditions for the possibility of any experience of world, and of any things in the world. These are Peirce's three categories: firstness—the possibilities of sheer sensuous qualities; secondness—the shock of perhaps chance encounters between actual existing things; thirdness—the weaving together of our experiencing through reasoning and sign action on various levels (to the extent that it is woven together). The categories are irreducible, not further explicable modes of being, because, he finds, they are presupposed in describing and explaining anything in, or about, the World as presence, as engulfing phenomenon (presupposed if for no other reason than there are three irreducible forms of judgment—monadic, dyadic, triadic). They are Inexplicable in the sense that they cannot be further explained, only shown to be inherent in all phenomena (including what's hidden in the first sense—insofar as we can detect it).[3] They are Immediate, in the sense that they cannot be shown to be the product of any mediation. And they are, in that sense, Unintellectual. Finally, they are more basic than are conceptions, for conceptions we can formulate and reformulate given our evolving needs, interests, discoveries; and in formulating and reformulating them we must presuppose the three categories.

The categories themselves are disclosed only through his patient and searching phenomenology. Again, we find we must assume them if we'd experience and know anything, e.g., about the brain and nervous system "the real effective force behind consciousness" that "brings about" that "mediation, which is the continuity" of the "continuous stream" of consciousness, "the sum total" of it. [237] (For more on categories, see Chapter 11.)

We may not be substances, but we *are*, we *be*, and with some luck, grit, passion, trust, and intelligence we can endure for a while and grow in a world that itself grows in continuity, generativity, regenerativity (see Peirce's "Evolutionary Love"). We can learn to love being part of it for a short time, despite the knocks, and the inevitable—death. As Peirce puts it, we may doubt just what the order of Nature is, but can we doubt that there is *some* order? Without some order we can't even effectively doubt. It must be that this adventure of minding our adventure is what kept Peirce going through decades of illness, poverty, advancing age, and persecution.

As we close we catch glimpses of the consequences of Peirce's thought: both on his own late, explicitly religious writings, and on the work of others. Also his resonances with what was "in the air." I think first of Edmund Husserl, with whose work Peirce resonates. Peirce's "imaginary experimentation" that leaves a residuum of belief unaffected is right in line with Husserl's "free variations" on phenomena, the purpose of which are to find what can't be varied without the phenomenon itself exploding. What is discovered is the invariable, what is essential to the phenomenon, its "essence." To be mentioned also is the distinction Husserl draws between the *Weltlich* (World) and the *Innerweltlich* (things within the world). The presence of the world is not translatable into a set of beliefs about it. We aren't sitting in a cozy catbird seat inspecting the world "out there"!

Here I think Peirce has the edge: he would never speak, as did Husserl at one point, of the domain of absolute consciousness which nothing can enter, nor of things as essences as correlates of this consciousness. The irreducible residuum for Peirce—World or Order of Nature—is always vague, evolving, open-ended, somewhat chaotic, and cannot be bound by the law of non-contradiction. (Which anticipates Niels Bohr's reported remark, "The opposite of one profound truth may be another profound truth.")

It is, of course, with William James that Peirce exhibits the most profound affinity.[4] Much of this affinity between them can be attributed to the much more precocious Peirce in his influence on James.

But some influence went the other way too. In an almost miraculous way the two thinkers complemented each other: where one was somewhat weak the other was strong. For example, James's ability to grasp the phenomenology of body-self—in, say, religious experience—complements Peirce's somewhat abstract and schematic idea of the self as an evolving idea, a moving nexus of sign-relations.[5] It is James, I think, who best "cashes" in terms of concrete experience Peirce's great idea of the vague residuum of belief that remains unaffected by our "imaginary experimentations" and variations.

James's *The Varieties of Religious Experience* was based on hundreds of actual accounts gathered by E. D. Starbuck. But James's book is best construed as a set of free variations on religious experiences, with the end of discovering the invariable residuum in all, or nearly all, of them. In a remarkable passage that fleshes out Peirce, parallels indigenous insight, leads into later American thinkers, and anticipates key elements in Whitehead, Jaspers, Heidegger, and Merleau-Ponty, James writes,

> Religion, whatever it is, is a man's total reaction upon life, so why not say that any total reaction upon life is a religion? Total reactions are different from casual reactions, and total attitudes are different from usual or professional attitudes. To get at them you must go behind the foreground of existence and reach down to that curious sense of the whole residual cosmos as an everlasting presence, intimate or alien, terrible or amusing, lovable or odious, which in some degree every one possesses. This sense of the world's presence, appealing as it does to our peculiar individual temperament, makes us either strenuous or careless, devout or blasphemous, gloomy or exultant, about life at large; and our reaction, involuntary and inarticulate and often half unconscious as it is, is the completest of all our answers to the question, "What is the character of the universe in which we dwell?"[6]

The religious experience is an involvement of the whole self in the whole cosmos residual in our experience, that is, it occurs behind the foreground of existence. By foreground is meant those things *in* the world that, to various extents, capture our attention in workaday life, particularly today. Not world as world-whole—its effulgent presence superseding thought and filling the whole life.

By this revealing move James casts a wide net over religious experiences, here and there, now and then. All the way from Black Elk, say, the Native American shaman and thinker to, yes, Charles Peirce, logician and scientist. Black Elk speaks of his visions as experiences of "the world behind this one."[7] The whole context of his speech shows that he does not mean a domain beyond Nature, but a depth of Nature itself which is accessible to us in certain of our states and attitudes within the Whole.

Peirce agrees, essentially. In "The Concept of God" he writes that he does not attribute existence to God, for existence he takes to mean, "to react with the other like things in the environment" (an irreducible element of secondness). Deity for Peirce is unique, for, after all, it must pertain to the World-whole as it involves everything in itself. Which includes ourselves as organisms evolving within the evolving Whole.

Surrounding, grounding, matrixing all reasoning is instinct, and however vague and ramifying may be its roots, it is—unless vitiated or poisoned—extraordinarily binding as well as releasing, constraining as well as probing and searching, extraordinarily undergirding and powerful. Hypothesis formation is the development of the instinct of guessing, an instinct without which the species would not have survived. We guess well when we take initiatives, of course, but in taking them allow the evolving movements of the world to lure us lovingly. That is, we belong in a world that ever more tends to integrate and develop itself within contexts in which chance plays a role, which means spontaneity. Perhaps this should be capitalized, Spontaneity, because all that is going on around and through us we can never know. We can only trust it as the unqualifiedly powerful, orienting, inspiriting. It is of mythic proportions—to use words demeaned in our culture today.

For Peirce the pragmaticist the question, Is Deity real? amounts to the question Is science as Peirce conceives it—in all its amplitude and in all its limitations—real? Both questions forecast identical consequences, and depend for their answers on whether these consequences occur. The question about science can be further unpacked:

> Whether the one lesson of Gautama Boodha, Confucius, Socrates, and all who from any point of view have had their ways of conduct determined by meditation upon the physico-psychical universe, be only their arbitrary notion or be the Truth behind the appearances which the frivolous man does not think of; and whether the superhuman courage which such contemplation has conferred upon priests who go to pass their lives with lepers and refuse all offers of rescue is mere silly fanaticism, the passion of a baby, or whether it is strength derived from the power of truth. Now the only guide to the answer to this question lies in the power of the passion of love, which more or less overmasters every agnostic scientist, and everybody who seriously and deeply considers the universe. But whatever there may be of argument in all this is as nothing, the merest nothing, in comparison to its force as an appeal to one's own instinct, which is to argument what substance is to shadow, what bed-rock is to the built foundations of a cathedral. [377]

Both science and logic in the broadest senses are, for Peirce, the use of any and all signs in any responsible way. All one's sign use presupposes some other being—actual or virtual—to whom the signs would be intelligible. These patterns of intelligibility don't depend on any actual, particular persons. They trail off and rest in the vastness of the pre-rational—or supra-rational?—cosmos. The universe has been in the process of interpreting itself for ages—through humans, other animals, and we know not what others. Peirce believes that the intelligible universe, opening out alluringly and bracingly before us, is inexhaustible and creative possibility, and that this is identical with God.

Peirce continues, pounding home the point that God is not a matter for argument; for wittingly or unwittingly, we are constantly presupposing God. "No: as to God open your eyes—and your heart, which is also a perceptive organ—and you see." Which recalls Emerson's remark that few persons really see the sun, for they see only with their eyes, not also with their hearts.

Peirce revels in the ever-burgeoning presence of the world in first person experiencing. God is this enrapturing world itself, as inescapable for Peirce at home in his first-person experiencing as it was for Emerson—who wrote in "Brahma," that is, wrote about the ultimate reality:

When me they fly, I am the wings

and in "The Sphinx":

Of thine eye I am eyebeam[8]

This trust, this experience of belonging within the world's presence, can fill the whole life, as Fuller put it. It both supersedes and matrixes thought and reason. Peirce remarks somewhere that no reason can be given for being reasonable. The very best we could say is that when and where reasoning has worked to further our needs and interests—insofar as we have discerned them—it has worked. We are incurably finite and fallible, both our weakness and—when acknowledged—our strength. For our knowledge and our lives are grounded in our limits. We can never be more than provisionally or practically certain of anything, because even if hypothesis H predicts events 1, 2, 3, and these occur, there may be another hypothesis not yet imagined which predicts these events and others which H does not predict. If found, this other hypothesis would expose H's limitations. In predicting the events it does, H tends to prevent us from imagining other hypotheses. But the ironical possibility—or probability—of better but unknown hypotheses can be acknowledged.

So, again, the very best we can say is that when and where reasoning has worked to further our needs and interests—insofar as we have discerned them—it has worked. But reason can also look out on what limits and grounds it, the pre-rational. Acknowledging this domain, it is also working, but in a chastened, allowing, deferential way. As indigenous peoples know, our kinship with the world is more than we can say, and makes possible what we can say. Kant said that he limited reason to make room for faith. Peirce has his own version of this insight.

Notes

1. "Some Consequences of Four Incapacities" was first published in *The Journal of Speculative Philosophy*, 1868. It can be found in the *Collected Papers of Charles Sanders Peirce*, vols 1–6, ed. Charles Hartshorne and Paul Weiss; vols. 7–8 ed. Arthur W. Burks (Cambridge: Harvard University Press, 1931–58. These references are typically noted "CP" with volume number, followed by paragraph number or numbers, divided by a period. Page references then follow. The materials used in my essay are, thus, 5.264–8, 280–317. One of the best and most easily accessible collections of Peirce's scattered writings has been assembled by the estimable philosopher Justus Buchler, *Philosophical Writings of Peirce* (New York: Dover Books, 1955). My page references will be to this volume, and will be given in brackets, in this case they are [230, 236]. We owe much to Buchler for this fine collecting of Peirce's often scattered remarks, particularly in the case of what Buchler places under the heading "Phenomenology." Peirce also used the quirky word *phaneroscopy*. Consult as well Richard Robin's *Annotated Catalogue of the Papers of Charles Peirce* (Amherst: The University of Massachusetts Press, 1967). See the index under "phenomenology" and "phaneroscopy." The Margaret Fuller quote is from the first paragraph of her *Summer on the Lakes*, to be found, for example, in Jeffrey Steele's *The Essential Writings of Margaret Fuller* (New Brunswick, N.J.: Rutgers University Press, 1995).

2. Under the rubric of "Critical Common-Sensism" can be included, CP 5.438–46, 453, 457; 5.505–8, 511–16, 523–25. Again, I benefit from Buchler's scholarship and patience and use page numbers from his volume.

3. See Buchler's painstaking arrangement of Peirce's "Synechism" [354]: "The synechist cannot deny that there is an element of the inexplicable and ultimate, because it is directly forced upon him; nor does he abstain from generalizing from this experience. True generality is . . . nothing but a rudimentary form of true continuity." See CP 6.169–73; 1.170, 171–75; 1.409; 6.101.

4. Though Peirce often became impatient with what he took to be James's inattention to concepts, and to the need in science—and to some extent in metaphysics—to discover law-like regularities in Nature, the universals, the long runs in things. James, Peirce thought, was tainted with nominalism, was too much fixed on one's own individual destiny.

5. For a much fuller account of Peirce on the self, see Vincent Colapietro, *Peirce's Approach to the Self* (Albany, N.Y.: SUNY Press, 1989).

6. The first section of James's strange and wonderful book, "Circumscription of the Topic," excerpted in my anthology, *William James: The Essential Writings* (Albany, N.Y.: SUNY Press, 1984 [1971]), 226. Critical edition, *The Works of William James, The Varieties of Religious Experience* (Cambridge: Harvard University Press, 1985), 36–37.

7. John Neihardt, *Black Elk Speaks* (Lincoln: University of Nebraska Press, 1988 [1932]), 85.

8. This is a line quoted by Peirce in "Phenomenology" [83]. CP 1.306–11. For the crucial influence of Emerson on Peirce, see Kenneth L. Ketner, *His Glassy Essence: An Autobiography of Charles Sanders Peirce* (Nashville: Vanderbilt University Press, 1998), 85–86.

Shamanism, Love, Regeneration

How do you know but ev'ry bird that cuts the airy way,
Is an immense world of delight, clos'd by your senses five?
—William Blake

In delighted regard Blake opens to the bird, flows with it, is buoyed by it. He opens ecstatically to its world of delight.

Ecstasy withers if Blake regards the classic five senses—his sight, hearing, touch, taste, smell—as merely inner sensations stimulated by five sorts of exteroceptor organs located on his body's surface. Trying to get to inner experience by objectifying the body is self-defeating. It is to detach in one stroke from the bird and from one's own surging, continuous, spiritual life.

In the previous essay we saw detachment's ill effects in the work of Steven Pinker: he found music to be anomalous. Music, that which augments, intensifies, clarifies our regenerative coursings, rhythmic modulations, ecstatic phrasings. That which is vividly adaptive, that which we experience when we live in the bird's life.

To detach from the bird is not to move freely on the earth and not to be open to the sky. Body-self takes in thought a position outside itself— objectifies itself in automatic abstraction and perverse ecstasy. Fixing on its exterior, the outer sense organs, body-self detaches itself from its other sense modalities, particularly the empathic viscera.

But this means it no longer incorporates in itself the bird's phrasings, coursings in space-time, the rhythmic beatings of its wings; it sees only the surfaces of a moving object in space. It tends to fill its emptiness with repeated ephemeral sensations, addictive fillers. Or with tedious but reliable mannerisms.

Two melancholy Danes, Hamlet and Kierkegaard, warn of being "sicklied o'er with the pale caste of thought." Kierkegaard speaks of the lunatic postulate: to abstract automatically from one's own immediate involvement and then to forget what one's done. To reduce one's self to an object in geometrical space that merely observes the moving surfaces of other objects is pathetic. One fails oneself at the heart of oneself, and other things at the heart of themselves.

This is a particularly modern sickness of detachment and loneliness, a malady that drives many to counselors or drugs. We even hear of what was unheard of a few years ago: the attempt—even by some of European lineage— to revive shamanism, the most ancient methods to heal when we go out of touch with the regenerative cycles of wilderness Nature in which we were formed.

With all our apparent prosperity and power, we are caught in a crisis of fundamentals. This leaves a huge opening for feminist critiques of the whole masculinist Western tradition. These aim to expose the dynamic that produces weird combinations of power and powerlessness, control and loss of control, efficient organization, startling communication, debilitating spiritual impoverishment and loneliness.

In a word, feminists locate the problem in the anxious attempt to prove that the male body is self-standing, almost self-sufficient, that it no longer needs mother and the regenerative systems of Mother Nature. That is, the male body objectifies and fixes itself as the fundamental unit, the model *individuum,* the template from which all of reality can be judged—calculated and manipulated as combinations of such units.

Grandly detached, the male body does not fear objectification and manipulation. The model object, it is safe, or so it thinks. Whatever longing for intimate participation and reciprocity, for a community of fellow subjects, it might feel—this can be safely repressed by its power and control. So it thinks.

Among the oldest images for grasping the regenerative earth are male and female divinities. These incite basal loops of creative and re-creative energies.

Specific dynamics of male and of female energies, and of the male/female relationship, mark a whole culture. Frequently found are Mother Earth/Father Sky, or Father Sun/Mother Moon. Although in ancient Egypt, for example, it is Mother Sky, Nut, and from early times in Japan, Mother Sun, Amaterasu.

In any case, the more ancient the source, the greater the tendency to regard the genders as complementary, and to allot them equality of power. The very ancient Chinese Nature religion, Taoism, depicts swirling Yin and Yang in dynamical interfusion and complementarity. And with respect to the most ancient healing traditions, a shaman is as apt to be a woman as a man. The near-violent reapportionment of power between men and women in North Atlantic culture today signals an attempt by the corporate body to rebalance, recalibrate, resynchronize itself.

In "Ways of Knowing" (Chapter 10), we saw how Western science is brilliant and grandly revelatory on one level, but on the human level of personal and interpersonal relationships—on its shadow side—it is constricting. Nowhere does this squinting mania to control show itself more plainly than in the eighteenth- and nineteenth-century exclusion of women from legal protections and civic opportunities. Scientific and technological constrictions coupled with theological animus pen women up. They are little more than their husbands' or fathers' property.

The masculinist Western bias collides with many women's aspirations in mid-nineteenth-century United States, and collides as well with traditional indigenous championing of the complementarity of the sexes.[1] Perhaps no other time or place of Western contact with the rest of the world better reveals how the world seems to be like an organism in some ways: thrown off balance it attempts to right itself (recall the speculations of James, Fechner, also James Lovelock's gaia hypothesis, and Black Elk's hoping against hope that The Great Tree of the World was not completely dead and could somehow bloom again).

The year 1848 fairly bristles with what it dates: social-democratic revolutions in Europe. Much less well known, nearly eclipsed by male-dominated history and journalism, is the first women's rights convention of that year held in Seneca Falls, New York, organized by Lucretia Mott and Elizabeth Cady Stanton. Nobody at that time could have foretold its immensely far-reaching effects; even today we are still trying to keep up with them and to predict what will happen. The feminist revolution interdigitates with the irruption of ecological indigenous consciousness, and prompts nothing less than a re-evaluation of what used to be called man's place in the cosmos.

The greatly perceptive and irrepressible Stanton noted that without the example of the Iroquois six nations living near her home at Seneca Falls, she would never have got the idea of a women's movement. The oppression she and Mott and others felt was very real: women could count on no legal protection for property, for the custody of their own children, for the protection of their bodies from abusive husbands or fathers. Of course they could not vote.

But it was the sight of indigenous women of the six Iroquois nations enjoying civil rights and powers that was the spark needed to touch off the rebellion. These women could, for example, veto a candidate for chief, withdraw their support from a war and typically stop it—as this withdrawal would be an ill omen—and inherit goods and will them in turn. Some of the native groups were both matrilineal and matrilocal. Women had their own mysteries and ceremonies. Stanton wrote:

> The women were the great power among the clan, as everywhere else. They did not hesitate, when occasion required, "to knock off the horns," as it was technically called, from the head of a chief and send him back to the ranks of the warriors. The original nomination of the chiefs also always rested with the women.[2]

If it were only for the women's movement, the confluence of European thought and ways with the indigenous world would strongly mark the uniqueness of American philosophical thought—primal and pragmatic.

On the forefront of feminist critique today, moving to the center of the issue, is Luce Irigaray, most emphatically in *The Sex Which Is Not One*.[3] As powerfully as anyone, she builds implicitly on pragmatists' critiques of oppositional dualisms, and their championing of continuity between different emphases in the whole. She prompts us to reengage with primal sources and resources of a dynamical community. She also suggests certain features of our own century's quantum mechanics, speculations that close this essay.

Irigaray does not deny that each of us is an individual in some fundamental sense. Without a firm sense of it, we fuse with anything we meet, imitate whatever comes close [209–10]. But she denies that this fundamental sense stems from an initial abstraction from the body that objectifies it and represents it "out there" and conveniently forgets what it has done (implicitly agreeing with Kierkegaard about the lunatic postulate and with James about the level of immediate involvement he called pure experience). She astutely

grasps the prerepresented and prereflective involved body that is both itself
and the other at the same time (although with different emphases in this
involvement at different times) [217]. Skillfully, phenomenologically, she
grasps the primal domain prior to representation and calculation, the
domain that cannot be owned as a unit and assigned to an owner. In this, as
we shall see, she recalls indigenous and shamanic ideas of "the dreaming,"
the zone of interfusion and primal power. Cuts apparently decisive between
self and other, now and then, here and there, youth and age, are washed out
[28, 216, 218]. She would find that energy—new as on the first day, as W. E.
Hocking put it.

Ever she undermines the key androcentric idea that one's body is a self-
contained unit that projects its calculations "in here" onto a world "out
there." "There is no need for an outside," she writes, "the other already
affects you. It is inseparable from you" [211]. Again, she does not deny all
individuality, but similar seemingly to Buber who asserts that the primal
name is I/thou, she writes, "You/I become two for (our) pleasure." "When
you kiss me, the world grows so large that the horizon itself disappears"
[210]. The "more" is with us, in us! Apparently fundamental distinctions
such as here/beyond, present/future, present/past—above all, yours/mine—
are humbled, sometimes expunged.

Ever she anchors thinking in the gendered bodies that think and in their
concrete situatedness. Thinking cannot catch itself up obsessively in itself,
occluding its own act of abstraction from the body. For example, to pleasure
himself a man must use an instrument, his hand, on the penis right there.
But moving certain ways in certain engrossing situations, a woman is already
pleasuring herself as moist labia move against each other. She is self and other
at the same time, and the whole bodily engaged situation is more the operant
unit than is her body objectified, her body understood as bounded by the
envelope of her skin. And there is no single or dominant erogenous zone,
but multi and multipotential mucosities.

Again, the sex that is not one—nor is it two, that is, two ones. The
woman is not pent-up, she flows, she oozes, she disturbs the male insistence
on excluded middles for thought (something is either A or not-A) and closed
categories for control. In *The Marine Lover of Frederick Nietzsche*, she
points out tellingly his androcentric biases that persist despite his genius:
His projection of himself onto the world, so he finds only mirror images of
himself—or sheer absences and dreadful loneliness.[4] He never really lives in
the life of the other. Most tellingly she finds not nearly enough water and
flow in his world, and his totem animals are land and air creatures, not water

ones. Thus again the rigid oppositions and exclusions of androcentric western philosophy.

The traditional denial of the female body connotes a world that cannot be trusted to regenerate us, that must be forced. The female pubic area is traditionally represented as a closed sector, the clitoris and vagina hidden and denied, something that must be forced open [201]. "The fantasy of the closed, solid virginal body" that, conquered, confirms the potency of the solitary male body. And the solitary society, male dominated, that preserves its purity and power by purging all that is alien, other. "Subhuman humans," wild animals and vegetation, oozing females of any species, all that obstructs the path of domination is co-opted or swept aside.

Only apparently paradoxically, the latest things—such as Irigarian feminism—point back to primal peoples. In fact, the most creative philosophical thought of the nineteenth and twentieth centuries does the same thing. I mean at least Emerson, Peirce, James, Dewey, Heidegger, Whitehead, Merleau-Ponty. This had to happen, I think, because the whole androcentric tradition of rampant, self-oblivious abstraction fairly obviously bankrupted itself the more irrepressibly modern it became. The only way remaining was to turn back and establish contact with our sources. Quantum physics also must be associated with this turn, as I will try to show.

Look for a moment again at James—that adorable genius, as Whitehead called him. His last decade is a creative frenzy. In 1901, sick in bed, he explores life in extremis in *Varieties of Religious Experience*. As we noted, the hither side of mystical or conversion experiences may be the human subconscious, but the farther is unclassifiable, "the more," the mysterious grounds of regenerative power: at moments we sense that there is an enormous domain that we do not know we do not know. Then in 1904 he is able finally to completely abandon the British empiricist charade of putatively basic "sense data in the mind." As we've seen, he advances a radical empiricism of pure experience, a level of encounter and interfusion in the world that antecedes the very distinction between self and other, subject and object. Some of his last work, *A Pluralistic Universe*, for example, repudiates "vicious intellectualism," the long-standing androcentric bias that what is not explicitly included in something's definition, neatly packaged in its alleged unitary being, is excluded from its reality. No, things constantly flow into what intellectualistic logic says they are not. So this logic, with its strangling verbalisms, must go. We must just look closely, feel clearly, and trust experience to take us where it will.

As we saw, the very same—numerically same—animal right in front of me figures in two contexts simultaneously: the history of the world at large, and my personal history as its perceiver. My perceiving it has antecedents and consequents unique to myself—the tone that is just my expectation arising out of my history as a body-self, the feeling that is just my enduring, the immediate taste of my body lived from within it, and the consequences for me alone—perhaps my fainting in the face of it, or remembering it in my own way much later. But the very same animal that lives and breathes in the world irradiates my life, informs me one way or other with its power. We used James's pure experience as a point of entry into shamanic healing.

Finally, finally, the psycho/physical splits—or complete mechanism and materialism—of mainstream medicine begin to lose their hegemony in the face of rampant, "untreatable" human malaise. How could a mind influence a body?—a phony question. A field begins to emerge hesitantly: psycho-neuroimmunology.

Let us look at some classic shamanic cures. In the cases I know best, the shaman happens to be male. As a matter of historical fact, a shaman is as apt to be female as male. This we should expect, since such healers are liminal beings, oozing right through the divisions that most people typically think of as fundamental: male/female; cultivated/wild; present/future and past; human/animal; life/death.

Levi-Strauss cites a pregnant woman with a blocked delivery who has appealed to a shaman (*Structural Anthropology*, "The Effectiveness of Symbols"). With the greatest patience, he enacts traditional "spirits" who enter and exit her room. As the woman fixes trancelike on these passages of spirits, she begins to be diverted from the pain that possesses her and blocks her delivery. Her womb and birth canal, apparently, begin to realign themselves in normal circuits of entry, conception, gestation, exit—delivery. In this case at least, the treatment works. She manages to give birth. She and the child are delivered.

Persons caught in mind-body dualisms are hard pressed to account for such a possibility, if they credit it at all. "How could sights and sounds in a mind possibly move the bodily machinery?" Again, the phony dualistic question, and the phony abstraction "in the mind." Following the leads of Irigary and James, who believe the other is already integral in the self, we have a conceptual model that can begin to account for it. The other is not just an image in my mind. When we are embedded together concernfully and mindfully in the self-regenerating universe, Circular power returns into itself. As the universe pours through that node of itself that is myself, it carries an

adjacent node, the other, through me. That is, envelopes of photons, phero-
mones, radiations, vibrations, sounds, all emanating from that organism—the
energic field without which others would not *be* themselves—pass through
me. In the case at hand, the other, the shaman, bodily and entrancedly enacts
entry and exit, entry and exit. In all encounters, particularly if I am open and
accessible, the other irradiates me, and I—a body-self—respond mimetically.
On one level of analysis, and restricting attention to my organism, it is
simply true that the world as perceived is a pattern of electrochemical events
in my body.

Hoping for greater vividness and specificity now, let us review Black
Elk's first cure of a very sick boy in an Oglala Lakota encampment around
1880. The boy lies in the northeast sector of the family's tepee. Black Elk
proceeds into the space through the entrance that faces south—the south,
believed to be, lived as, the source of heat and life. Four virginal young women
accompany him, as does a male colleague who carries the sacred pipe and a
four-rayed herb. He offers the pipe to the Six Powers—the four cardinal
directions and the heavens and earth. Then he passes it, and all who accompany him smoke. Someone beats a drum as another offering to Wakan Tanka:
this engages them. Black Elk carries a wooden cup full of water and a few
flakes of red willow bark, and proceeds on the outer perimeter of the inner
space until he faces west—the west where the sun sets each day and dies, as
each of us must do some day. He addresses the Grandfather of the West with
the sacred pipe. He then proceeds to the north, "where the white hairs are,"
where the cleansing cold wind of the north teaches endurance, and addresses
the Grandfather there.

At about this point, the sick boy smiles at him, and Black Elk, who had
been unsure of himself, feels power come up through Mother Earth and
through his body—"I could feel something queer all through my body,
something that made me want to cry for all unhappy things, and there were
tears on my face."[5]

He drinks from the cup with the red willow bark and instructs one of
the virgins to give it to the boy for him to drink also. He walks to where the
boy lies and stamps his foot four times. After some incantations in pulses of
four, he puts his mouth on the pit of the boy's stomach and sucks the cleansing wind of the north through his body—the wind that teaches endurance.

He arises and proceeds to address the east and the Grandfather there—
the east, the source of light, heat, and understanding. He then instructs one
of the virgins to go to the boy and to assist his rising and walking. This the
boy does, with great difficulty. Black Elk then exits to the south, having

completed the cycle through the Four Directions and the Six Powers, and not waiting to monitor any further progress by the boy, not wanting to suggest any possibility of failure.

He relates that the boy lived until thirty.

Roughly, Black Elk's diagnosis: an organism sick because disengaged from the regenerative cycles of the universe. The prescription: a massive, visceral dose of immediate engagement with felt regenerative totality. Tympanic communication from body to body via the drum; drinking from the same cup of water and vegetable matter used by the healer; the power of the ancestors, the Grandfathers—and from every direction and all beings—summoned into the tepee where the boy lies; the presence of virgins, that is, the palpable power of possibility; and what seems to be the consummating moment, Black Elk sucking on the boy's abdomen and drawing through it the cleansing power of the north wind that teaches endurance. Black Elk is a channel for the mobilization of the regenerative powers of Nature.

It is at least very interesting that a recent article in *The Journal of the American Medical Association* reports that persons with strong and extensive social networks are less apt to catch colds when injected with cold virus than are those with weak and restricted ones. Christiane Northrup, M.D., speaks of such networks as supportive structures of the immune system.[6] Attentive philosophers and scientists may learn things from indigenous peoples that were previously unimaginable. The domain of what we do not know we do not know is unimaginably vast and replete with regenerative potential. New possibilities, new alternatives, are sudden and perhaps shocking openings in the experienced world.

But how are we people brainwashed with psycho/physical dualism and mechanism to really understand how such healing might happen? A skeptic thinks, "Surely this sucking of the north wind through his body is only symbolical? There are probably in fact no gusts of wind from the north inside the tepee that a meteorologist's instruments might detect."

And here we are yet again, back in the "merely symbolical," back inside the mind, that is, back inside a fiction. So conceived, shamanic cures are improbable or impossible.

But it is prejudicial to conceive things this way. There is more to the reality of north wind than particular gusts from the north at particular places and times. The north wind must include how that sort of event figures in the habituated human nervous system in a culture over time. As the north wind works on, in, and through directly perceiving and memorializing humans, it leaves a potent residue in the body that communicates and radiates directly from body into body in the ritualized situation. To conceive the north wind nominalistically as only "particular gusts in themselves" is to say it is really only what it is minus our organism's mindful participation in it. But, again, this is a partialization, compartmentalization, abstraction that forgets itself—the lunatic postulate. Black Elk does suck the north wind that teaches endurance through the boy's body—it's true, I believe. It can be seen to be so *if* we can see what it *means* to say this. (Recall Essay 3 above.)

But what exactly and concretely might it mean for us in our situation today? It is extraordinarily difficult to grasp this. Almost inevitably we are distanced from the phenomenon of healing by our psycho/physical dualism, or by deep skepticism, or by an aura of exoticism and romance—far-off places and times, shadowy figures, spirits, and so on. Or we are lodged in mechanistic frameworks of interpretation so tightly that a vast range of human possibilities is concealed.

What if I concentrated on our daughter, Rebekah? The obstetrician believed she gestated eleven months. Nobody I have ever known looked more at home in the water. She swam by undulating her whole body under the surface like a porpoise. I would kid her, "But can you swim like a human being?" She could, but didn't like to. Even as a baby, when her diaper was wet she would seldom cry, but just coo in her crib in a sort of liquid way. She developed some cradle cap, encrustations on the scalp. I actually took leave of my obsessive work, sat her in a pan of water in the sink in Indianapolis, and began to soften it up and scrub it off. It took several sessions over several days. Only rarely would she wince or complain as she played in the pan full of warm water.

Her rapport with living things was phenomenal. Her childlike being-in-communion grew along with her. She—about eighteen at the time—my wife, and I were walking in the Lake Country of England. Noticing a horse in a pasture, we stopped. Fortunate to see it at all, for it stood stock still under a tree, looking out at us from under boughs. All alone, the animal looked forsaken. Standing at the rail fence, my wife and I tried various appeals to lure the creature toward us. For several minutes this went on, the horse keeping its frozen stance, baneful and pitiful. Our daughter made a few little sounds in her throat, and the horse came over. When she was little, she collected small animals, rabbits and abandoned cats and kittens. One apparently undistinguished rabbit was so handsomely groomed and nourished that the judge at the local fair created a special category for an award: General Rabbit. I referred to it as such at every opportunity. Her cats roamed the house and formed our daughter's most intimate family, which amused me. But I did not relish them roaming the bedroom as I slept. So each night, however tired, I tracked them down and deposited them, a bit roughly at times, in the furnace room.

One of her cats—as undistinguished by all "objective standards" as any cat could be—Charcoal—became sick and emaciated. She dragged her paralyzed hindquarters. Clearly she would die soon. One evening late, while all others slept, she looked up at me and made a sound. I found myself kneeling beside her and holding my head against hers. Astonished and elated, I said Goodbye to her.

About five years before this, when Rebekah was about thirteen, we were phoned at midnight that she had been found passed out at surf's edge in New Jersey, about sixty miles from where we lived. A nearly empty bottle of Vodka lay beside her. When we arrived very early in the morning at the hospital, she lay on a sheet-like hammock. I looked urgently into her eyes and asked her, "What are you doing?!" She blurted, "I'm just a little kid."

She implied that she would learn. And she did. But aided by removal from a circle of friends desperately seeking adulthood and not knowing the way. Distanced by thousands of miles, living with my youngest brother and his wife, she discovered the singing and music that would so distinguish her. Very likely, a deep memory lingered of her mother singing to her a lullaby every night before crib time. Earlier than that, nested in her mother's singing and dancing body, she must have heard singing all through herself and felt the movement of her mother.

Two years she was gone in California. I would often ride my bike many miles. Happening to pass a cemetery, I noticed a monument to a child inscribed, We miss you everywhere. Yes, that was it. She occupied a realm with animals and avian and marine beings that circulated timelessly all around me but never quite through me. It was a dreaming zone in which I was not secure. A few years ago—she was thirty-one, married, and on the verge of stardom as a singing actress—I had said to her as I left their loft in Brooklyn one night, "I miss you, Bek." As if she were a visitor from some realm come to beckon me for a time and then depart.

Our daughter died in 1997 from complications from a fall from a horse in Central Park. We brace ourselves day by day to prevent falling into the abyss. We buried some of her ashes near the shore of Puget Sound, her husband's home, where they would go some day to settle down and have children. Many came there, and many more to her requiem at Trinity Church in Manhattan.

Came from all over, the many people she touched deeply in her thirty-one and a half years. A friend from Sarah Lawrence College days, Tamara Lindesay, came from England, and gave us this poem:

Birdsong

It was in Woolworth's in Yonkers,
before forty ruffled parakeets rattling their cage
in the pet department, that I first saw you sing.
It was as if you had flown through the door,
their long-lost mother brought back to them
in human form, to ease their restless fluttering,
bring them a moment of peace. And sure enough
within minutes, your singing had coaxed
each and every one of them to sleep.

I wonder if all those parakeets found
owners to love them, liberate them
from Woolworth's, bring them home,
give them names. Maybe they carried your song
on their travels, taught it to their children,
maybe it's known to birds all over New York.
I'd like to think they have the power
to conjure you here, your voice lingering
on the air for an instant, before it disappears.

Another friend from college, a tall woman like our daughter, told me at the requiem about skulking self-consciously on the periphery of a party one night. She related that Bekah sidled up to her and said, "Isn't it great to be tall!" The friend said, "It changed my life."

In that summer I was visiting my middle brother in California. He is an extraordinarily staid and self-contained academic historian. As I turned away to leave that night, he said, "I have something to tell you."

I had heard him talk for sixty years, but never in that tone of voice. I turned abruptly to see him smiling in an odd way. Afflicted with stuttering since childhood, nevertheless now he spoke fluently and calmly. He said, "I was gathering up exams in a large lecture hall, but thought a few students hadn't finished. Sometimes students will slump down in their chairs, perhaps pouring over a dictionary, trying hard to finish. I checked each row. There were no students left. Still, I believed someone was present in the room. I suddenly looked at something in the room and said, 'Bekah, is that you? Bekah, is that you?' She seemed to be taken aback that I would doubt it. She said, 'Tell dad not to worry.' She stood there a moment looking at me, and then was gone. . . . I thought you should hear about this. I didn't know her very well, but that's about what happened, as near as I can tell you."

Rebekah's mother-in-law—a quiet, unexcitable woman—told us of hiking near Zermatt, Switzerland, the next summer. She said she heard someone coming up behind her on a bicycle, and then, "It was Bekah. She flashed by me, saying, 'Isn't this fun!'"

Bekah's mother, returning from two weeks abroad, opened the front door of the house, and it was if a wind swept past her and out of the house. "It was Bekah," her mother said.

Recently I was returning home in my car after a workout at the gym. I recalled a snapshot I had happened to see of myself as a young man holding Bekah on my knee. Just for a second it registered (my wife had the photo out—I cannot bear seeing pictures of her). She was only maybe five months old. The picture caught an expression of hers I remembered instantly: a kind of odd, old-woman's expression on her baby's face. Maybe she was a spirit-child, I now said to myself—trying to figure out what that could possibly mean.

Then I thought, She may be on the front porch waiting for me. I didn't believe it exactly. I didn't not believe it either. What I thought of—and my thought itself—were oddly placeless and timeless, a state of mind I never recall having before.

When I drove up the driveway, I was not surprised. She was not sitting on the porch. But something was on the porch. It was in the mailbox, an unexpected letter from our friend, Calvin Martin. My wife had sent him and his wife Tamara's poem. The letter read,

> Nina keeps marveling that Bekah could calm those birds with her singing. More than that, that she would even *think* to do this, and that she would do it in a public place. This is an extraordinary person indeed.

> Somebody with that kind of spirit doesn't die. Let me tell you emphatically: that spirit cannot die. I lived too long with Eskimos to think that people like this, like Bekah, merely come and go. No. They don't. These people house a spirit that is immortal, that is earthy. . . .

Something (I purposely use this mythic word, "something," to keep it unspecified, plenipotential, powerful—what in quantum language is known as "superposition") dwelled in her. The late poet and anthropologist Stanley Diamond said that writing a poem is like experiencing a mysterious arrow: it comes from somewhere we know not whence and passes right through us on its journey. . . .

But it had to continue on its trajectory. And so it did. But it is not gone, nor dead, nor even remote. It is there with those parakeets in Woolworths; it is there in the lives of her friends and those who heard her sing; it is there with you two and her husband and brother. It is out there on the dawn, there in the path of the moon. . . .

I don't know if you understand what I'm saying. You mourn . . . imagining her death was trivial or accidental. . . . It's like saying that the trivial and accidental would happen to Ulysses or Persephone or Diana—that it could happen to some being who housed the power of the universe.

The inclination to dismiss all this is nearly irresistible. A grieving parent indulging in wishful thinking, allowing himself to be cozened by well-meaning and grieving others, and by his own odd experiences, conveniently overlooking obvious explanations of these strange "appearances" of Rebekah: Namely, they are dreamlike experiences, although somewhat unusual ones. As one may dream of being attacked by a tiger and not be attacked by a tiger, so one may dream of one's dead daughter without her being alive. Oughtn't a professor of philosophy ensconced within a great research university at the end of the twentieth century be embarrassed by all this?

Perhaps. But I think one ought rather to be more embarrassed to be deterred from thinking by a feeling of embarrassment. First, history bristles with instances of "obvious explanations" that later proved false. Second, the scientistic idea that dreams are simply the mind spinning crazily when proper sensory input is suspended has waned in the face of Freud's and Jung's revival of ancient practices of interpreting dreams. But finally, and most important, the strange experiences above are different in salient respects from both night dreams and daydreams.

Unlike night dreams, one doesn't lie down, disengage, with the intent to sleep, then go to sleep. Unlike daydreams, one doesn't drift off from a boring situation, say, or impelled by smoldering resentment or lust, for example, slide into daydream reverie. The motivation for the strange experience, the motivating situation, doesn't seem to be there. *That is, the strange experience is much more discontinuous with one's ordinary locatedness in time and space than are either night or daydreams.* But, then, aren't they *more out of touch with reality* than are night and daydreams—at least as scientistic thinkers have traditionally derogated them?

Let's develop Calvin Martin's suggestion about superposition and quantum physics. Let's speculate in a way that might conceivably account for the phenomena, "save the appearances," as Plato put it. Superposition, or what interests me as much, nonlocality—what does this mean? David Bohm puts it this way: Entities that have originally been combined show a peculiar nonlocal relationship "which can best be described as a non-causal connection of things that are far apart."[7]

Physicist John Bell hypothesized that when one of a pair of subatomic particles once joined undergoes a change, the other will undergo the same change instantaneously, no matter how far it now be from the other. This was later confirmed by Alain Aspect. It was a notion that Einstein had thought to be absurd.

But surely this applies only in microreality, only with regard to subatomic particles that *are* at some distance, and not the gross macroreality in which we live our lives? Surely on the macrolevel odd quantum events are evened out, averaged out, concealed, and have no significant impact on us? So it was—and still is—widely thought.

But a disturbing set of books appeared in 1988 and 1994 by the eminent physicist, Roger Penrose (*The Emperor's New Clothes* and *Shadows of the Mind*). He directly challenged conventional brain science's assumptions (1) that the ultimate units of brain functioning are neurons and their connections, and (2) that all of the mind—and its corresponding brain functioning—can be understood on the model of computational processes (somewhat analogous to computer processing). No, for Penrose, neurons are individuals far too crude. We must begin to understand the microtubules of neurons and their possible interfusions across the brain. In this expanded but still microdomain, quantum effects might be of decisive significance for human experience. We need a new physics, he declares, the outlines of which we only partially discern.

Penrose detects what he takes to be a noncomputational level of mental experience, to which, he believes, must correspond a noncomputational level of brain functioning. I appropriate this as follows: When we enter a room full of people, say, we immediately intuit, usually, the felt quality of the whole situation. No computation is required. We do this because we are minding and feeling bodies, while computers are not. To this minding and feeling must correspond a noncomputational level of brain functioning, Penrose believes, and for this a new quantum physics of microtubules is required. Perhaps, if we had it, quantum events in an individual's brain would be seen to be involved in fields of events or beings beyond our present capacity to imagine.

The strange experiences of Bekah's presence outlined above would seem to be noncomputational as well as nonlocal. How could we possibly be computing anything about any situation? The experiences come unbidden and unpredicted—feel completely real, both located *and* utterly disconnected from preceding local situations in which our locatedness in time and space is typically so pressing and inexorable: for example, we are repulsed by an attractive woman and drift into a daydream of some sort.

The big question is this: Is there a noncausal connection between entities—or persons—once connected that is not subject to our computations? Must it simply be immediately felt? Do we exist "even now" at some level, nonlocally, beyond space-time as that is ordinarily conceived, even in relativistic physics? Recall Hocking's questioning in the 1930s and 1940s whether space-time as ordinarily conceived is the only system of space-time.

According to the latest cosmological thought, this palpable universe of space and time, of locatedness, emerged from a big bang in which space and time *were created.* A nonspatiotemporal reality—a *fons et origo*—seems to be imagined.[8] Perhaps the influences of this nonlocalized background universe still permeate ours, but usually masked out by the foreground noise and pressure of ours? With Bekah's death she ceased to be in one pressing local situation after another: the reality that had so flooded our attention as we cared for her through the years and later visited her and attended her concerts. Does nonlocal reality have a chance to emerge into the focus now, abruptly, completely unpredictably?

Perhaps the embarrassment of appearing to believe in ghosts comes back to inhibit us. Do we really believe in ectoplasmic emanations and concretions in space and time, in ghosts that flit from place to place and time to time!? No, that's precisely what we needn't and shouldn't believe, I think! For we are *trying* to imagine a level of reality that is not spatiotemporal at all—as that is typically conceived—but is just suddenly with us. It is practically impossible to imagine this, so profoundly conditioned are we by the quotidian spatiotemporal world in which we either adjust or die.

Beyond all this, the truly ultimate question, Why is there any universe—

or universes—at all? Nobody who thinks claims to know, not even Stephen Hawking. Are we connected even now to a Source that we cannot begin to imagine, so beyond our conceptions of space and time and localities is it? Isn't this what the world's religions have tried—however fumblingly, variously, bludgeoningly—to introduce us to, so that we will not be torn to pieces or numbed into oblivion by the everyday world—so closely and relentlessly pressing around us? To which we must respond or we die?

It is easy to say that Bekah is dead and gone. She is dead—God knows that's true—but I don't exactly know what "gone" means. Something remains to teach me endurance, at least so far, and maybe someday delight in just being. And surely, if love means finding one's rhythm in another—as someone has said— then I love her, and keep on loving her, more than anything I can imagine.

Postscript: It is now three years since our daughter died. To my knowledge there were no "reappearances" after five or six months. This agrees with certain indigenous peoples' observations that the soul lingers for awhile on the earth. Which suggests that the organisms of the living—longing for the deceased and expecting her—spontaneously, viscerally reproduced her body-self as that had irradiated their own body-selves, flowing through them for so long. Something like a photographic negative left in the body that fades in time? If a nonlocality phenomenon occurs, it may be only of limited duration?

I turn again to Hocking's speculations on immortality, but the words do not come with which to judge and respond. Nor does Henry Bugbee's insight into depth of affirmation, anteceding all reasons, feel completely right.

I do feel her energy in my work. No reason now to putter around! Strange sadness, strange excitement.

Notes

1. Sally Roesch Wagner, *The Untold Story of the Iroquois Influence on Early Feminists* (Aberdeen, S.D.: Sky Carrier Press, 1996).

2. Wagner, *The Untold Story*. 33. Concerning indigenous cultures in general and their contemporary relevance, see *Ayaangwaamizin: International Journal of Indigenous Philosophy* (Thunder Bay, Ont.: Lakehead University), esp. 1, 1 (1997), "Some Thoughts on Articulating a Native Philosophy," by the editors, D. McPherson and J. D. Rabb. They approach Kant's moral philosophy from a fresh and revealing angle.

3. (Ithaca: Cornell University Press, 1985 [1977]). *Page references are given in brackets.*

4. (New York: Columbia University Press, 1991), particularly 3–73. See also Irigary's *I Love to You: Sketch of a Possible Felicity in History* (New York: Routledge, 1996), especially the chapters "Human Nature Is Two" and "Sexual Difference Is Universal."

5. See Chapter 3, note 4 above. Although the pragmatic and phenomenological traditions open the way to an understanding of indigenous ways of knowing and being, practically nobody has exploited it. Eugene Gendlin is an exception. He has developed an awareness of the body as knower, an awareness that most Westerners would not count as conscious, certainly not as cognitive. I believe Gendlin could make something of Black Elk's, "I could feel something queer all through my body." If we are properly attuned, we can learn from the body's subconscious or preconscious adjustments to, and sensed openings in, the world around it. A deeper belonging of the body in the ever-regenerating world, a deeper fit, may be signaled by a queer feeling throughout the body. If we are attuned to this clicking into place—better, falling or moving into place—we can know palpable reality beyond the ability of fully conscious and articulable minding to imagine. *Focusing* (New York: Everest House, 1978). Though the connection to indigenous ways of thought and being is clear to me, Gendlin is not explicit about the matter.

6. Her newsletter for October 1997, "Health Wisdom for Women," Rockville, Md.

7. *Wholeness and the Implicate Order* (London: Routledge & Kegan Paul, 1980), 175.

8. I should say that this hypothetical reality is not spatial or temporal in any way we might directly perceive (or even that most of us can confidently imagine!). See, again, Brian Greene's *The Elegant Universe,* in which he explains how physicists suppose spatial dimensions in excess of the usual three, dimensions "curled up in themselves" so minutely and compactly that incredibly great energies can be released. What implications such putative dimensions and their force potentials might carry for understanding how dead persons might leave an active residue in living ones, I do not know. But I think it likely that things are going on that we can't imagine.

Index

Abbey, Edward, 96
academic philosophy and professionalism, x, 10, 12, 154. *See also* analytic philosophy
addiction and obsession, 20, 26, 98, 104, 114, 147, 191–206, 220, 228
Alexander, F. M., 22, 102, 111ff., 122, 148, 203
alienation, 18, 191–206, 209
Amaterasu (goddess, Japan), 221
analytic philosophy, 7, 12, 78, 86, 141, 146, 154, 158–60, 199, 201–2
animal grace, 92, 104
anthropology, 193, 205 n. 6
APA (American Philosophical Association), 199–200, 203
Apaches, 30
Apffel-Marglin, F., 196, 206 n. 10
archaic, 107, 110, 113
archaic-ecstatic, 108
archetypes and archetypal, 101–2, 109, 113, 115, 124–25, 135, 146, 188; and genetics, 134
Arendt, H., 122
Aristotle, 60, 84, 127, 176, 192–93
Arnold, Mathew, 203
art and arts, 97, 99–101, 166, 169, 172
Aspect, Alain, 233
awe, 157, 164–66, 173

Bacon, Francis, 16, 165
Barrett, William, 158
Basso, Keith, 32 n. 13
Beaseley, Conger, 58
Beckett, Samuel, 21
Bekah, 228–35
Bell, Hannah, 32 n. 9, 221
Bell, John, 233
Bergson, Henri, 160
Berlin, Isaiah, 201

Black Elk, 4, 15–44 (frequently quoted), 46, 63, 95, 100, 105, 155, 165, 226; ritual enactment and theatre, 167
Blake, William, quoted, 219
Bode, Boyd, 87 n. 7
body, 148–49, 184, 236 n. 5; contempt for, 97; and television, 103; being with, 113; objectified, 219; male, 220
body-mind or body-self, 8, 97, 104, 111, 148, 184, 195, 219
Bohm, David, 27, 233
Bohr, Niels, 108, 215
bonding or kinship, 58–60, 69, 91, 93, 187
boredom, 95
Borges, J. L., 200
Boydston, Jo Ann, 115
brain science, 43, 233
breathing, 59, 63, 99, 127
British empiricism, 8
Buchler, Justus, 119 n. 8
Buddha, 100, 215

Cather, Willa, 57, 200
Cavell, Stanley, x–xi
chance, 183, 215
Charcoal, the cat, 229
chimpanzees, 194
Christians and Christianity, 18, 30
Colapietro, V., 217 n. 5
Conant, James, 201
concepts, 56–57, 62, 72–73, 75–77, 80–84, 146, 207–8, 217 n. 4
Confucius, 215
consciousness, 35, 51, 55, 62–63, 73, 99, 111, 126–29, 144
continuum or continuity, 127. *See also* Peirce, C. S.